# STEVE WAUGH

## NO REGRETS

# STEVE WAUGH

## NO REGRETS

**Harper**Sports
An imprint of HarperCollins*Publishers*

**Harper*Sports***
An imprint of HarperCollins*Publishers*

First published in Australia in 1999
By HarperCollins*Publishers* Pty Limited
ACN 009 913 517
A member of HarperCollins*Publishers* (Australia) Pty Limited Group
http://www.harpercollins.com.au

HarperCollins*Publishers*
25 Ryde Road, Pymble, Sydney NSW 2073, Australia
31 View Road, Glenfield, Auckland 10, New Zealand
77-85 Fulham Palace Road, London W6 8JB, United Kingdom
Hazelton Lanes, 55 Avenue Road, Suite 2900, Toronto, Ontario M5R 3L2
and 1995 Markham Road, Scarborough, Ontario M1B 5M8, Canada
10 East 53rd Street, New York NY 10022, USA

National Library of Australia Cataloguing-in-publication data:

Waugh, Steve, 1965–.
   No regrets: a captain's diary
   ISBN 0 7322 6452 9

1. Cricket captains – Australia – Biography. 2. Cricket
players – Australia – Biography. 3. Cricket – Australia.
I. Title
796.358092

Printed in Australia by Australian Print Group on 115gsm Matt Art
Front cover design: Bluecork
Design and finished art: Brevier Design

6 5 4 3 2 1
99 00 01 02

# CONTENTS

## DEDICATION

We called Australia's World Cup campaign the 'No Regrets tour' and throughout the tournament associated our motto, 'No Regrets', with the declaration that …

*Every sacrifice we make is a down payment on the acquisition of the World Cup.*

This book is dedicated to all the Australian cricketers and support staff, from the Test and one-day squads of 1998 and 1999, whose sacrifices and great effort made Australia's 1999 World Cup triumph a reality.

## NICKNAMES

Throughout *No Regrets*, a number of Australian players and support staff are referred to by their nicknames. These players (and their nicknames) are as follows: Michael Bevan (Bevo), Adam Dale (Chippen), Damien Fleming (Flem), Jason Gillespie (Dizzy), Ian Healy (Heals), Brendon Julian (BJ), Justin Langer (Lang), Darren Lehmann (Boof), Stuart MacGill (Magilla), Glenn McGrath (Pigeon), Damien Martyn (Marto), Colin Miller (Funky), Tom Moody (Moods), Ricky Ponting (Punter), Paul Reiffel (Pistol), Gavin Robertson (Robbo), Michael Slater (Slats), Mark Taylor (Tubs or Tubby), Shane Warne (Warney), Mark Waugh (Junior), physio Errol Alcott (Hooter), coach Geoff Marsh (Swamp), fitness co-ordinator Dave Misson (Misso) and team manager Steve Bernard (Brute).

## ACKNOWLEDGMENTS

Special thanks to my wife Lynette and daughter Rosalie, for their unstinting love and support throughout the last 12 months. I cannot stress enough just how important and appreciated are the help and encouragement provided by our families.

I am also extremely grateful to everyone in the Australian cricket squads of 1998 and 1999, for their friendship, support and dedication to the cause. Thanks also to:

- Geoff Armstrong, who has worked with me on each of my seven books, and diligently managed this project from start to finish. Without Geoff's commitment and support, the end product would not have been possible.
- Kylie Prats from Brevier Design, who must be just about the best in the business when it comes to maintaining the quality of her product *and* meeting impossibly tight deadlines.
- Jake Causby from Bluecork, for the front-cover design.
- Ian Russell, for once again producing a comprehensive statistics section.
- The people who contributed to the text — Tom Moody for the foreword, Lukey Sparrow for his prelude (and his support of the Aussie team in recent years!) and Chris Ward, for his piece on the Australia–South Africa semi-final.
- The magnificent photographers, management and staff of AllSport, who have provided many of the photographs in this book.
- HarperCollins*Publishers* for giving me the chance to publish this book.

*The editorial and design processes for* No Regrets *were managed by Advantage International, 10/37 Nicholson St, Balmain East NSW 2041 (tel: +61-2-9810 8188)*

# FOREWORD

## By TOM MOODY

ONLY TWO CRICKETERS were playing members of Australia's two World Cup-winning squads — the teams of '87, in India, and '99, in the UK. One, of course, was Steve Waugh. The other, I'm very pleased to say, was me.

I must say that being involved in these World Cups, at the extremes of my career, gave me two very different emotional highs. Both, though, were fantastic. In 1987 I was a very green, very fresh-faced newcomer to the game at the top level. Twelve years later, I was a man who had played a lot of first-class cricket — in England and Australia — with a sprinkling of Test and one-day cricket thrown in. I was not so green, perhaps better described as 'ripe', with the benefits of many years' experience in my cricket kit.

At the start of the 1987 World Cup Allan Border's Australian team was considered to be one of the underdogs of the competition. However, history has demonstrated that such status can be an advantage more often than not. I remember the squad as being young, eager and fit. We were also fearless and had a very high work ethic, ingredients that proved to be the recipe for a world champion team.

I have so many fond memories of that sub-continent adventure, but what really sticks out for me was the strong bond the team had, and how that sense of team evolved during our journey to the top. This spirit came from many sources, from the hard work we put in at training to the way we enjoyed the victories that occurred along the way.

After our first win, over India in Madras, we had a party that set the tone and established the unity between all the members of this team. We all piled into the manager's room and drank, sang and laughed, but more importantly, we enjoyed each other's success and company. Then we quickly got straight back to business on the training track the next day. A combination of great times and hard work led to a very successful tour and the beginning of an upturn in Australian cricket. A lot of players grew in confidence on the international stage together and Australia became a dominant force in world cricket once again.

From this point on, Steve and I knew of the great pride and pleasure a World

Cup can bring — personally and as a team. This is something that you can only discover by going through the experience.

The World Cup of 1999 was always going to be big, especially as it was being played at the 'Home' of cricket. For every Australian there is a real pride in representing Australia in England. Our squad in '99 was a team of experience, recognised as possessing a lot of talent — a major contrast to 1987, where many of the guys were relatively new to international cricket and as such had little top-level form on the board. However, the superior-on-paper credentials of the 1999 side actually became something of a stumbling block, because the expectations were a great deal higher than they'd been 12 years before. As the guys struggled early on to justify their high ratings, we had a lot of trouble finding that momentum which is so critical in a tournament of this magnitude.

Consequently, despite countless team meetings and much soul searching, the side came to the point of exiting the World Cup much earlier than anyone could have anticipated.

But then came what I feel developed into one of the crucial moments of our tough journey. A meeting was sprung on us by our coach, Geoff Marsh, the day before our match against Pakistan at Headingley, during which he pointed out some real home truths to the squad. Geoff was not backward in his criticism. He then asked everyone to give their thoughts on where the team was going and why things were not working out as we'd planned. The result was a meeting in which some valuable points were made, and the team responded to them. We'd been stuck in a 'zone of doubt', but straight after this meeting we snapped out of our lethargy and started to perform to our abilities, as individuals and, more importantly, as a team.

Of course, we had magnificent leaders in our fightback. One was our captain, Steve Waugh, the other being his deputy, Shane Warne. These guys invariably lead from the front, particularly when the team is under great pressure. The next day we lost narrowly to Pakistan, but we fought hard and might have been a touch unlucky to lose. And from that point onwards we got better and better as a team, to the point that it was all just meant to happen. The two best examples of this sense of inevitability came in the now-famous clashes with South Africa, first in the Super Six part of the tournament, then in the semi-final. Both of these games could have gone either way, but it was the team with the 'mental edge' that came out on top when the real pressure was on.

By the time we reached the final against Pakistan, we were very much at the peak of our powers, and Pakistan would have had to have a real day out to knock us off our course. We remained focused and hungry, and as a result they were no match for a team that was quite rightly crowned world champions.

My personal highlight of the 1999 World Cup would have to be the Super Six game against South Africa at Headingley. This match was another 'must win' encounter for us, our fifth in a row to that point, and I was fortunate enough to be involved in the final stages of our run chase. This was, without doubt, one of the most intense passages of play I have ever experienced. To help the team and Steve Waugh complete a famous victory gave me more satisfaction, I think, than any other personal achievement in my career.

While Steve and my World Cup adventure in one sense began 12 years before the 1999 Cup final, for the Australian players who were at Lord's on June 20 it started, in many ways, at the Commonwealth Games in Kuala Lumpur, in September 1998. That was when the 1998-99 one-day squad first came together, and not surprisingly that is where Steve begins this book. For it was at the Games, and then on through Pakistan, Bangladesh, Australia, the Caribbean, and on to England that the team spirit and camaraderie that were a feature of our performances developed. Steve was very keen to build a pride in the Australian one-day cap, and a sense of tradition and great ambition in the way we go about things, and I believe we managed that. I certainly appreciate the way Steve's pride in the team and in Australian cricket comes through in the pages of this book.

Being part of both the 1987 and 1999 World Cup victories has been the highlight of my cricket career. And they have given me memories that will last for a lifetime.

Thank you for the opportunity.

# INTRODUCTION

**By STEVE WAUGH**

THIS IS THE STORY of a very arduous, usually exciting, sometimes controversial and ultimately richly rewarding 'year' of cricket. In fact, in terms of days and weeks, it was a little less than a full year, but many times it felt like much more than 12 months' worth, as the cricket calendar asked us to be in a succession of countries — Malaysia, Pakistan, Bangladesh, Pakistan again (with a brief stopover for coach Geoff Marsh and I in India), home to Australia, then the many nations of the West Indies, finally England and Wales — from mid September 1998 to late June 1999. It was certainly more than a 'season'; at times when I'd been separated from my family and home for weeks on end it seemed like an eternity.

The 'Road to Lord's' we called it, for Lord's was where the final of the Australian one-day team's ultimate target — the World Cup — would be played on June 20. In a sense, the one-dayers from the Commonwealth Games to the Caribbean would be preliminaries; all important in their own right, but all to be used to rehearse methods and eliminate faults and weaknesses before the Cup competition began.

Once in England, I introduced a new title — the 'No Regrets Tour' — which reflected what I wanted from myself and all involved. Nothing left to luck, no 'what ifs' or 'if onlys', simply a concerted, full-on team effort that would maximise our chances of victory. Hence the title of this book. But there was the odd hiccup along the way, especially early in our Cup campaign when we found ourselves only one defeat away from elimination. However, we regrouped, remembered our goals and believed in each other, to fight back in a manner that typified the character of the side, and the quality of the lads who made up this very Australian cricket team.

Since the start of the 1997-98 Australian season, there have been, as many critics like to put it, two Aussie sides — the Test XI and one-day team. But although some players have become, for want of a better term, 'specialists' in one form of the game or the other, the two squads remain in essence the same. They are both fiercely patriotic, both determined to win every time they play, both totally committed to doing everything in their power to be fully prepared for the battles ahead, traits that have allowed us to remain at the head of the pack, as one of the most feared cricket nations in the world.

As a member of both squads, it would have been totally inappropriate for me to focus solely on the one-day matches in telling this story of our road to the World Cup. For one thing, the two sides feed off each other's successes — learning from innovations that work and developing strategies, training drills, mental preparation techniques and facets of game plans useful in all forms of the sport. And the three Test series involving Australia during this period produced a streak of records, great achievements and often thrilling finishes. We won a Test, then a series, in Pakistan for the first time in 39 years. Mark Taylor matched The Don. Then we won a sixth straight Ashes series, a feat unprecedented this century and never before achieved by Australia. Then, following Tubby's retirement, I was honoured with the Test captaincy, the prelude to a remarkable four-match series in the Caribbean that just might have included the greatest Test match ever played.

In truth, if I had tried to cover in detail all the things that happened between our first encounter in Kuala Lumpur and our victory in the World Cup, I could have published three or four books. So what I have done is divide the book into five parts — the Commonwealth Games, our tour of Pakistan and Bangladesh, the Ashes summer, our Caribbean adventure, and finally the World Cup. In the first four parts, I have provided a summary of all that went on, followed by a selection of photographs — many from the lens of my own camera, some others from the magnificent AllSport photo library — to give a feel for not just the cricket but also some aspects of the nations we journeyed through and the people, rich and poor, who live there. I've also tried to show aspects of an international cricketer's life that the TV cameras and newspaper pages can't always reach. For Pakistan, the Ashes and the West Indies, I have also ripped a page or two from my diary, to focus on major days, or occasionally — such as when Justin Langer, Steve Bernard and I visited the squalid but amazing Trench Town district in Kingston, Jamaica — to give a pen-picture of lives and lifestyles that had a major impact on me.

And then to the World Cup, where I return to the diary format that has been the basis of my cricket books from the 1993 Ashes tour to our return to England in 1997. This time, I've added the occasional feature (such as my notes from some pre-game team meetings and our poems, each written by a member of the tour party especially for the next challenge that confronted us), but I must also confess that once or twice one day's diary entry has been swallowed up into two or three. This was due to the extra demands on my time that come with being captain, which as the World Cup reached its dramatic finale became incessant and draining. But also rewarding, as the fact the phone was always ringing reflected the fact that we were going all right.

Thanks to Ian Russell, who has compiled the statistics sections for all my books, *No Regrets* ends with a comprehensive record of all the matches we were involved in. All up, I hope the book successfully captures the excitement and passion of one of the most fantastic periods of cricket that I have had the pleasure to be involved in, and produced a worthwhile souvenir for all the people who supported and kept faith in the Australian team throughout an extraordinary journey.

# PRELUDE

By **LUKE GILLIAN (aka LUKEY SPARROW)**

WHEN LANCE KLUSENER clubbed the ball to the fence, leaving South Africa one run from four balls to claim a berth in the 1999 World Cup Final, I lost the plot. I remember telling myself, as I jumped and thumped about the terrace, 'That was it.'

For the first time in my years of supporting Australian cricket, I conceded that we could not win. But then, in that moment of desperation, I recalled the brilliant victory against South Africa at Headingley. Clutching my mate Darren's arm, through gritted teeth and with blood curdling, I roared, 'A tie will see us through. It's not over, mate. It's not over. We go for the tie ...'

'Go Australia!'

Cricket is one of those rare games where no team is ever totally winning. So you can never give up. A match is only ever decided with its last ball and no-one ever knows when that ball will be — until it has been delivered. That, for me, is the beauty of the game. That was the beauty of the semi-final.

Having had the opportunity to support Australian cricket around the world, I've witnessed matches that could not have been scripted. Games such as the semi-final against South Africa will always reduce the game before to relative insignificance. Immediately afterwards, you believe a match cannot be bettered, but invariably it is. Consequently, I look to the next game as something special that will be remembered, and that's what keeps me going. I've supported Australia in the West Indies in 1995 (first day, March 16), the World Cups of '96 and '99, South Africa and England in '97, Pakistan '98 and now, as I write, Sri Lanka '99. The Zimbabwe tour that follows will be my eighth tour.

Cricket isn't just about the winning, losing or flag waving, but being there. And I always remember where I'm from and why. We travellers face sacrifices every day, but I don't regret those I've made so I can enjoy this 'cricket tourist' lifestyle.

Before heading to the Caribbean in 1995, I worked as a chef in Melbourne, and afterwards travelled around Europe before going to the '96 World Cup in India and Pakistan. On my return to the UK, I became one of the privileged few to score a position on the Formula One Grand Prix circuit. However, I have a preference for cricket, so I decided to leave my 'greatest job ever' after seven months; not easy knowing the first race of the '97 F1 season was in Melbourne. I often wondered who in their right mind would walk away from an all-expenses-paid job in favour of flea-pit dormitories, hitching, hiking, death rides on public transport, insects, and disease-ridden food and beverage. But just like the F1, the cricket has been fantastic. I could be earning my wealth on F1 but that does not compare to supporting Australian cricket.

Unfortunately, there comes a time when money is required. So, despite the hurt, I returned to F1 midway through the '97 Ashes campaign. It still hurt in early '98, when the Australian team was in India ... but I wasn't. The 1998 F1 season was exceptional, so the decision to leave again for the cricket was not taken lightly. However, waving the flag for Australia in Pakistan was more important to me than being in Japan for one last Grand Prix.

I sometimes miss the cash, but look at what I've seen! Australia's triumph and Steve Waugh's 200 in Jamaica in 1995. Steve and Greg Blewett's 385-run partnership in Johannesburg and Mark Waugh's century in Australia's victory in the second Test in Port Elizabeth in 1997. Mark Taylor's 334. The amazing victories in the 1996 World Cup quarter and semi-finals. Ian Healy's world record. And, after an ordinary win against Scotland and losses to New Zealand and Pakistan, Steve Waugh raising the '99 World Cup.

Touring doesn't have to be expensive, but it can be difficult. I remember most vividly, in Pakistan in 1998, when I survived a scheduled one-and-three-quarter hour flight, full of people using their mobile phones, that took two-and-a-half hours (the plane, I was told, was tired). There was no safety demonstration before we took off, no life jackets, no oxygen masks, and the flight ended with the airport shuttle bus crashing under the plane. Then I endured a 42-hour train journey (should have been 25) without food, but with stripped body searches, armed bandits and child births, all before seeing 22 days of cricket that featured food, rocks, refuse and verbal abuse being thrown at me every five minutes. Steve Bernard (the Australian team manager) said afterwards that he didn't think it was such a good idea for me to stay for the one-day games and I was the first to agree. On the other hand, though, as I mentioned, I did see Mark Taylor score 334 and Ian Healy claim his world record. And I was there when Australia won for the first time in Pakistan for 39 years. So it wasn't all bad.

I was disappointed to leave before the tour was through. My experiences in Pakistan had been a one-off; shoestring travels aren't always hair raising and some of my most memorable times have been hitching from game to game. Holding a cricket bat and waving the Australian flag will usually guarantee a trouble-free ride and cricket-rich conversation — meeting the locals is one of the best ways to learn about a country, especially about its cricket heritage.

Hitching around, surviving internal flights or sitting on trains for days over the length and breadth of the Indian sub-continent — it's all part of the adventure. From our first experiences together in the West Indies in 1995, travelling with my mate, Darren Moulds, has not only made the hard times bearable, it has also given me someone to play cricket with, and someone who can help pass the time. And there are the other Australians I've met who follow our religion. I journeyed through most of the Caribbean with Dave and Duff from Tasmania, who were there when I carried the drinks for Australia in St Kitts (soon after, Dave became the first Australian supporter to field — just one over — for his country in a first-class game).

That night, we were 'invited' to the team's rum punch party, and made ourselves known. During proceedings, I mentioned that it was unlikely that I would be able to get to Trinidad for the third Test, and Steve Waugh immediately said to Tim May and Ian Healy, 'How do we get Luke to Trinidad? He can't not be there!'

Those words I'm not likely to forget, or the Test that followed, even though it was over in three days. Thanks fellas!

Unfortunately, Dave and Duff have not been able to join another tour, but Colin 'Bomber' Dale, Cath Bahr and Bradley Wooding, all of whom I met for the first time in the Windies, have been. Darren, who had toured with Bomber in South Africa in 1994, fronted again for the World Cup in '96. Following Australia to the final with these guys and a handful of other 'faithfuls' was brilliant, and eased the pain of the end result. We got together again in South Africa a year later and continued on to England for the Ashes series.

How did all this begin? My employer, Kevin Hawking, said to me one day in 1991, 'Before I go to the grave all I want to do is follow an Australian cricket tour of the West Indies.' After watching on television the '91 tour, I decided that Kev was right, so I immediately began looking forward to '95. 'Soon' after, as the plane banked over Barbados, I was taking a photograph of Kensington Oval. I have always promised Kev that I'd thank him if I ever write my book and although this is not mine, it's an opportunity to say, 'Thanks Kev. Wish you were here'.

Steve Waugh has always showed an interest in stories from my side of the fence. During the Ashes tour in 1997, I gave him my 'South African Tour Diary' to have a look at, but he lost it the moment I gave it to him! And then he found it in a most unlikely manner. At Lord's, during the second Test, Steve went out to bat but then marched straight back, one ball later, given out lbw. In his anger following this dismissal, he threw his left pad against the dressing-room wall and my diary appeared! When I had given the manuscript to Steve he had put it in his pad, to protect it from the English rain, and duly forgot where he put it. I laughed when he told me and remain proud knowing that, whatever I achieve in life, a part of me has been out to bat in an Ashes Test at Lord's.

I can't imagine what I'd be doing now had I not followed Kevin Hawking's dream and pursued my love for cricket. Worse still, what would I have missed? The celebrations and commiserations. Crushing victories and defeats. Friends, locals, match tickets and near death experiences. Most importantly, I would have missed acknowledgment from the team for all the support — support that can take so much out of you but is worth every effort.

# COMMONWEALTH GAMES

Steve Waugh

*Title page: Three East Hills Boys High School lads, one (Ian Thorpe) half the age of the other two and an infinitely better swimmer too, at the team get-together before the Commonwealth Games got underway.*

*Left: The great Kieren Perkins leads the Australian contingent, including, for the first time, Aussie one-day cricketers, into the main stadium at KL.*

*Below: Gavin Robertson and I are seen here mixing with our new-found friends, Aussie swimmers Chris Fydler and Kieren Perkins.*

# A TEAM WITHIN A TEAM

FROM THE MOMENT it was first whispered that cricket was to be in the Kuala Lumpur Commonwealth Games of 1998, the Aussie cricket team couldn't wait to be involved. Our desire to be a part of the 300-plus strong Australian contingent was so strong we managed to reverse the Australian Cricket Board's original idea that perhaps the Games should be a tour for the Second XI, or even an Australian Cricket Academy side. And once we were there, nothing could dampen our enthusiasm to be a part of the opening and closing ceremonies and march around the stadium with the rest of the Aussies, as well as all the other competing nations.

I can honestly say that our Commonwealth Games cricket experience was as good a two weeks as I've ever had in sport. Why? Having the opportunity to mingle with top-class sportspeople from across a broad range of disciplines was a real learning curve for all the guys. To see the dedication and application these athletes put into gaining that extra, split-second advantage over their rivals was inspirational.

Things such as having the odd beer, being able to venture out at night time in cold weather, eating whatever you like … these are things international cricketers take for granted. However, if someone is trying to win a Gold medal in a track-and-field or swimming event, getting a cold or not having enough carbohydrates in the body can ruin years of sweat and toil when another, fully-fit competitor prevails by a couple of hundredths of a second. The many sacrifices on display for us to observe and learn from were enough to make sure that we not only came away from Kuala Lumpur with a collection of fond memories, but also with a new-found meaning to the words 'dedication', 'commitment' and 'determination'.

What, I believe, we gave in return was an increased awareness to many of the athletes who compete strictly as individuals as to what it means to be a part of a team. The enjoyment we get out of seeing each other succeed, and the way we revel in our team atmosphere, was something of an eye-opener for many.

One evening during the Games fortnight, we extended invitations to various teams and individuals to come and spend some time with us. Our motivation was not just to meet our new comrades, but came from a desire on our part to feel a part of the bigger picture — the Australian team. To our almost disbelief, such get-togethers hadn't really occurred before, probably because there are a lot of younger athletes in the various teams and the rules regarding 'after hours' activities are consequently very strict. As it was, people from the swimming and track-and-field teams couldn't have a drink, even if they had wanted to, as to do so would mean that they were breaking their contracts.

Nevertheless, we entertained many of our new-found team-mates and while doing so we were like kids in a candy shop, picking these young champions' brains as to how they train, what motivates them, what it's like to win a medal, what's in and out of their diets, who their toughest rivals are, and so on. The most common question asked in return was, 'How come you're staying with us in the village? We thought you guys would want to stay in the usual five-star accommodation.' A close second was, 'Where are you blokes eating? You won't be in the mess hall with us, will you?'

For some reason, we were seen by many as being a poor man's 'Dream team' who wouldn't be able to survive in the 'amateur' world of the Commonwealth Games. US basketballers on million dollar salaries, we quickly explained, we are not. The myth was quickly dispelled as the beers and twisties acquired for our little get-together went down nicely.

Competing while living in the four-to-a-room accommodation was like a breath of fresh air for everyone in the cricket squad, as — believe it or not! — was the fact that we weren't earning a cent. This newly-discovered status and freedom was in a way uplifting, as we wandered, almost incognito, around the village and to the many other sporting events. However, having to live basically as bachelors threw a couple of the lads off balance, particularly the fact that you had to do your own washing and organise enough food and water so that your room was self-sustainable. The other occupants in the dormitory I was part of were Tom Moody, whose bed was about half a metre too short for him, Gavin Robertson, who became like a mother hen to all of us, and Mark Waugh, who in regard to domestic duties was, it must be said, probably our weak link.

Getting used to the fact that the usual support staff of concierge, room-service attendants and housekeeping weren't at our beck and call was a bit of a stumbling block early on. Mark quickly experienced reality as an amateur sportsperson when, upon waking up from his first night's sleep, he wandered to the front door, opened it up and then spun around and exclaimed, 'Where's the morning paper?'

Probably the best part of being at the Games was the chance to see other sporting events at close range and to support the athletes in the green and gold. We became regulars at the swimming, talking our way into the sold-out venues for which we didn't have passes. On one occasion, Gavin Robertson tried to persuade the officials that we were actually running late for our swimming events and did such a good job that, of course, we were immediately waved on through. The only problem was that we ended up among the race officials and competitors in a hallway leading out to the pool deck for the next event. A bit of ducking and weaving and fortunately we stumbled across the Aussie support crew and immediately blended in by donning the zinc cream and joining in the 'Aussie, Aussie, Aussie, Oi, Oi, Oi' chants.

Other events to fall prey to our freeloading were the men's and ladies' hockey, weightlifting, athletics, synchronised swimming and netball. We couldn't believe our luck actually being able to compete for a Gold medal as well as being right in the thick of things as a spectator.

From a cricket point of view, a pre-tournament concern about the quality of wickets proved to be unfounded, although the bowlers certainly held the upper hand on pitches that took plenty of turn. To keep the surfaces together, the groundsmen began applying wood glue to the soil, then letting the glue set, then rolling it. This proved to be a masterstroke, as the tracks stayed in one piece and played reasonably true. They certainly were to our liking, as we raced through the preliminary rounds, disposing in ruthless fashion of Canada, Antigua, New Zealand and India, before lining up against a South African side, minus a few of their big guns, in the final. But in the end they were too good, winning by four wickets.

The enjoyment factor was probably the aspect that let us down in the final. Not that we didn't have a good time on the field, rather that our lack of discipline off the ground let us down in the final analysis. By not setting ourselves for the big game, and by following our pre-game instructions abysmally once the final began, we paid the ultimate price — the squandering of a Gold medal.

To make matters worse, this may well have been a one-off opportunity, as it was strongly rumoured during the competition that cricket would be a sport that would be cut out next time the Games come around, in Manchester in 2002. The Poms must take responsibility for this tragedy. They were the team who showed no respect for these Games by refusing to come; I can't help thinking this contributed to cricket's downfall as a Games sport, if that is what occurs.

To have a Silver medal around our necks was punishment enough for us, and a reminder that next time a big match comes around, hopefully in the World Cup, we will need to be more professional. In saying this, I mean no disrespect to others who gained Silver or Bronze medals or did not even get on the dais, but Silver, quite simply, was a loss for us and not acceptable, considering the standard of our opposition.

After the closing ceremony had concluded, it felt like we had lost something but I couldn't quite put a finger on what it was. Maybe it was the fact we would never have this opportunity again. But, in reality, we have to be eternally grateful that we at least got one chance at it.

At that closing ceremony came a special moment, something that made our trip to Malaysia doubly worthwhile. The King, Kieren Perkins, walked over to us and said, 'You guys have been great for the whole team.' And then he continued …

'Your enthusiasm and energy reminded us all that we shouldn't take anything for granted, and that the Commonwealth Games are a special event.'

That they are.

Steve Waugh

*Above: After sweltering in stifling Malaysian humidity for over an hour while we waited for a replacement bus to arrive, after our original vehicle broke down, we lost hope and headed for the shade of a newly-constructed overpass. At this point in time we weren't so sure that life as an 'amateur' athlete was as exciting as we had hoped.*

*Below: Gavin Robertson in the heat of KL, T-shirt over head, icepack on the shoulder, another bottle of water in his bowling hand.*

Allsport

Steve Waugh

*Above: There's one thing that's virtually guaranteed on any tour … there will be no spare room on the bus. If we have a touring squad of 16, the hosts will provide a 15-seater, just to give us a little test. Mind you, our packing skills are pretty ordinary and neatness is not one of our strong points. Robbo (Gavin Robertson) had better hope that there are no sharp turns in the road ahead or else we might never find him under the rubble.*

Allsport

*Right: A quick acknowledgement after reaching three figures against India.*

*Opposite page, top: After putting on a 171-run partnership against India in extreme heat and humidity, Moods and I sat in the cold shower for a good 20 minutes, trying to bring our body temperatures back to normal and stop our heads exploding. After being in the middle for a couple of hours with temperatures lurking around 40°C, it's vital to look after yourself. Getting enough water in you before games is extremely important, but this was unfortunately forgotten by the Indian batsman, Amay Khurasiya, who fainted while fielding during our innings and was taken off to hospital for the night.*

*Opposite page, bottom: One of the most exciting things about being a part of the Commonwealth Games, besides having the chance to win a Gold medal, was having the opportunity to watch all the other athletes at close quarters. Getting this close to the start of the men's 100-metres heats was a real highlight, something Gavin Robertson and I will never forget.*

*Below: In the end South Africa were too good for us in the final, but we came away with a valuable lesson learned and a strong ambition to reverse the result the next time the two sides met. Here I'm shaking hands with South African captain Shaun Pollock after the Gold-medal game.*

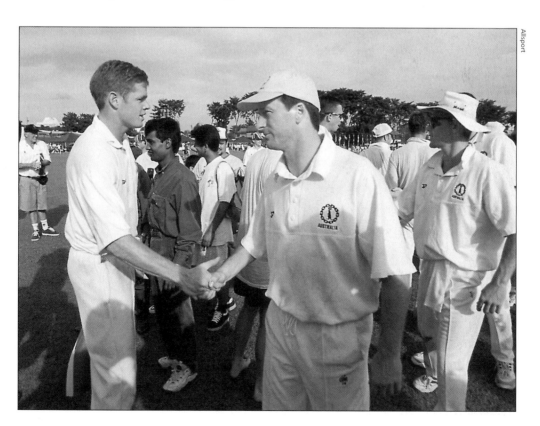

Allsport

*Above: Michael Bevan, Darren Lehmann, Michael Kasprowicz and Andy Bichel accompany Scott Volkers, swim coach for, among others, Susie O'Neill and Sam Riley, into the Commonwealth Games Main Stadium for the closing ceremony. This was the ending of two of the best weeks of our lives, and after being a part of the Aussie party in Kuala Lumpur, the boys are offering their services as cheer squad members for the Sydney Olympics, just to be part of the experience again.*

*Below: The winning Australian women's 4x100-metres track relay team, (left to right) Nova Peris-Kneebone, Sharon Cripps, Lauren Hewitt and Tania Van Heer, after their win on the final day of track and field. I'd managed to sneak in to support the Aussies.*

# PAKISTAN
# BANGLADESH–PAKISTAN

Allsport

*Title page: A sweep shot during my century in the first Test, at Rawalpindi.*

*Above: At the gateway to the mystical Khyber Pass, we were heavily flanked by both security and a gathering of locals in traditional dress.*

*Below: Just a couple of days before Mark Taylor (far left, with Ian Healy to his left) completed his historic 334 not out, the famed regiment of the Khyber Rifles took us to their training grounds in the mountains bordering Pakistan and Afghanistan. Maybe it was all the target practice that got Tubs' eye in for the Test.*

# RUNS AND RECORDS

THE TASK AHEAD was daunting — the last time an Australian team had won a Test series, or for that matter a Test match, was way back in 1959–60, when Richie Benaud's team was successful. This, to many critics, seemed an impossible assignment but to the determined squad of which I was a part it presented a challenge, a chance to turn things around and dispel a few myths. And so we went out and won the Test series, and after a brief, unsuccessful sojourn in Bangladesh we went back and dominated the one-day series, winning three out of three — a feat never before accomplished by any touring side.

The secret to our undefeated tour of Pakistan in 1998 was a shift in attitude we've adopted towards touring life on the sub-continent. In my first, disaster-laden tour to this sometimes mysterious country, back in 1988, we adopted a 'siege mentality' before we had even touched down at Karachi Airport. We feared the crowds, the umpires, the wickets, the people, the food, everything that Pakistani culture entailed. Since then, as individuals and collectively as a team, we have moved on to become a more mature, worldly and accepting group. It was a conscious effort by all to try and embrace the culture of the locals, and to actually try to enjoy ourselves. In my early touring days to India and Pakistan we used to count down the days left on tour, starting from our second day; nowadays on these tours we look forward to our next challenge.

A team touring the sub-continent can do two things — you can allow the country to tear you apart, due to homesickness, poor health, a habit of locking yourself indoors and becoming reclusive as well as a general poor attitude, or you can grow strong as a unit, helping each other through the difficult periods and getting out and seeing the place and experiencing a lifestyle that is so different to what we are used to. This squad took the latter option, making a significant move towards learning about the culture around us. We also ensured that we enjoyed ourselves, while at the same time we worked hard to achieve our objectives.

One of the highlights for the squad was travelling up the famous Khyber Pass and joining the legendary Khyber Rifles at their shooting range. A cultural show was also organised at their headquarters, involving sword juggling, dancing troupes and various other local specialty acts. On another occasion, quite a few of us ventured up to Murree, in the beautiful mountains encompassing Rawalpindi, for a day of sightseeing. It was here that we got a feel for the way the local people go about their day-to-day lives, as we strolled down back alleys and through the marketplaces.

Another marked change from previous tours was the arrival of quite a few of the players' wives for the Karachi Test. Not only was this initiative successful from our point of view, it also showed the locals that we are no longer suspicious of their country, that instead we were trying to enjoy it.

It was no coincidence that we played tremendous cricket throughout. Our victory at Rawalpindi in the first Test was a stunning achievement, especially considering that the home country produced a wicket tailored to their strengths. Playing against three spinners, two of whom were world class in Saqlain Mushtaq and Mushtaq Ahmed, was a supreme test of our technique and mental capacities — as demanding in its own way as facing a relentless barrage of four West Indian quicks. The only difference is that pace and bounce is replaced by turn and unpredictability. Michael Slater and I played as well as we've ever done in this match, while Stuart MacGill grew in status enormously, losing nothing to Shane Warne on this occasion.

Without doubt, Ian Healy's breaking of the world record for most Test dismissals by a wicketkeeper was the highlight of this Test (Wasim Akram, caught for 15 in Pakistan's second innings). Here was a fitting reward for one of Australia's all-time great cricketers and an inspiration to all of us who know him and play alongside or against him. For Colin Miller, in his debut Test, to bowl the ball that gave Heals his record was enough for him to hang his hat on for the rest of his career. Col reckons he'll be a happy man just to be in the highlight package whenever the record-breaking dismissal is replayed in years to come. The Test, however, was a bit of a personal disaster for Mark Waugh, whose New Year's resolution was to never let Glenn McGrath score more runs in an innings than he did. Unfortunately, Mark's duck was three less than our famous, but ever-improving No. 11 managed.

If we thought this was as good as it gets then we were mistaken, for Tubby pencilled his name alongside the immortal one, Sir Donald Bradman, when he climbed the summit at Peshawar by scoring a colossal 334 not out. Tubby's innings was a masterpiece of concentration and willpower, together with skill and technique, and all those who saw it will never forget it.

It was also here that Justin Langer announced himself as Australia's No. 3, with a debut century that proves that if you work hard and want something badly enough, you will eventually succeed. It was superb to see, but if umpire Steve Bucknor had adjudged him to be lbw first ball, which he could quite easily have done, Lang's career may have gone down a different path. Either someone's looking after Justin, or this was a reward for all the great things he's done for the team over the years or for the endless hours he's spent in the practice nets.

This was a Test series that saw many tremendous individual efforts, but our biggest strength was our unity — we refused to let Pakistan take control of the contest at any stage. In fact, we dominated to the point where the locals had to play superbly to avoid more than just the first Test defeat. This is something very few teams touring Pakistan can lay claim to.

Another record was created during the one-day series, when, thanks to the brilliance of Ricky Ponting and Adam Gilchrist, in the third game we chased and achieved the highest winning total ever made by a side batting second in a one-day international. I honestly believe this single victory will be the making of our limited-overs team — we now know we can reach any target and win in any conditions that confront us. To win 3-0 against a highly-rated outfit such as Pakistan was further proof that, as a team, the one-day side was starting to come together. This fact, coming after the slow start we had when the Test and one-day sides first took on their separate identities, made our performances in Pakistan extremely significant.

Making the achievements of this tour even more memorable was the nightmare everyone had to live through that was the Pakistan bribery scandal. Immediately after the first Test, Mark Taylor and Mark Waugh had to drive down to Lahore to face the judge in charge of the inquiry and to answer questions in what was supposed to be a confidential environment. This turned out to be completely the opposite, with even Salim Malik, the Pakistan player at the centre of the allegations, able to watch proceedings. The whole affair was certainly a distraction throughout the tour but, just as we overcame the fact that Shane Warne was missing from the tour due to injury, we overcame this hurdle and grew as a team.

The only downside to this tour was our short and unfortunate foray into Bangladesh for a 'mini World Cup'. At 4.30am on the morning after the last Test, we boarded a flight — well not quite, it was delayed four hours — only to see the Pakistani team in business class while we were squeezed in down the back of the plane in economy. After finally arriving late in the day, we snuck in a training session and a charity coaching clinic before bedding down in a pretty knackered state. Worse was to follow the next day, as Sachin Tendulkar smashed his third successive one-day hundred against us, in another masterful display, before we gallantly fell 44 runs short.

It's never good sportsmanship to cry foul, but our lack of preparation here directly led to our downfall. It felt like we had been dudded. But life goes on and hopefully we can all still learn from the mistakes we made.

Steve

*Above: The moment all the hard work paid off! Lang sweeps his way to his maiden Test hundred, with an anxious Mark Taylor backing up, at Peshawar.*

*Below: Mark Taylor at Peshawar, during the innings of his life.*

Allsport

*Tubby gets to 300, only the second Australian captain to reach that score in a Test (after Bob Simpson's 311 at Old Trafford in 1964). Soon after he went past Bradman's 304, then Bob Cowper's 307 (the previous highest by an Australian left-hander in a Test match), then Simmo. Only Bradman's mystical 334 was left among Australian landmarks …*

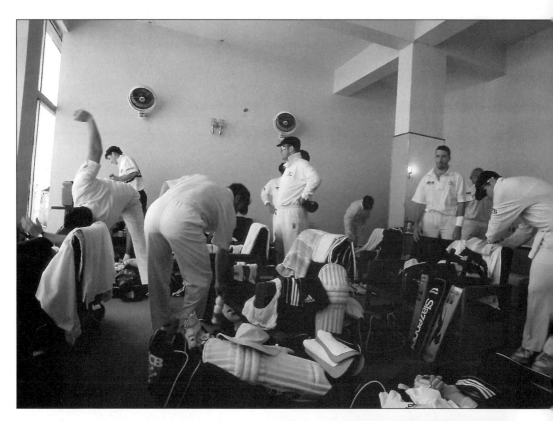

Pics: Steve Waugh

*Above: This photograph was taken moments before taking the field in Rawalpindi, where the opportunity was in front of us to become the first Australian XI to win a Test in Pakistan for 39 years. The man in the middle is the boss, Mark Taylor, while the quicks limber up nearby among the other lads who are also making their final preparations.*

*Right: This little fellow came straight from Fantasy Island to take up the concierge job at the most prestigious hotel in Murree, high up in the hills outside Rawalpindi. I couldn't resist lining Pigeon up next to him — and I'm sure Glenn wouldn't mind having a bowl against him either!*

*There were very few options to get your clothes washed and laundered in the Commonwealth Games village, unless you wanted to wait a couple of hours in the hotel basement for a washing machine to become available. The best option was the bathtub and a cake of soap. I'm not sure how successful the outcome was, but it certainly reminded us of our newly discovered 'amateur' status.*

*Left: Brad Young has just taken a hat-trick in our Commonwealth Games semi-final against New Zealand.*

*Below: This was supposed to be the bus that would take us to a pre-match training session, but after the driver set out down the motorway like Michael Schumacher we ended up broken down and camped by the roadside for a couple of hours. The only saving grace was the fact we had a Sherrin footy in our midst and many a 'speckie' was taken before our new bus finally arrived to get us where we needed to go.*

*Right: This is cricket's version of the Aussie 'support crew', in among the swimming team's usual band of loyal team-mates and fans. We'd tried to look as patriotic as we could in our green and gold zinc.*

*Below: The Australians in KL, after the medals presentation.*

Pics: Steve Waugh

*Above: The boys are checking out an anti-aircraft gun used only once during a skirmish between Pakistan and Afghanistan. The setting is the famous Khyber Pass, with our guide being a member of the legendary Khyber Rifles Regiment.*

*Below: After our quarter-final loss to India in Dhaka, the team had a two-day break before heading back to Pakistan for the one-dayers. During this time, coach Geoff Marsh and I journeyed to Mumbai in India to accept, on behalf of the Australian team, a trophy for being the international team of the year. While I was in Mumbai, I again took the time to take in the extraordinary Mahalakshmi Temple, where there are invariably crowds, the sound of gongs, and worshippers offering prayers to Mahalakshmi, the Goddess of Wealth and Plenty.*

Pics: Allsport

*Michael Slater (above left) reaches another Test hundred, this one at Rawalpindi during a 198-run partnership he shared with me for the fourth wicket. Stuey MacGill (above right) at Rawalpindi, spinning through the much-vaunted Pakistani batting line-up.*

*Below: Darren Lehmann batted superbly at Rawalpindi, missing out on his first Test century by just two runs.*

*Above: Ian Healy catches Wasim Akram off Colin Miller, to break Rod Marsh's world record for the most dismissals by a keeper in Test cricket.*

*Below: A moment for contemplation as Heals reflects on his newly-acquired status as a world-record holder. On the wall to Ian's left is our team mission statement — 'The Aussie Way' — which provides us with a checklist and reference point as to how we want to play, train and carry ourselves on and off the field. Its contents come from input from all players and, as such, each team member must sign off on it and be responsible for ensuring it is implemented.*

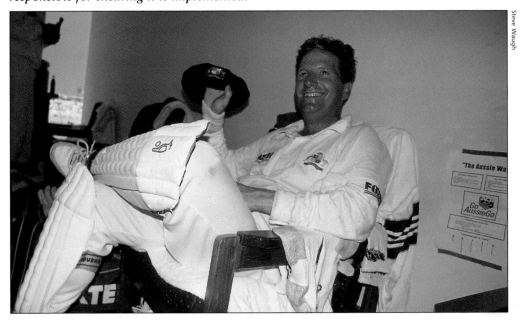

*Above: Bartering with the main man at the chicken markets. The choice of product can be alive or freshly killed, with every possible piece of chook being made available to buy. Less encouragingly, the flies are thrown in free of charge.*

*Below: You certainly wouldn't want to live with this guy, as his specialty is selling garlic. As you can see, he is totally surrounded by the stuff and, one assumes, consumed by the fragrance.*

No Regrets **39**

*Above: During an attempted shopping excursion to the local mall in Dhaka we were bombarded by fanatical locals, who had rarely seen cricketers in the flesh. The result, inevitably, was chaos, and the shopping trip became a short-lived affair. Once on board our bus, I decided to empty one of my lolly bags and as you can see the kids had a great time trying to catch them, while the local policeman didn't seem to mind either.*

*Left: This is one of my all-time favourite photos. A Pakistani carpet salesman in Murree cradles his granddaughter. Both sets of eyes are mesmerising, especially the grandfather's. He looks as if he's experienced plenty, while the little girl's eyes glimmer with the sweet innocence of youth.*

# The Waugh Diaries

OCTOBER 22, 1998 — KARACHI

In my opinion, if you can make 300 in the backyard you must be a good player, so to make 300 in a Test match makes you very special.

Mark Taylor's effort in Peshawar was phenomenal. To concentrate for such an extended period of time was fantastic, but I thought the aggressive manner in which he batted made the knock even better. He was back to his very best form of 1989, always looking for runs, always taking to the bowlers with a very straight bat.

I remember that the West Indian Courtney Walsh once wore a T-shirt which carried the message 'Form is Temporary, Class is Permanent'. Tubby's performance reminded me of that line.

Obviously, I was disappointed to get only 1 in our first innings. I might have been unlucky to be given out, but I probably wasn't as switched on as I should have been when I finally arrived in the middle. Sometimes it's tougher to go out to bat when the score's 3-20 than it is when it's 3-500. Instead of having adrenalin pumping through my system, I was half asleep and paid the price.

I knew, like everyone, that the pitch in Peshawar was very flat – Mark was probably right when he suggested the only thing missing was a white line down the middle. Even so, the Test might have been winnable if we'd bowled as well on the third day, when we took just two wickets, as we did on the fourth, when we took seven.

Now we find ourselves in Karachi, where Australia has never won a Test and the conditions are completely different.

We have really enjoyed ourselves on this tour, and are well prepared and very positive about this Test match. Off the field, in many ways touring life here is akin to that on a tour of South Africa or the UK. The hotel here is excellent, the restaurants (such as the Chinese downstairs and the Italian across the road) are very good and we've got cable TV in the rooms. And five of us have our partners with us, too, the first time this has occurred in the sub-continent. Cricket-wise, we're determined to break the long run of Aussie series defeats in Pakistan that stretches back almost 40 years, and to prove to future generations of Australian Test cricketers that we can win over here.

We don't want to have to leave that responsibility to someone else. We want to be the guys who turned it around ...

Pics: Steve Waugh

*Above: A weary but triumphant Mark Taylor speaks to the press at the end of the day's play, after equalling Sir Donald Bradman's record score of 334. As you can see, he had lost quite a bit of weight due to fluid loss, but it was his courage and determination that were an inspiration to all who witnessed the extraordinary innings.*

*Below: While a typically laidback Colin Miller chills out on the window ledge, Stuart MacGill handles the media during the Karachi Test. Behind the scrum, our long-time scorer Mike Walsh is tucking into another bowl of his beloved ice-cream.*

Pics: Steve Waugh

*Above: With one-day cricket having taken a stranglehold on the public's attention on the sub-continent, the longer version of the game now struggles to attract the spectators. During this match in Karachi, the opening game of our tour, the police presence certainly outnumbered the paying public. Fortunately for the players, the security boys had the target firmly in their sights (on scoreboard).*

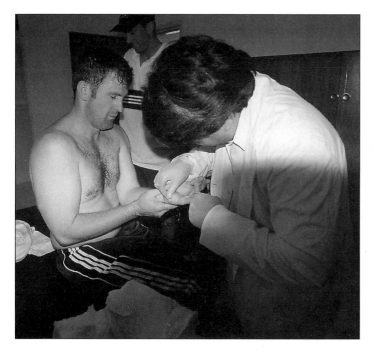

*Left: Not many people know that Tubby had to have a couple of stitches inserted into his hand two days before his famous innings, after he slipped while trying to jump a fence at the venue of our previous tour match in Rawalpindi. Now Tubs is a man notoriously gun shy of needles, and my presence certainly didn't help his frame of mind when the doctor reached for his bag full of surgical implements.*

No Regrets **43**

# The Waugh Diaries

## NOVEMBER 11, 1998 — LAHORE

One thing we have been stressing over the past few months, as the one-day team has grown as a unit, has been that if we want to be considered one of the best teams in the game, then we need to be able to win the matches we're expected to. This, more than anything else, is what made our big win yesterday, in the third and final match of the series, so enjoyable.

We'd already won the first two encounters, in a style that made us solid favourites for game three. But in the past, in such situations, we have lacked a bit of intensity and often fallen short. Not yesterday, though, and this has left us with a feeling of great satisfaction. While we realise there are still some very important dates ahead, to get where we are now represents the culmination of a lot of hard work and planning.

If what we've been told is right, this was the first time Pakistan have ever been swept in a one-day series at home. So, how did we go about breaking the world record for the highest winning score by a team batting second in a one-day international? The truth is that there was no set plan, as our approach, however the game is going, is governed by the principle that each member of the squad is smart enough to adjust to any situation and think for himself. But between innings, we spoke of the need to get a good start, and to keep wickets in hand for a final assault. With the outfield outrageously quick and the Pakistanis not being the greatest fielding team of all-time, we felt confident about getting 80 or 90 in the last 10 overs, provided we had wickets in hand. As it turned out, Adam Gilchrist and Ricky Ponting were superb and, by the time the 41st over arrived, the required run rate was down below six runs an over. With seven wickets still in hand, we felt we were just about over the line by this point.

After yesterday's game, the Aussie journalists who have travelled with the side presented us with a 'trophy' they'd purchased on the streets of Lahore. This was their compensation for the fact that there was no official trophy awarded to the winning team. How can I describe it? Let's just say it was a local antique, suitably inscribed. After this ceremony, we headed to the local McDonald's, one of the few in Pakistan and probably the biggest, and then it was on to Lahore's 'American Club' for a few drinks. For this part of the journey we were without Michael Kasprowicz and Andrew Symonds, who are dashing back to Cairns in North Queensland to take on the touring Englishmen. For the rest of us, it's a morning flight to Karachi, then a night departure back to Australia, via New Delhi and Kuala Lumpur ...

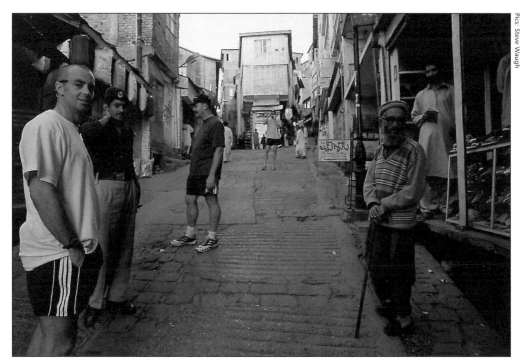

*Above: Colin Miller (far left) in an alleyway in Murree. But who is the lanky fast bowler with the camera, a little bit further up the road?*

*Below: The lads are running out of patience as they wait for our official team photo to be taken, at the fort in Peshawar.*

*Above: The food markets of Karachi provided Gavin Robertson and me with hours of entertainment. While the operations of the various vendors and their methods of displaying their products were an eye-opener, I certainly couldn't see myself making any purchases from the lads selling these chickens. Unfortunately, they don't have the benefit of refrigeration or air conditioning, and their produce was smothered in flies. To fully appreciate the overall scene, I'd need to somehow include the pungent smell, which was overwhelming.*

*Below: Families gather on a street kerb in Karachi to sell their nuts and spices. Even though they lead a difficult existence, their smiles are infectious.*

Pics: Steve Waugh

*Above: Closer to me is a Muslim woman, dressed traditionally in a manner that reveals nothing of her features but her hands. Behind her a colourfully decorated, packed-to-capacity bus, adorned with chains and trinkets, is heading towards Peshawar. They reckon the best spot to sit on a bus such as this is on the top — where there's more room, fresh air and the option to jump off if the bus looks like running into misfortune.*

*Below: The village butcher displaying his fresh cuts of meat, which I'm sure are very popular with the locals. But the lack of hygiene to me was a bit of a worry.*

*Left: Despair in Dhaka, as the little Indian maestro, Sachin Tendulkar (foreground), slams another superb one-day hundred against Australia.*

*Below: I took this photograph as we made our way into the stadium in Dhaka. It was the gigantic load of 44-gallon drums the poor chap was carrying that caught my eye, so I popped my head out and got lucky with this image.*

# THE ASHES
## 1998–99

*Title page: With the man-of-the-series trophy, after the fifth Test, in Sydney.*

*Above: Before the opening Test of the series, in Brisbane, our captain Mark Taylor was honoured on reaching 100-Test match appearances.*

*Below: The 187-run sixth-wicket partnership I shared with the redoubtable Ian Healy in our first innings of the first Test was one of the most enjoyable stands of my entire Test career, given that my partner was one of my closest allies from many a tough on-field battle and one of my best off-field friends. This also represented a significant landmark for me: my first hundred in an Ashes Test in Australia.*

# CRICKET'S OLDEST BATTLE

THERE'S NOTHING LIKE a contest to fire up the imagination of the average Aussie. For an Australian cricketer, the adrenalin rush thinking about lining up against the oldest enemy of all is one of life's great joys. And although we seem to have earned a vice-like grip on the little, tattered, old urn of late, each time we line up against England we expect a tough battle. It was no different in 1998-99, especially because, on paper, their squad looked to be talented and experienced.

When Ian Healy and I joined forces on day one of the first Test, at the Gabba in Brisbane, it seemed our expectations were going to be realised. The score was 5-178, and we were being asked to defy an upbeat and spirited Pommie unit. However, by the end of the day we had swung the pendulum back in our favour (the score at stumps was 5-246), but it could have been so different had Nasser Hussain and Angus Fraser not dropped straightforward chances. Even more disastrous for England had been Alan Mullally's earlier, unnecessary intervention of a shy at the stumps from Alec Stewart that seemed sure to hit the target and would have found me well short of my ground.

Scoring a hundred each in the same Test innings was a special moment for Heals and me. We're good mates, who have been through many ups and downs; as players we're pretty close to being soulmates. Personally, it was my first ton in Australia against England and, as such, represented the fulfilment of a goal I was determined to achieve during the series.

Our overall performance as a team during this Test was very impressive, until rain and 'earth-ending' skies full of hail thwarted our hopes late on day five, just as Stuart MacGill was torturing their middle and late-order with another Warne-like display. This guy is a super talent, capable of turning the ball as much as anyone and possessing an impressive array of deliveries. Sometimes you take things for granted — which maybe we do at times while Warney, a gift to anyone who watches cricket, is in our midst. Then, along comes Stuart MacGill, who could possibly be another great leggie in the same era.

With our confidence high but the series still level, we made our way to Perth. We were minus MacGill, who had been 'dropped' (or more accurately rested), to make way for the extra quick to bowl on the world's best fast-bowling-friendly deck at the WACA. Many critics said it was a poor selection, but in fact I believe it was a smart one — Stuey now had a chance to play a four-day game for New South Wales and keep his form intact, rather than sit on the 12th-man's bench and possibly lose his momentum.

As it was, he wouldn't have been required much anyway, as we steamrolled the English batting line-up, who in this Test didn't seem prepared to get in behind the line of the ball and do the hard yards. Consequently, our pace trio of Jason Gillespie, Glenn McGrath and Damien Fleming had the time of their lives, destroying the opposition in less than three days and setting up the series exactly as we wanted it to take shape.

For England, though, it wasn't all bad news because young quick bowler Alex Tudor made an impressive debut, showing enough pace and venom to let everyone know he's going to be a force to be reckoned with.

One big bonus of such a comprehensive win was that it allowed all the squad to go home for a couple of days, to get to know their families again and spend some quality time together.

Adelaide for me is always a highlight. I regard the Adelaide Oval as equal to Lord's — the best place in the world to play cricket. It has its beautiful, old, wooden scoreboard on the grassy hill, and is surrounded by peaceful yet striking cathedrals. The ground also has the world's premier playing surface, but perhaps its greatest feature is the low-key, unobtrusive stands that blend into each other and give the place a warm, friendly feel.

This calmness was much needed after the controversy involving bookies, the providing of information and the alleged involvement of Shane Warne and Mark Waugh broke two days before the Test was due to start.

This was, of course, disruptive to the Australian team, and highly embarrassing and damaging to our team-mates, who had inadvertently been implicated and confused with the real villains — players who had taken money to influence the outcome of games.

As expected, all the boys rallied around Mark and Shane and gave them our 100 per cent support, in the knowledge that it was a mistake made with no intent to hurt the team or cricket.

It was a relief to finally get on with the game, after the media frenzy of the previous few days, and it was here that Justin Langer put his hand up with a beautifully crafted innings of 179 not out. In doing so, he reminded everyone of how David Boon used to go about his business as Australia's No. 3 with distinction for so many years.

And, proving to many that he is a mentally tough player capable of overcoming the most difficult obstacles, Mark Waugh played with great poise and courage to score 51 not out in our second dig, which helped set up a decisive victory and ensured we'd come away from the series with the Ashes for a record-breaking sixth time in a row. It was a great feeling to be a part of all six of these victories, as had Heals and Tubby.

In accordance with our team motto, we play hard, but when we achieve something worthwhile we like to enjoy ourselves. In my view, this is why we are the best side at the moment, because we enjoy our cricket and successes more than any other team. As one member of a successful unit, these are the times you always remember with great fondness.

With the Ashes retained but pride on the line, we travelled to Melbourne for the Boxing Day Test. As always, this is a time when the families travel with the players to celebrate Christmas as a family. To see my daughter Rosie's face on Christmas morning, as she opened her presents, made me realise how important family is. It also underlined all the sacrifices that are made by our families in order for us to pursue our careers, a debt we can probably never repay.

This Test match, from a spectator's point of view, was a beauty, seesawing back and forth until its conclusion four-and-a-half hours into the last session on day four. It was a match that provided me with every possible emotion, ranging from ecstasy and elation to pain and grief.

Scoring 122 not out in the first dig and putting on 88 with Stuart MacGill for the ninth wicket was a wonderful experience. I find batting with the tail to be a real challenge but highly enjoyable, as you can visibly see your partners grow in confidence and stature with the increase in responsibility that I like to give them.

I believe this policy of taking each run as it comes and therefore giving my late-order colleagues the strike if the chance to take a single or a three comes about has worked pretty well in the past. This is an assertion backed up by my involvement in 19 partnerships of more than 50 runs with tail-end batsmen during my Test-match career.

Occasionally, this policy can backfire and unfortunately for the team and me it did in the second innings of this Test, when I took a single off the first ball of a Darren Gough over with 14 runs needed to win and two wickets in hand. If I had my time again, maybe I would have tried to take a single off the fourth ball, but on my mind was the fact that Darren Gough had bowled 11 overs straight, and hadn't taken a wicket all day.

Stuey had just come off a 43 in the first innings and the whole English team had been on the field for well over four hours during this extended session. But, sure enough, Goughie went straight through MacGill's defence before cleaning up Glenn McGrath to claim a famous win and leave me to answer quite a few in the media who wanted to know why I'd taken that run.

To be fair to these observers, that is their job and they have to call it as they see it, and I was given plenty of kudos for my first innings exploits. I just had to wear their criticism and get on with life.

Some even suggested I was selfish. I'd like to think that my show of faith in my fellow players could have been seen in a better light, but I also know you can't please everyone.

It was then on to Sydney and a chance for England to square the series. However, in our minds there was only one result that was ever going to happen. Our great asset over the last decade or so has been our ability to play well under pressure and to win the big games. England, on the other hand, tend to fail when the stakes are at their highest. And they know that we know that.

In the end, we achieved a comprehensive victory, with Stuey MacGill continuing his amazing progress by claiming 12 wickets — all taken with the master at the other end in his comeback Test match. Warney managed to take two himself in a promising return.

Mark Waugh and I have relatively poor records on the SCG, our home ground, so it was gratifying for us to put on a big stand on the opening day. Mark scored an impressive ton, while the older brother claimed a somewhat unwanted world record — that of finishing in the 90s (out or not out) for a record ninth time in Test cricket. In our second innings, Michael Slater put in a sensational performance, scoring 123 out of 184, which put the game out of our opponents' reach. But it could have been so different had the third umpire ruled against him after a direct hit was obscured by the English fieldsmen. It seemed pretty obvious that Slats had been struggling to make his ground.

The Test was also notable for Darren Gough's hat-trick, late in our first innings, and Tubby's world record 157th Test-match catch, in what turned out to be his last Test match.

In my opinion, the final scoreline for the series of 3-1 was a fair indication of our dominance — something which would continue in the one-day World Series competition.

*Damien Fleming (left) in Perth, in the middle of his first five-wicket haul in Test cricket.*

Allsport

*Left: Darren Gough, of England and Yorkshire, in the nets in Adelaide. No-one could dispute Goughie's intensity and desire, as he bravely led the English pace attack throughout the Australian summer.*

*Below: After every Test-match win or one-day series victory the media have five minutes to get the footage and photos they need. Invariably, this involves a celebratory spraying of beer and champagne all over them and their gear. Here, after the third Test, we thought it was time to point the lens in the other direction, and Errol Alcott grabbed my camera and caught them in action.*

*Perhaps it was the fact we'd retained the Ashes in Adelaide that made hometown boy Jason Gillespie (far right) so animated.*

Steve Waugh

# The Waugh Diaries

**DECEMBER 17, 1998 — ADELAIDE**

It's a bit strange, the Ashes having been retained this early in the series, even before we head to the Melbourne and Sydney Cricket Grounds. But for us, there is still much work to be completed as we see winning the series against England as being our most important goal. The job is only half done.

We realise we're approaching a few records, in terms of winning successive Ashes series. The record is seven, won by England between 1884 and 1890 (after they squared a four-Test rubber in 1882-83), but this involved only one five-Test series, plus three three-Test series, one two-Test series and one series that featured just a single Test. In 1934, Australia regained the Ashes that had been lost in the Bodyline series, and then held them for five more series (1936-37, 1938, 1946-47, 1948 and 1950-51), but one of those, 1938, was drawn. Australia matched that six-series feat by winning the Ashes in 1958-59 and retaining them for five more series, but they won only two of those five, drawing in 1962-63, 1965-66 and 1968.

So if we can win a sixth straight series we'll become the first Australian side to do so. At present, much of the talk is about England's lack of success, but I reckon 10 or 20 years from now our wins, especially if we can make it six (or even more), will be recognised for the big achievement they represent.

I think the critics might have been a bit unfair in their assessment of the Englishmen. Sure, they've had their problems, but I think their bowling has been very good most of the time and Nasser Hussain and Mark Ramprakash have batted well. But they've rarely had decent starts, which has put a heap of pressure on the lower order and the tail, and they have dropped too many catches to keep up the pressure on us.

One other thing that has annoyed me is the suggestion from some quarters that Ashes cricket has lost its importance. I still think it's the No. 1 battle for Australian cricketers, though I will concede that other confrontations — such as Australia v the West Indies and Australia v South Africa — have grown in stature in recent decades. The Ashes is not the only big one any more, as it was 50 years ago, but it still matters. And it always will.

We had a decent party after winning in Adelaide, but it wasn't too big. For many of us, we were restricted by the fact we had commitments the next morning, but we were also slowed by the knowledge that any BIG celebrations can't happen unless we win the series ...

*Above: Our much-anticipated trip to the Khyber Pass took days to organise, and we needed the blessing of the local tribesmen who control the area before we were allowed to travel along the windy, single lane road up to the famous landmark. This guard is on the lookout on our behalf and seems to have everything under control.*

*Below: The gypsy street kids of Karachi are searching for an unsuspecting tourist, on whom they can ply their trade. These kids' innocent, sweet looks are a trap, and apparently many victims fall for their wicked skills.*

No Regrets **57**

*Above: There is always a great deal of conjecture when we check out the wicket, especially the day before the match, as was the case here in Karachi, venue of the third Test. This was quite obviously a flat, dry wicket more suited to the slower bowlers.*

*Below: The groundstaff at Peshawar, making sure their cricket pitch is as perfect as it can be.*

*Mark Taylor, in total control on his way to equalling The Don.*

*Above: The view from the Australian dressing room as Tubs reaches 300.*

*Below: At stumps we formed a guard of honour to welcome our exhausted captain into the record books.*

*Above: Seeing sights like these makes you realise how lucky you are to live in a great country like Australia. From the comfort of our quality hotel in Dhaka this was the view that confronted us — a ramshackle collection of huts, engulfed by a foul-looking, smelly expanse of water. But even in these terrible living conditions the spirit and character of the children is the same as anywhere else in the world.*

*Below: The moment the tourists realised that they had saved the first Test, in Brisbane. The storm that arrived minutes after this photo was taken was so ferocious we were lucky to get out of the ground unharmed. Sports psychologist Sandy Gordon (left) and coach Geoff Marsh (centre) survey the angry scene*

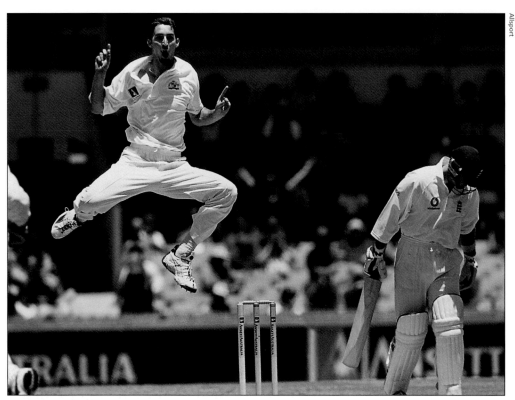

*Above: Jason Gillespie, highly animated on his return to Test cricket, celebrates capturing the wicket of Darren Gough.*

*Below: Retaining the Ashes was special for the team, but even more so for Heals, Tubs and me, as we became the first guys to ever be a part of six consecutive Ashes triumphs.*

*Above: Michael Slater, as exuberant and innovative as ever, slashes another four during his second-innings century in Adelaide.*

*Below: To reach my century in Melbourne I had to resurrect my long-abandoned hook shot from out of the bottom of my kitbag. Fortunately, I got the ball safely behind square for the needed runs, to complete one of my most rewarding Test hundreds. The support I received from the MCG crowd made the moment even sweeter.*

Two views of the world-famous Sydney Harbour Bridge.

Above: Members of the Australian one-day squad on the forecourt of the Sydney Opera House at a sponsor's launch for our World Cup campaign.

Left: Earlier in the season, the New Year's Test in Sydney had given me the opportunity to bring my family into the team motel, which overlooks the best harbour in the world and the best-known landmark of Australia.

Pics: Steve Waugh

*Justin Langer celebrates his century in Adelaide, a brave unbeaten knock that finally silenced those who doubted his game at the highest level.*

Pics: Steve Waugh

*Above: As part of the family Christmas lunch at the Hilton Hotel in Melbourne, clowns, choirs, magicians and face painters came in to entertain the kids. Both Rosie Waugh (right) and Laura Healy seem to think it's a pretty good idea.*

*Left: This is now just about the normal Waugh family Christmas. Melbourne's Boxing Day Test has taken me away from home for Christmas on 13 of the last 14 years, and my wife Lynette and I now bring our own Christmas tree on tour, along with a cricket bag full of presents, to ensure this is still a special occasion, especially for our daughter, Rosie.*

# The Waugh Diaries

**JANUARY 5, 1999 — SYDNEY**

I've played in a lot of Test matches, but I'm pretty sure that I've never played in better back-to-back Tests than the last two. Melbourne was a fantastic game of cricket, and as I write this diary entry, on the morning of the final day of the series, it seems Sydney might well develop into something just as exciting.

If you forget the result — which is very, very hard to do — the fourth Test was brilliant, and a real triumph for the game of cricket. Personally, I was delighted to bat as well as I did. My hundred in the first dig was, technically, just about the best innings I've played in Test cricket. Until Stuart MacGill came to the wicket, I had hardly played-and-missed at all, and then the period up to my hundred became almost a 'one-day' situation. It was exciting to get to three figures this way — a bit of improvisation, even a hook or two — and then to continue on with Stuey with what we thought at the time would be a Test-winning partnership. I've rarely felt as pumped after a big innings as I did after this one, for which I need to thank Stuey, who batted very well and very sensibly, and the MCG crowd, whose support was loud and fantastic.

The emotions after our second innings were obviously totally different, although the cricket was even more dramatic. When Justin Langer and Mark Waugh were together, and doing it easily at 2-103, we even thought we might win by eight wickets. But then Mark Ramprakash took a brilliant catch at square leg to dismiss Lang, Graeme Hick took another good one in the slips to get rid of Junior, and Dean Headley and Darren Gough did the rest.

Our decision to take the extra half hour wasn't a difficult one. We needed 14 to win, with three wickets in hand. The light, despite what some commentators have said, was fine. Sure, the Ponsford Stand's shadows had extended onto the pitch, but the light was even and extremely playable. The Englishmen had already been in the field for more than three hours, were clearly weary and clearly wanted to go off. And Matthew Nicholson was batting well. However, Headley and Gough raised one more remarkable effort, and in no time at all won a great victory for England.

I'm aware there has been much comment on my decision to expose Stuart MacGill to Darren Gough when we needed 13 to win on the final evening. I can see both sides of the argument, but all I can say is that, in the same situation, I would do the same again. No-one was complaining when Stuey and I were adding 88 for the ninth wicket in the first innings.

So to Sydney, where I was again very happy with my form … until I got a

Continued next page

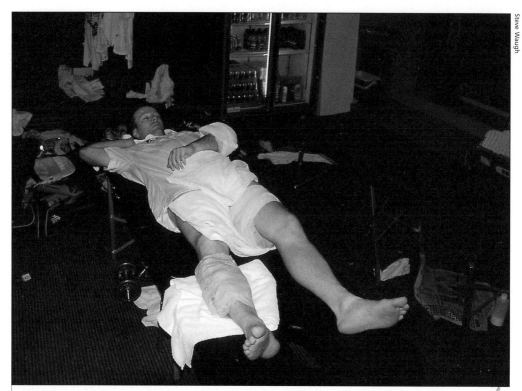

*Above: I've been caught by my own camera, lying in the dressing room after scoring 122 not out in Melbourne. The ice packs on my right leg are to counter the cramps that plagued me late in the innings, the ones on my left hamstring for a slight strain, while my left elbow is the one that Darren Gough had targeted earlier and then honed in on.*

Continued from previous page

pretty good ball from Peter Such which knocked me over for 96. I enjoyed batting with brother Mark, who made a superb century — one of his best — but was a little less thrilled with the knowledge that I've now scored more 90s (out and not out) than any other batsman in Test history. This, I guess, is a record that's both bad and good. I'd love to have turned them all into centuries, but 90 in a Test match is still a fair effort, especially on a pitch such as the one we're playing on at the SCG.

It was tricky on day one; now it's very tough. It's a bit crumbly and turning a long, long way. If you play defensively to the spinners, it's only a matter of time before you'll fall; much better to be aggressive, as the Englishmen were yesterday afternoon, and hope for a bit of luck. This was how Michael Slater went about things during his brilliant century, one of the great Test innings. He demonstrated how much he has worked on his technique against the spinners, and played a heroic lone hand, which we hope will prove to be a series-winning effort ...

Pics: Allsport

*Above: With shadows ever lengthening and the clock well past 7pm, England win the fourth Test by 12 runs, after Stuart MacGill and Glenn McGrath failed to handle Darren Gough while I was stuck at the bowler's end. I copped a mountain of criticism after this result, much of which I thought was unfair, especially the rather sinister suggestions that I was more concerned with protecting my own wicket than sheltering my late-order team-mates.*

*Right: The highly exciting and often excitable Michael Slater reaches three figures in Sydney, during one of the best Test-match hundreds it has been my pleasure to see. He was finally out for 123. Incredibly, the next highest score in our innings was Mark Waugh's 24, after that, 8.*

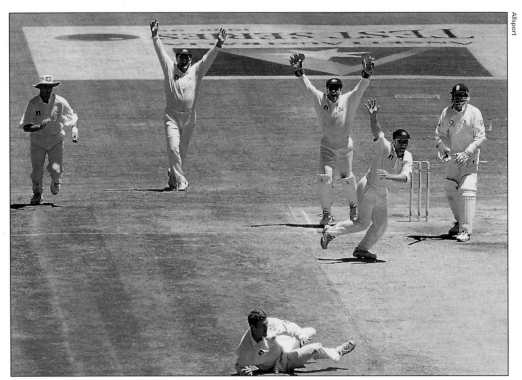

*Above: The end of the series, as Stuey MacGill takes a spectacular caught and bowled from England No. 11 Peter Such to end the tourists' second innings in Sydney. The ball had deflected off the leg of Michael Slater, fielding close in on the off-side.*

*Below: In my view, the gathering of the two teams at game's end remains highly important. Here at the SCG, Yorkshire team-mates Darren Gough (centre) and Darren Lehmann (to Gough's left) are catching up, as are one-time Essex comrades Mark Waugh (in cap), Nasser Hussain (to Mark's right) and Peter Such (sitting at right).*

# A Change at the Helm

Tubby tried to contact me on the morning he made his retirement announcement. Unfortunately, I wasn't at home that morning, but he left a message.

Obviously he wanted to speak to me in person, which I appreciated. But I was almost certain, even before I heard his message, as to what was going to happen. Once we heard he had called that press conference, I think most people had the feeling he was going to retire — you don't call a press conference to announce you're going to keep playing.

It's strange feeling. We expected him to retire, but when he did … it was so final. Tubby Taylor won't be touring with the Australian side any more. This is going to be a big change.

He seemed pretty happy with the decision, as calm and relaxed as you could be. This, I'm sure, is a good thing. I've seen a number of players in a very emotional state as they go out of the game, as if they're not really sure what they're going to do with the rest of their lives. Mark Taylor, on the other hand, seems to have things pretty well planned.

Is there one stand-out example of his ability as a captain? That's a tough call, there are so many. I think the gutsiest call he made as captain came when he won the toss before the Third Test, at Manchester, in 1997 and batted on a green wicket. Remember, we were one-nil down in the series at that stage. A lot of people thought he was mad.

I think if you had asked 99 per cent of the people there — players, commentators, groundstaff and spectators — they would have bowled first.

As it turned out, it was a great decision because we got through a tough first day's batting, scoring quite a few runs in the process, and then the pitch began to turn sharply. Our spinners took over and we ended up winning the Test to square the series.

The first time I thought Mark would make a captain was back in the early days, when we played together as teenagers and when we'd go away as NSW players to play in the Toohey's Country Cup.

We often had input into the way we approached those games, and it was soon clear that Mark had good ideas about how we should go about things.

We actually captained some of those country teams occasionally. Mark showed a liking for that role and also demonstrated that he had a good command of tactics and the need to look after his players.

I've always reckoned you can tell at an early age whether someone's going to be a good captain, and it was pretty obvious, even at 18 or 19, that Mark was going to a good one.

The thing I think the Australian team is going to miss most by Mark Taylor not being there is his calmness on the field and the steadiness and confidence he gave the side, as a player and captain. Everything always seemed to be in control. In this sense, he was like a good umpire — you don't notice the good umps very much; they just do their job.

Good captains are the same. They just go about their business without any fuss, and then the game's over and you've won and you're thinking, 'Why did we win so easily?'

You've won because the captain managed the game, looked after it, and didn't let anything faze him or his team.

That was Tubby Taylor. Always calm, always in control.

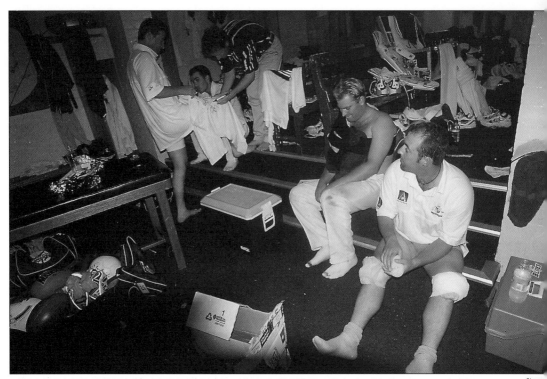

Steve

*Above: On this day during the fifth Test, the home dressing room at the SCG looks more like a casualty ward in a hospital, with Warney and 'Boof' Lehmann applying the career-enhancing ice packs. After each day during a long season most players end up with the ice being applied to a problem area, just to keep the inflammation and soreness under control. Mark Waugh, Justin Langer and Ian Healy are in background.*

*Below: Because of injury, I was unable to play in any more than two of the World Series matches that followed the Ashes series. However the boys seemed to cope reasonably well without me, decisively winning the final over England in two straight games.*

Allsport

# The Waugh Diaries

FEBRUARY 12, 1999 — MELBOURNE

When I was first picked for Australia, back in late 1985, the music guru and keen sports fan, Molly Meldrum, founder and inspiration of the old Countdown shows on the ABC and now seen on Hey, Hey, it's Saturday, came up to me and said, 'Son, one day you'll captain Australia. When you do, I'll give you my Don Bradman bat.'

As I parried the media's stream of questions during my first press conference as Australian captain, I couldn't help thinking, 'Molly, it's time to pay up!'

Of course, this is a very busy period for me, with a countless rush of interviews and meetings, shaking hands and photo opportunities, meetings and interviews. But I'm not complaining, not one bit. Instead, I'm sailing though with a satisfied smile. I'm truly honoured to be given the chance to captain my country, and eagerly looking forward to the challenges ahead.

Through my career I've played with and against a number of captains, some excellent and inspiring, some okay, some not so good. When I do the job, I'll try to use things I've picked up from the winning captains, from the leadership of men such as Allan Border and Mark Taylor and also from my NSW skippers, Dirk Wellham and Geoff Lawson, who were very aggressive and very successful.

It's interesting thinking of my situation now, compared to the state of the Australian teams when AB and then Tubby took over. Of course, Allan got the job in ordinary circumstances, when the team was struggling following the retirement of Lillee, Marsh and Greg Chappell and the West Indies were at the very height of their powers. The way AB and coach Bob Simpson toughened the side and eventually restored Australia towards the top of the cricket tree left an indelible mark on me.

In many ways, because of Allan's efforts, Tubby's task was easier than AB's, although the side was still in something of a state of transition in 1994. Allan, Dean Jones and Merv Hughes had just departed, others such as Terry Alderman, Geoff Marsh and Bruce Reid were also not too long gone and David Boon and Craig McDermott were approaching the end of the careers. That the Aussie team under Mark hardly missed a beat, continued to play aggressive cricket and kept winning despite these great players' farewells, is in my view one of his finest achievements. Another thing I'll be taking on board is the way new guys in the team were encouraged to play their natural games, to play for Australia in the same way that had got them in the team in the first place. I think this has been a critical factor in the continued run of success we've had in recent years.

Right now, there is so much to do. Looking back on the past few days, since Mark retired, there was preparation and planning I would like to have begun, but there was no way I was going to pre-empt the Board's decision on the captaincy. So now I want to catch up on our opponents, to try to develop a strategy for the Tests ahead. I need to talk to Geoff Marsh and I want to chase up video footage from the West Indies' recent series in South Africa, and also locate some footage of our recent Test-match adventures against the Windies. I'm sure there'll be some interesting lessons to be learned from the former, and some inspirational moments to be remembered from the latter.

And I also want to savour the moment. Even though my childhood dreams were pretty ambitious, I never envisaged that this Bankstown boy would play 100 Tests for Australia, score the runs I've done, take the wickets, meet so many classy people, see so much of the world. Now, can you believe it, I'm captain of Australia. To be honest, I don't really want to think too much about the history and the tradition and the great names who have held this position in the past. To borrow a cliché, which for me is very, very appropriate at the moment, I know I've got to keep my feet on the ground. Tonight, I'll get together with a few close friends and have a small celebration. Tomorrow, I know already, will involve a series of media appointments. Somehow, by Wednesday I'll be packed and on a plane for the Caribbean.

It's going to be a frantic few days, but I can't wait.

# THE
# WEST INDIES

*Title page: So many different emotions are going through my head, all of them positive, as I proudly lead the Australian Test team onto Queen's Park Oval at Port of Spain in Trinidad to begin my first Test as Australian captain.*

*Above: The hamstring strain that had kept me out of the World Series one-day competition in Australia was still a slight concern when our Caribbean tour began, so as a precaution I didn't play in the first match of the tour, in Antigua. But I was certainly fit enough to act as the drinks waiter for the guys during this break in play.*

*Below: Adam Dale has just claimed a West Indies Board XI scalp, one of seven he took (for 24) as our opponents were decimated for just 55 in their first innings.*

# A CARIBBEAN ADVENTURE

MUCH WAS EXPECTED of the Australian squad when we touched down in Antigua to take on a supposedly ailing West Indian team. The Windies were coming off a 5-0 Test series drubbing during their recent disastrous tour of South Africa, and this result was seen by many as a forerunner to what lay ahead for Brian Lara's team at the hands of the No. 1 ranked Test-playing nation. What had been overlooked in this equation was the fact that the West Indies had only lost one series at home in the previous 26 years ... and that had been our historic 2-1 victory on our last foray to the Caribbean back in 1995.

Adding an extra dimension to this series was the news that Lara's captaincy was under close examination from the West Indies selectors, so much so that he was only appointed for the first two Tests. He was also instructed to communicate more with his players and toe the line in regard to discipline. From my point of view, it was a huge honour to lead my country in a Test for the first time, and something of a relief that all the focus was on Brian and not myself in the lead-up to the first Test.

And what a Test it was for us, as we bowled the West Indies out for a record low score of 51 in their second innings. Both Jason Gillespie and Glenn McGrath were magnificent, and if not for two lots of four overthrows and a steepling bouncer that went for four byes, the total may well have been around 40!

The overall winning margin was emphatic, but had it not been for a career-best century by Michael Slater in our second innings, and some gritty, grafting work by Matthew Elliot and Greg Blewett in our first innings, the result may have been very different. The turning point was no doubt short leg Justin Langer's run out of Brian Lara in their first innings, just when it appeared they had gained the ascendancy. From this wicket on the Windies batsmen failed to adhere to the basics and put up very little fight — much to the annoyance of the local public and media.

But such is the pride and tradition cricket commands in the West Indies, we should have known that they would come charging back at us, which is exactly what they did in Kingston, Jamaica. After winning the toss and electing to bat, I was making small talk with Brian Lara as we strode back to our dressing rooms to let our teams know what was happening. I'll never forget the last words from my adversary before he went his way ...

'Well, this will be the last five days of this for me.'

Of course, he couldn't have been further from the truth. After we were bowled out for 256 with around an hour to play, we had the Windies on the ropes again at 4-37 at close on day one and sensed another major collapse was on the cards. But day two of this match would be one of those days that turns a Test match, even a Test series, on its head, and for us was one we immediately wanted to wipe from the memory banks.

My century in our first innings brought for me a mixture of satisfaction and relief, because, after scoring just 14 and 0 in my debut Test match as Australian skipper, quotes had already begun to surface along the lines of 'the captaincy always affects the captain's form'. However, Jamaica holds special memories for me, especially after my 200 here in the deciding Test of the 1995 tour. On that occasion I had to rely on Glenn McGrath to reach the double-hundred milestone, after he joined me with my score on 195. This time I was on 95 when Pigeon arrived at the crease. Both times he got me across the line and both times I then got out on him — not surprisingly he reckons I've cost him plenty of runs, and owe him big time.

Day two. Six hours of toil and we had absolutely nothing to show for it. After nightwatchman Pedro Collins retired hurt at 4-56, Lara and Jimmy Adams batted the whole day without ever really looking to be in any trouble. Our double leg-spin attack had trouble coping with the left-handers, but our options were somewhat limited as the day wore on. Lara's batting was the stuff of a genius, doing virtually what he wanted in the last hour. Upon reaching 200 he ran off the field. It seemed he feared for his safety, perhaps because of the many threats he had endured leading up to this match. He had been targeted in these parts as the reason why West Indies cricket had gone downhill.

However, it was our cricket that went downhill on day three, after we got off to a promising start by bowling out the Windies in the morning session. McGrath was again magnificent, claiming another five-wicket haul, while Gillespie's growing reputation was enhanced still further. But our second-innings batting collapse was feeble, and unfortunately it was not the first time that we'd played poorly in this type of situation. It must be said that if we have a weakness as a team it must be our second-innings batting. To lose by 10 wickets was a real wake-up call and a signal for us to get down to some serious work.

It's now history that the Barbados Test will go down as one of the greatest Tests, if not the greatest Test, ever played. There were some excellent individual perform-ances, such as Punter and I putting on 281. Ricky batted with maturity and an even temperament associated with the champions of the game, while my 199 was as worthy of a dig as I've ever played — I'll never forget the effort involved in trying to survive one of the great spells from Ambrose on the opening morning. To fall one short of the double-century milestone was a little frustrating, but it seems I'm destined to collect these nice but unwanted stats.

Again, we had the Windies on the ropes at 6-98 chasing 490, but some spirited batting by Sherwin Campbell, Ridley Jacobs, Nehemiah Perry and Curtly Ambrose got the Windies to 329 and back in the game.

And again, we collapsed in the second innings. The lion-hearted Courtney Walsh took five wickets, but it was the run out of Michael Slater that proved decisive. With hindsight, this was probably the turning point of the game. With the home side chasing 308 to win, the odds looked heavily in our favour, but Lara had other ideas and played the knock of his life, guiding and cajoling the tailenders as he steered his team to a one-wicket victory after all seemed lost. His 153 not out was a masterpiece, especially considering that they needed 60 runs to win when the eighth wicket fell. At this point Lara had only Ambrose and Walsh left to bat.

When the winning four was struck, absolute delirium broke out around the ground and throughout the Caribbean.

For us, McGrath was once more inspirational, bowling 77 overs and taking nine wickets for the match, while the courage of Gillespie in dragging himself off the bench, where he was treating a severe back ailment, to bowl like a champion was legendary stuff.

This loss was such a let-down. Then the Windies celebrated in a motorcade through the streets to the airport, which was hard to take. To try to come back in the final Test would be our greatest test of willpower and self-belief ...

To overcome these disappointments something special was needed and it came from Justin Langer and Colin Miller. Before all this, though, there was the huge issue of Shane Warne being dropped, which I must say was one of the toughest decisions I have made or will ever have to make. But the gut feeling of Swamp and myself was that we had to do it. Lang's hundred in the second innings was a courageous one and proved once again that hard work does pay off, while Col's 43 off 38 balls in the first innings was significant — not only for its value to the team's cause but also because he twice hooked Ambrose over the fence. One of his hits sailed out of the ground, to the absolute astonishment of the non-believing Ambrose.

Lara's 100 off 84 balls in this Test was a joy to watch for the spectators, but in reality it was an innings in which he rode his luck at times. But at other times his genius shone brightly once again. Still, in the end it was not enough to prevent us completing a decisive 176-run victory. To come back and level the series was a fine achievement, and a show of our pride and resilience, but overall we had all expected better things. Some hard lessons must be learned from this series.

The one-day competition that followed turned out to be a thriller, full of exciting cricket and outstanding individual efforts, but disturbing field invasions and interruptions marred the matches.

Game five in Guyana turned into a farce. A crowd invasion of massive proportions saw all six stumps missing after Warney and I tried desperately to scramble a match-tying third run off the last ball of the game. As I raced towards the bowling end, the Windies' Keith Arthurton was trying to find a stump to dislodge the bails and win the game. For me, the 72 not out I finished this game with was a pretty good effort, but I was unhappy not to have scored the six runs needed from the last over for victory off the part-time spin of Arthurton.

The final decision for a tie was made by the ICC-appointed match referee, the former England opening batsman, Raman Subba Row. And it was one that led to Aussie team manager Steve Bernard and I copping physical threats from angry spectators who trailed us back to the dressing rooms after the inquiry. The game's conclusion left everyone with a sour taste in their mouths, but the circumstances that led to it emphasised again the complete lack of concern shown by officials towards player safety in these circumstances. Not for the first time, I commented that it was only a matter of time before a 'Monica Seles-type' scenario occurred.

We didn't have to wait long for this prediction to nearly come true. An accidental collision between Brendon Julian and local hero Sherwin Campbell in Barbados led to the batsman falling over and being run out. This was the signal for anarchy to take over, with bottles covering the entire outfield and chants for the batsman to be reinstated singing out amid a chorus of booing against us. We had no option but to leave the field and it was here that a bottle, thrown by a prominent local identity from the top deck of a stand, missed my head by centimetres.

The rest of the story, unfortunately, can't be told, as I currently have a defamation writ against me in regard to comments I made regarding the security of the grounds. This writ was served on me in the days immediately following the match. We remained in Barbados for another six days, to rest and recuperate before the World Cup, so that by the time we boarded our plane, bound for England's Gatwick Airport, we were ready and eager for action.

Overall, this was one of the most physically and mentally gruelling tours of my career. However, it took me on a huge learning curve and for that I'll be forever grateful.

*Lunch on the deceptively serene banks of the Potaro River — only seconds away is a thunderous 220-metre drop to a foam-filled gorge below.*

*Two press conferences ... two captains! Above: Mark Taylor announces he won't be leading the Australian team to the West Indies. Below: The 40th Australian Test captain is introduced to the media.*

*Above: Colin 'Funky' Miller in Antigua, showing the locals a thing or two about the niceties of beach cricket.*

*Below: Immediately in front of me was a hilltop cemetery, and in the distance was a luxury liner cruising into the beautiful Caribbean port of Grenada, scene of the second one-day international of the tour.*

*Above: This is not exactly the most picturesque setting for a cricket field. In fact, it is a ground owned by an oil refinery company located about an hour outside of Port of Spain, the capital of Trinidad. Slats is seen practising here after we wrapped up our tour game well inside the allotted time.*

*Below: No, it's not Elvis. Or John Travolta. It's Funky Miller enjoying life to the full as he mingles with the Aussie supporters after our first Test triumph in Trinidad. Team manager Steve Bernard and scorer Mike Walsh are along enjoying that winning feeling.*

Just looking at these pictures makes me nervous, especially with Pigeon standing behind me (left) and a 226-metre (741 feet) drop in front. The view would have been nice if I could have relaxed and taken it in, but this was difficult with the big quick's hand grabbing hold of me and rocking me to and fro ...

Pics: Steve Waugh

The awe-inspiring Kaieteur Falls, near the border of Guyana, Brazil and Venezuela, feature the largest single-drop waterfall in the world. Deep in the rainforest, surrounded by lush tropical growth and a wide variety of animal and bird species, the falls are outrageously dramatic. There is no guard-rail at the top, and you can feel yourself being drawn over the edge. Of course, Pigeon wanted to see it from the most dangerous vantage point possible — much to the horror of our tour guide (pictured below with Glenn and me), a man who has spent most of his life in the Amazon basin.

Our guide admitted to almost suffering a heart attack when he saw where we were headed — we wanted the very best view we could find. He explained later that no-one had ever risked edging to that position before. When we had safely returned from the precipice and he had regained his composure, our guide enthralled us with tales of seven-metre long anacondas, but, thankfully, we didn't stumble across any here. What we had found, though, was a truly wonderful work of nature.

*Above: This is probably my favourite photo of the last 12 months. For me, the striking feature is the joy on the faces of these schoolgirls as they skip down the street in front of this mural of famous Jamaicans. Their happiness is in complete contrast to the dilapidated state of the buildings and the grey, sombre mood of their environment.*

*Below: Experiencing life in Trench Town, Jamaica, was an enormous learning curve for we Australian cricketers and the locals. The mother with the Don King hairstyle was more than happy to pose for a photo, but her son had just seen a white man for the first time in his short life and didn't like what he saw.*

Pics: Steve Waugh

*For both Brian Lara and myself, the third Test in Barbados was excellent from a run-scoring point of view, but only Lara (right), whose unbeaten masterpiece on the final day won the match for the home side, was in any mood to celebrate after the game.*

*Above: Given the way our one-day international in Guyana finished, there's a certain irony in the advertising hoarding. But most cricket lovers in the Caribbean are friendly people, who love their sport, the atmosphere at the big matches and the people who play the game.*

*Below: Here I'm in earnest discussion with match referee Raman Subba Row, as Aussie coach Geoff Marsh looks on, during the crowd trouble in Bridgetown.*

*Right: Who is this Australian cricketer? Actually, it's Michael Slater, taking a quick breather while exploring the seaworld off the coast of Trinidad.*

Pics: Steve Waugh

*This is life in the comfort, or rather very squeezy fit, of the team's minibus.*

# Team Meeting — the Captain's Notes

## Antigua, opening of 1999 West Indies tour

It's an honour to be captain — well done Warney, as vice-captain, and all the players selected. You can judge a squad by the players left out — such as Darren Lehmann and Michael Kasprowicz. In my view, all 15 players in the squad are in line for a Test spot. This doesn't mean success is guaranteed — this tour is a great challenge, and a great opportunity.

1. No one else has beaten the West Indies at home for 30 years (they play on pride and egos).
2. Everyone expects us to win — they lost in South Africa 5-0, but that doesn't count.

I also expect us to win. We're the No. 1 side in the world. Why we are No. 1?

1. We love playing for Australia — pride in our performance — little things (baggy green, tattoos, team song).
2. We enjoy each other's success, and celebrate a win.
3. We work harder than other teams, practise better, simulate game conditions in practice — our training sessions are quality and intense.
4. We usually win the big moments in games.
5. We enjoy pressure situations.
6. We stick to the basics the best — such as line and length, partnerships, catching.
7. We have the most talent and the best techniques.

But we do have some weaknesses. Every time in recent years that we have lost a series or a match, it has been due to one or both of two things ...

1. Complacency — such as in the final Test of England '97, at The Oval (we were too cocky).
2. Poor preparation — such as in New Delhi (when we didn't do the hard work).

Now is the time to switch on — start preparing for the first Test. Each player should be prepared to play and to do whatever they need to be ready, such as throw downs, fitness work, etc.

I see the first Test as being crucial to the whole tour ...

• First morning — first day — will set the tone

It won't be easy — Ambrose, Walsh, Lara and Hooper are all capable of being match winners — but if we stick to our game plan and stay hungry, we will succeed.

Allsport

*Above: Not a bad start! My first Test as captain has just ended in a sensational victory for Australia.*

*Below: There's nothing better than a winning dressing room after a Test match, even more so when you've just bowled the West Indies out for a record low of 51. Here the chief destroyers, McGrath and Gillespie (or as we call them — 'Lloyd Christmas' and 'Harry Dunne' from Dumb and Dumber) take it easy with Funky (Colin Miller), Bic (Andy Bichel) and Magilla (Stuey MacGill) before the celebrations move into top gear.*

Steve Waugh

*Above: We've all heard that line ... when a batsman's smashing the bowlers around the commentators will inevitably say, 'He's on fire!' Consequently, after Pigeon made his invaluable 39 in the Trinidad Test, he quickly called for a couple of ice cubes to cool down his smoking blade, while Slats caught the moment.*

*Right: The Windies have just been bowled out for 51, to the delight of dual destroyers McGrath (wearing cap, back to camera) and Gillespie.*

# The Waugh Diaries

MARCH 9, 1999 — PORT OF SPAIN

At the toss, my first as Test captain, I thought the wicket looked pretty good. With two quality spinners in our side (given Shane's class and Stuart's lead-up performance, how could we possibly have left either of them out?), and a strong expectation that the pitch would deteriorate, there was never any doubt that I would bat first if the coin came up heads. And so it proved.

There was the odd butterfly in the pit of my stomach on that first morning, at least until after the toss and we were on the field. But from that point I was pretty relaxed, with a great faith in the guys and in the game plan we'd been developing over the previous fortnight. Our intention was to grind them down, and take advantage of the fact we had included four genuine wicket-takers. The pitch, we knew, was very different to the lethal greentop of four years ago; this time we were playing on a pitch that was slow and a bit two-paced from the start.

Four days later, and I feel very lucky and very proud to be leading this team. The highlights for me were the extraordinary bowling of McGrath and Gillespie on the fourth day, and the great batting performance of Michael Slater in our second innings, and from our lower order in both innings.

It's not every day you bowl out a Test side for 51, especially on their home turf. We're all very happy and looking forward to a good time tonight.

It was a great feeling to be out there in the middle during the carnage of the Windies' second dig, watching our quicks perform so superbly. In fact, the Windies could have been out for anything — even 30 or 40 — so well did Glenn and Dizzy bowl. This was one of those days when we bowled the right line and length, got a few lbws and held our catches. Everything went perfectly — a thoroughly professional performance.

I admit I was confident we'd win the Test, but not like this. However, once we got two or three quick wickets, I started to think we could get them for a small total. Ironically, I'm convinced that four or five of their lower-order batsmen are very susceptible to our leggies, but the spinners weren't even needed today. Still, we must remember we're only one up in a four-Test series — we can't take too much out of this success. I've been around long enough to know that one win doesn't make a series.

Although our final margin today was emphatic, in fact we slowly wore them down over the four days. On day one we did really well to get close to 200, so tricky was the pitch and so slow was the outfield. Some slick work in the field on day two — especially Justin Langer's effort to run out Brian Lara — and good, persistent bowling kept them down to 167, a lead for us of 102. And then Slats produced his masterpiece ...

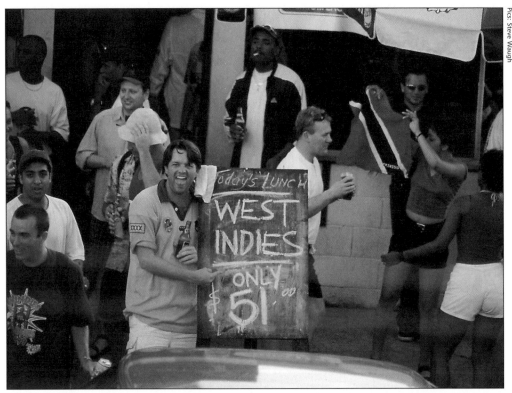

*Above: The sports bar where the Aussie supporters congregated after each day's play in Port of Spain was directly across from our dressing room window. And bowling the West Indies out for a record low total of 51 was enough for one of our ardent supporters to sabotage the board on which the bar promoted its lunch menu.*

*Below: Matthew Elliott tries to relax before the second Test match, in Jamaica, using his new form of meditation, possibly with a prayer or two thrown in.*

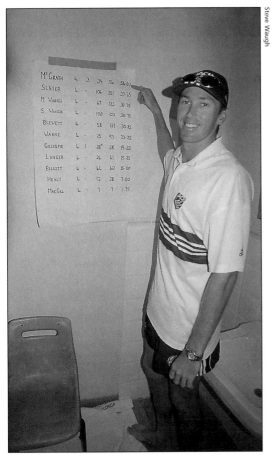

| | | | | | |
|---|---|---|---|---|---|
| McGrath | L | 3 | 39 | 54 | 54.00 |
| Slater | L | - | 106 | 151 | 37.75 |
| M. Waugh | L | - | 67 | 123 | 30.75 |
| S. Waugh | L | - | 100 | 123 | 30.75 |
| Blewett | L | - | 58 | 121 | 30.25 |
| Warne | L | - | 25 | 93 | 23.25 |
| Gillespie | L | 1 | 28* | 58 | 19.33 |
| Langer | L | - | 21 | 61 | 15.25 |
| Elliott | L | - | 44 | 60 | 15.00 |
| Healy | L | - | 12 | 28 | 7.00 |
| MacGill | L | - | 7 | 7 | 1.75 |

*Left:* I'd be happy to talk about Glenn McGrath's bowling all day, but I'd rather steer clear of his batting — every interviewer I met during the first two Tests wanted to know when Pigeon was going to be moved up to No. 10! Someone told me that after the first Test Glenn now had more Test runs than wickets, which I knew would please him. We've always maintained that 20 for Glenn is like a century for a more accomplished batsman, so he nearly made a double ton in the first Test (when he hit 39 not out), to go with his first 10-wicket haul in Test cricket.

However, we were still not convinced he'd done enough to go any higher in the batting order than one after Stuart MacGill. But by the end of the second Test, Glenn did sit atop the Aussie Test batting averages. As you can see, he was pretty happy about this fact.

*Below:* Brian Lara at his exquisite best, during his fantastic 153 not out that won the Windies the third Test.

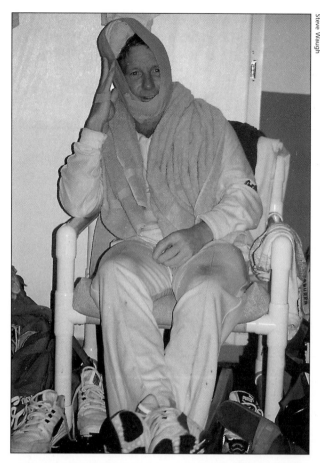

*Left: One of the dangers of the wicketkeeper's trade is copping the odd stray bat from an over-extended pull or sweep shot when you're standing up to the spinners. Here Heals applies some ice to a wound suffered in the opening game of the West Indies tour, from the bat of the free-swinging Jamaican, Wavell Hinds. I'm sure it wasn't amusing for Heals but the rest of the lads saw the funny side of his newfound headgear.*

*Below: A quick game of touch in Antigua, with Heals, a former junior rugby league halfback of some repute, trying to break clear of the despairing clutches of Andy Bichel (right).*

# The Waugh Diaries

MARCH 17, 1999 — KINGSTON

In the end, our defeat in Kingston in the second Test came down to the simple fact that we didn't bat well enough. I'm sure the pitch would have turned for Shane and Stuart on the fourth and fifth days, if only we'd given ourselves enough runs. But we were about 100 short in the first innings, and then sold ourselves well short when we went back in.

Perhaps if we'd been able to turn a couple of half chances into wickets, things might have been different, too. They would, after all, have been around 6-120 if a couple of tough catches had been held around lunchtime on the second day. But credit to the Windies, especially Brian Lara and Jimmy Adams, who both batted very well. And their bowling was excellent, too.

Brian Lara played a magnificent innings — perhaps not quite as good as his famous 277 against us in Sydney in early 1993, but still superb. Then, on the third morning, our bowlers got us back into the game. The pitch was good — once you'd settled in there was a real opportunity to make a big score — but we batted poorly. Not enough value was placed on each wicket.

People have talked about a gigantic turnaround between what happened here and what occurred in Trinidad. But, in truth, neither Test was as one-sided as the scorebooks suggest. In Port-of-Spain, the Windies' low fourth-innings total masked the fact that for most of the first three days it was a tough, tense match which both sides could have won. And here, after day one, most pundits had us well in front. I reckon there are still some interesting and exciting stories to be told in this Test series …

I'm confident, though, that we can come through, so long as out batting improves. The Aussie bowling, especially Glenn McGrath and Jason Gillespie, continues to shine. As for Lara, he is clearly the key to their hopes, but he can nick them like everyone else. The battle between the Windies skipper and McGrath should be one of the highlights of the final two Tests. And we mustn't forget they have some other matchwinners in their ranks, not least their two great opening bowlers.

Then again, we must also not forget that we can play this game very well, too. At the top of our game, we know we have the artillery to win the most difficult Test match.

Courtney Walsh and Curtly Ambrose remain extremely difficult bowlers to counter, always at you, always threatening. Perhaps they've lost a metre in pace, but all they've learned over the past few years in Test cricket adds up to them still being as good as anyone around ...

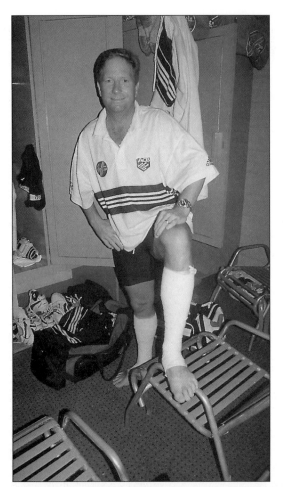

*Left: Here's Heals showing off his bound-up calf muscles before the start of play in the Barbados Test. He was in doubt right up to the night before the game because of slight strains in both legs and, as a precaution, Adam Gilchrist, due to arrive anyway for the one-day series that would follow the Test, had flown in early as cover in case Heals didn't respond to the physio's treatment.*

*Below: A moment of immense satisfaction, tinged with a hint of regret — I've just been dismissed one short of a double century. It was an innings that I'll look back on with much fondness, as I'd come in at 3-36 against a rampaging Walsh and Ambrose on the first morning of the third Test, but survived to add 108 for the fourth wicket with Justin Langer and then 281 with Ricky Ponting for the fifth.*

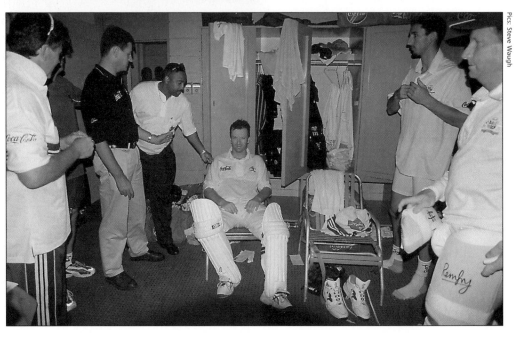

*My first Test-match coin toss.*

# The Waugh Diaries

**MARCH 22, 1999 — ST JOHN'S**

O'Neil Gordon 'Collie' Smith might have been one of the finest batsmen in West Indies cricket history. His third game for Jamaica was against Ian Johnson's 1955 Australians, and he scored 169 — against an attack that included such names as Miller, Lindwall, Johnston, Davidson and Benaud. A few days later, Collie began his Test career in the first Test against the Aussies and made 44 and 104. On the Windies' 1957 tour of England he batted at No. 6 in a batting order that also included Sobers, Worrell, Walcott, Kanhai and Weekes, and scored more runs in the Test series than any of his comrades, including 161 in the first Test, at Edgbaston, and 168 in the third, at Trent Bridge.

In the fifth Test against India in 1958-59, Collie scored his fourth Test century, an even 100, and took eight wickets for the match, bowling off breaks. A three-Test series against Pakistan followed, and then Collie headed to the north of England, to play for Burnley in the Lancashire League. This, tragically, was to be the last cricket Collie Smith ever played.

In September, Collie Smith was killed, dead as a result of injuries received in a car crash, which also involved his great friend Gary Sobers. Collie was 25, and had been asleep in the back seat, Sobers at the wheel, the fast bowler Tom Dewdney in the passenger seat, when they tried to avoid a truck travelling in the opposite direction. Collie Smith's body was taken back to Jamaica, where an estimated 60,000 people attended his funeral.

Collie Smith had come from a world of poverty, but early in his life he had come under the influence of a social worker, cricket enthusiast and Methodist minister by the name of Hugh Sherlock. The Rev. Sherlock had developed a club for youngsters from the ghetto on the western side of Kingston, which he called 'Boys' Town', and Collie became a student there. Boys' Town became famous throughout Jamaica and beyond for the manner in which it was able to rescue hundreds of young boys from the crime and misery that was ghetto life. Today, Collie Smith remains the most notable man to emerge from Boys' Town; but for his death he may well have been a West Indian captain, a forerunner to Clive Lloyd, Viv Richards, Richie Richardson and Brian Lara.

The environment around Boys' Town today is different, even more brutal and devastating than it was when Collie Smith was a boy. Last Thursday, a friend of Steve Bernard had arranged an invitation for Steve, Mike Walsh, Justin Langer and me to visit the Boys' Town Cricket Club, which is situated in a place called Trench Town, in Kingston, Jamaica. Consequently, I was able to see first-hand just what the school and its surrounding districts looks like today and learn of the work Boys' Town continues doing for the unlucky and underprivileged children of the poorest parts of town.

A large photo of Collie Smith on the wall of the Assembly Hall pays tribute to their greatest hero, as does his name upon the Honour Board. We learned of other Boys' Town 'graduates', such as those who had made it all the way into the Jamaican national soccer team.

However, the lead story, the thing that has dominated everything around Boys' Town in recent times, is the violence. Without our escorts there is little chance we would have got out of there alive — this is an area that in the 1990s has been engulfed by guns and gang warfare, death and bloody violence.

For months before a recent ceasefire was called it was unsafe to set foot on the Boys' Town playing fields unless you were meant to be there; one violent gang occupied one side, another callous group the other. The cricket and soccer fields were just about a 'no-go' zone, especially for the uninvited or uninitiated. If the gang leaders wanted play stopped, then play stopped. Instead of barracking, you heard gunfire. We learned that around 900 people were killed in the area in 1997 alone, when the fighting was at its peak.

Things are slightly better now, though you'd be mad to pop in uninvited, especially if you're white. But as invited guests, we were warmly greeted, and got to see first hand the history of the place — including a peek at one of the first homes of the late Bob Marley — as well as the insatiable grins on the faces of the kids from the school and the keen cricket minds of the locals, youngsters and street-wise adults alike. We learned we were not the first Australian cricketers to visit the place — an old photograph showed Bill Johnston, the great Victorian left-arm swing, seam and spin bowler, being presented with a memento in 1955. This time, though, they wanted to know more about the current stars, Warney, Lara and Glenn McGrath. Lang's digital camera had them fascinated, and before we departed we'd been presented with Boys' Town T-shirts and many, many extraordinary memories.

Despite the gang warfare and the injustices that violence creates, I know now that Boys' Town still offers an education and a chance for the underprivileged kids of the ghetto, the Collie Smiths of today. We were privileged to get the chance to see that Rev Sherlock's great vision and charity is still hard at work. Inevitably, I compared these kids' lot to the struggles of the children of Udayan in Calcutta, the home for the children of leprosy sufferers that I support. The unsettling climate and the poverty may be inspired by different forces, but the smiles on the children's faces — and their optimism and ability to make the most of the chances their shelter provides — are very similar.

*Above: The image of the much-revered Bob Marley adorns many buildings in the country of his birth, Jamaica. This street mural was in Trench Town, a district in the backstreets of Kingston, where he once lived and featured in the lyrics of his songs.*

*Below: Lang in Trench Town, looking for a high five from one of the local heavies.*

Pics: Steve Waugh

*Above: It's amazing how happy these kids are, considering what few material possessions they have. The building behind was actually Bob Marley's house in his formative years — and in the future hopefully a tourist attraction that will provide much-needed income for the community.*

*Right: This was the only success to come our way during a four-hour trip off the coast of Trinidad — a 20lb Wahoo landed by an excited Glenn McGrath. Not in picture is the victim of the world's worst ever case of sea sickness. Matthew Elliott was probably responsible for the capture of this fish, thanks to his endless supply of berley during the voyage.*

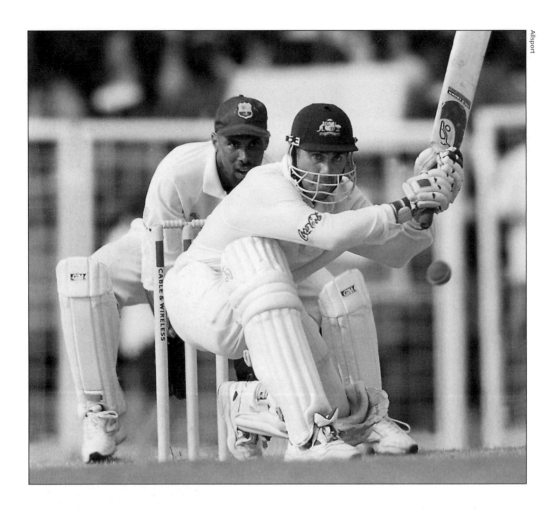

*Before the Test series began, I sat down on a one-to-one basis with all the squad members and as part of the exercise I gave them a one-pager outlining how I hoped they'd approach the upcoming matches. This is what I put to Justin Langer ...*

- Enjoy the challenge — this is where the hard work pays off.
- This is your chance to test yourself against the best.
- Give the team the solidarity it needs — play your own game
- Know your game plan; eg: hooking or not, attaching the spinners, etc.
- Intimidate them — use good body language
- Keep up the great attitude, looking after your mates and team
- Make the No. 3 position yours.
- Don't waste good form — make them pay, same as Adelaide, stay hungry and focused
- Energy in the field — make them feel your presence at short leg.

Be ruthless!

*The photograph above was taken during Lang's disciplined century in Antigua. The manner in which he grew in style and confidence through the four Tests against Courtney Walsh and Curtly Ambrose — clearly enjoying the challenge! — was one of the features of the series.*

*Right: It was no wonder Brian Lara was celebrating with a cigar — he'd just won a Test that no one thought the West Indies could win. And that victory had come about largely because of his astounding double century. Behind Lara and Greg Blewett (right), these stairs led to the players' dining room, which was located directly outside the dressing rooms.*

Steve Waugh

# Team Meeting — the Captain's Notes

## St Vincent, before the one-day series

- Welcome and well done — especially Pistol, Moods and Flemo, back from injury.
- Excellent squad — I couldn't have been happier with the 15 chosen.
- This is the start of a chance of a lifetime — the pinnacle of a one-day cricketer's career — seven games in the Windies, then on to the World Cup.
- Our goal is, of course, to win this series (four games out of seven) but ultimately we will be judged on the World Cup.
- I look back to our win in 1987 and why we did so well …
  We were hungry for success.
  We did it for each other.
  We worked harder than any other team.
  We had the best team spirit.
  We did the 'one per cent' things — sacrifice, contribute to the team on and off the field.
  Winning became a habit — which is what happened to us last year
  Watching from the sidelines, you could see that we wanted it more — our team looked composed and players looked confident under pressure. That comes about by knowing your own game, keeping it simple and following the team plans.
- Keep the pressure on these guys and they'll falter.
  RESPECT …
   Respect yourself first
   Respect from each other

*Right: Darren Lehmann in Grenada, where he hit a superb 110 from just 92 balls and with Michael Bevan established a new fifth-wicket partnership record for Australia in international one-day cricket.*

*Below: An interesting view of the new cricket stadium in Grenada, scene of the second match of our one-day series in the Caribbean. This was the first international match played at the ground, and the first played in this beautiful little part of the world since 1984. The local Prime Minister, a cricket addict, had declared the day a public holiday for the island's 94,000 inhabitants. There's no doubt that this is definitely a potential Test match venue, although it probably wasn't quite ready for big cricket when we played there. However, that didn't stop 16,000 people turning up to enjoy the day out.*

Pics: Allsport

Allsport

*Below: The moment of truth as the match referee, both captains and managers, plus Sir Clyde Walcott, Sir Garfield Sobers and a security representative discuss the possible options after we were forced from the field when the crowd reacted violently to the controversial dismissal of Sherwin Campbell (left) during the final one-day international of our Caribbean tour. In the end, it was decided that there was only one option — to reinstate Campbell — as our safety couldn't be guaranteed if we decided not to go back on. The side then debated what we should do, with quite a few having reservations, especially the guys who would have been required to field on the boundary. In the end we all agreed that, for the sake of cricket, we should go back on.*

Steve Waugh

Pics: Steve waugh

*This was the scene in our dressing room, moments after being forced from the field in Barbados when the crowd rioted.*

*Left: During our time off at the conclusion of the West Indies tour, the lads who didn't have their partners with them went out and hired mopeds for the week. Miraculously, considering the daredevil, precision moves we were making, there were no major accidents. Here we can be seen puffing our chests out on one of Barbados' famous beaches. Unfortunately, with the exception of Brendon Julian I reckon our futures as potential subjects on a 'Men of Cricket' calendar look pretty bleak. Left to right: Shane Lee, Shane Warne, Damien Martyn, BJ and myself.*

# THE WORLD CUP

Steve Waugh

# MAY 2  Gatwick Airport to Cardiff

THE FLIGHT FROM BARBADOS took seven and a half hours, and as usual with air travel there was no sleep for me. Instead, I watched a few movies, never missed a meal, and tried to make the time pass as quickly as possible. But in all honesty it was a little boring counting down the minutes to touchdown.

When we arrived at Gatwick Airport, at around 8.30am, we were taken to an airport hotel for what developed into a surprisingly tame press conference. I found myself in front of 20 to 30 journalists, with vice-captain Shane Warne, manager Steve Bernard and coach Geoff Marsh by my side. Inevitably, most of the questions pertained to the World Cup, but there were also questions about the Police Commissioner's defamation writ. Unfortunately, I couldn't comment on that particular issue, as I am legally bound not to say anything. It seemed, though, that the legal happenings in Barbados were of secondary concern to the news hounds, whose principal interest lay in the future of Warney's international career. How had he reacted to being left out of the fourth Test match in the Windies? Was his shoulder okay? Would he have a successful World Cup? Obviously, after his performances in the one-dayers in the Caribbean, Shane's very confident and he told the press so.

Was the team weary? 'No,' I replied. 'We're physically and mentally prepared, and we have a good chance.'

Then to the team bus, to be greeted by the same bus driver, Huey, we have had on our last two Ashes tours. We've got the same baggage man, too, a bloke called Tony Smith, who's carried the bags of Australian cricketers for the past 27 years, and hasn't lost a single piece of luggage.

From Gatwick, Huey's bus set off on what proved to be a three-and-a-half hour trip on the motorway to Cardiff. As with any tour that involves a bus, as soon as you get on the bus for the first time, that seat is your seat for the entire tour. This was no different. The only time the boys left their new-found spots was when, inevitably, we stopped to satisfy the lads' interest in a Burger King and a KFC outlet.

Before that pitstop, a card school had started down the back, some guys were watching movies, a couple were catching up with the latest UK news. One of these was our manager, a man with an unmatched ability to study every column of every page. I have never seen anyone devour a newspaper as thoroughly as Steve Bernard, from front to back — in this case over 200 minutes of non-stop reading.

(During a fines meeting on the Caribbean leg of this arduous campaign, 'Brute', as he's known throughout the Australian cricket community, was found guilty of a misdemeanour and given a particularly cruel sentence. Not a monetary penalty; rather he was barred from reading the Sunday papers — a ruling that nearly sent our manager stir crazy, much like, I imagine, a junkie going cold turkey.)

The weather was surprisingly warm in Cardiff as we checked into our hotel. Unfortunately, my name wasn't on the team list — not a good start for the captain. Perhaps they assumed I'd be staying in a Barbados prison cell. Eventually, the hotel staff found a room on the ninth floor but it was so small it only had sufficient space for one quarter of my bags. So it was downstairs again, to try to change rooms, which I did, finally.

In the afternoon, we headed for what has been designated as our team room, to sign 150 bats for the English and Wales Cricket Board (ECB) and collect all our clothes for the Cup competition. Our gear is unbelievably yellow — bright yellow tops, yellow training pants, yellow tracksuits, yellow everything. No-one is going to miss us on the training park, and I just hope Sylvester the Cat doesn't mistake us for a group of Tweetie Pies.

Unfortunately, the organisers must have thought the Cup was going to be held in India, because among all the gear we've been given there is nothing that is going to keep us particularly warm. Ironically, when you do go to India, you generally get two jumpers and tracksuits, fleecy-lined tops, pants that are heavy and hot, the works. In England for the 1999 World Cup, however, we've received stuff that's see-through thin, and no jackets. We'd put in orders to the ACB for long johns, warm training shirts, even bomber jackets, but to no avail. We can only hope that some commonsense prevails and some protection against the elements finally arrives.

We had a team meeting tonight, where first up we went through the horrend-ous schedule of functions we are facing over the next week. There are at least 10 functions in the first seven days. On top of this, I'll be facing a succession of press interviews. In short, my first week is filled with obligations, so it's going to be difficult to fit in the cricket, even though that should be our priority.

The importance of prioritising effectively was reinforced before the meeting, when we had a chat with our sports psych, Sandy Gordon. I believe Sandy's input will be extremely helpful, as respected psychologist Dr Rudi Webster has aided the West Indies side, and he gave us what should be some good advice on how to stay focused and alert while effectively handling our off-field obligations.

After the team meeting, BJ, Darren Lehmann, Paul Reiffel, Shane Lee and I went out for a feed at a nearby Italian restaurant. We then tried to get into a local bar, but because tomorrow is a holiday over here, the place was packed and we couldn't get in. Just as we were accepting the fact that we'd have to come back another day, Jonathan Davies, the former Canterbury-Bankstown rugby league player (and former Welsh rugby legend and Great Britain league star), noticed us and kindly got us in. But by 9.30, a mild dose of jet lag was starting to have an effect, so we went home to bed.

We have a training session at 8.30am tomorrow. In fact, this leg of the 'Road to Lord's', Australia's 1999 World Cup adventure, starts tomorrow. Today was simply a day for acclimatising.

This campaign will probably be my last World Cup adventure — same for a few of the other Australian guys — so we're really looking forward to having a successful campaign, as individuals and as a team.

# MAY 3 Cardiff to London

AS FAR AS AUSTRALIA are concerned, the Road to Lord's on June 20 began as much as two years ago, with our defeat by England in the Texaco one-day series before the 1997 Ashes series. Following that loss, Australia's approach to the abbreviated form of the game was marked by a significant change of policy ... and captaincy, with me taking over from Mark Taylor and 'specialist' one-day players being given their chance. The past 24 months have seen outstanding players such as Adam Gilchrist, Adam Dale, Brendon Julian and Shane Lee take their opportunities and continue to grow and improve as the team has evolved.

I can honestly say that this is the best-balanced one-day squad I have ever been part of. We have individual match winners such as Michael Bevan, Shane Warne, Glenn McGrath and Mark Waugh mixed with the youth of Ricky Ponting, Damien Martyn, Lee and Julian, and a wealth of collective experience of playing here in the UK.

We have certainly not come here to do anything other than take top place. However, in my opinion, South Africa are entitled to be favourites after their consistently good one-day results over a long period. They have a strong sense of togetherness — such camaraderie will be the single most important factor in deciding who lifts the trophy. With most games likely to be close and tough, it is the team who holds together and fights the hardest under pressure that will pull through.

The next six weeks has the potential to see the most keenly fought World Cup ever staged. The way the competition has been organised suggests that consistency will be rewarded, and if the weather holds I see no reason why the cricket won't be of a higher standard than we have ever seen before.

The conditions at the Cardiff Cricket Centre, where we held our first practice this morning, are satisfactory, with two centre wickets available. They were a little bit wet, which assisted the bowlers, but a good session was had by all. Before we went out to loosen up, I had a quick five minutes with the lads, going through a summary of all I hope we can achieve during the tour. I've given the tour a theme of 'No Regrets'. I want every guy to say, when our World Cup is over, that he gave himself and the team every opportunity to play their best cricket and that we all made the necessary sacrifices to enable each of us, and the team, to do well.

Steve Waugh

*Here's our ever-alert coach dreaming of glory as we head off down the motorway. Meanwhile, behind Swamp, the 500 school of Bernard, Bevan, McGrath and Dale is probably striking more controversy, as the experienced veteran, Brute Bernard, again runs out of patience with his 'wet behind the ears' partner Chippen Dale.*

I'm sure all of the guys are going to do just that.

Reflecting our ambition, and our desire to make the sacrifices needed to ensure an optimum performance, we have also introduced a midnight curfew and an alcohol ban, that will be in place throughout the tour, except for the days when we play our matches. On those occasions, after the games, we'll be able to have a drink and the curfew may be extended, but otherwise we're going to be pretty strict about this aspect of our preparation. I've pondered for a while whether it was time we included a bit more discipline into the side.

On to practice. As I said, the bowlers got a lot of assistance out of the wicket, which may be a precursor to some difficulties all batsmen will face during the tournament. The white Duke balls tend to be harder than the Australian Kookaburra balls. They're smaller and they've got a bit more 'rope' (seam) on them, which means they dart about a lot. Consequently, I believe that in this World Cup the opening batsmen are going to have to play a different role, be a bit more cautious, and see the new ball off. Otherwise, the middle-order batsmen are going to have a bigger influence on the outcome of the tournament than they have had in some previous one-day tournaments. The bulk of the runs in this competition might be scored by numbers 4, 5 and 6, who'll be in early on, compared to most one-day internationals of the recent past. They'll be batting in conditions that will be a bit easier than what had confronted the openers.

Our training session went for two to three hours, after which five of the guys headed off for a coaching clinic. I went to the hotel pool, for a private fitness

# Team Meeting — the Captain's Notes

## First meeting

### The No Regrets Tour '99
- Any sacrifice we are going to make is a small one in the overall picture.
- We've already experienced the pain of the Commonwealth Games.
- I need everyone to give thought as to how they can become a better player and how we can become a better team.

Ways that we can make sacrifices ...
- alcohol — the amount you consume or none at all.
- social life (especially time at nightclubs and bars) — I don't expect you to turn into monks but cricket results are the priority.
- be prepared to help others with their problems, whether it be lack of form, technique, homesickness, or just needing a chat.
- make time for your own game — extra net sessions, fielding practice, studying opposition players (don't leave it to team meetings), watching videos of your game.

- Make a commitment to giving your preparation your full attention — all successful sportspeople put their game first; things such as extra sessions, maybe fitness work, maybe just thinking about game ahead.
- If you find yourself losing track or just struggling to motivate yourself, dig deep. It must come from within.
- Don't be afraid to be different, to be the best, or to improve your game — take Heals, the way he practises with a golf ball in car parks.

session with Dave Misson, where we did eight warm-up laps, then 10 lots of two laps, then five lots of four, then eight lots of one. It was a heavy workout, especially given that the pool was as overheated as this one was. It was like swimming in a bath and my head felt as if it was about to explode — tough work! — but it was also definitely what I needed, given that I put on three or four kilos during that one week of relaxation in Barbados.

I spent the afternoon on a train to London, off to a pre-World Cup captains' meeting at Lord's which will take place tomorrow. With delays for work on the line, the journey evolved into a three-and-a-half hour trip, then a half-hour wait for a cab to my hotel. Then, when I reached the hotel, they weren't expecting me. The room hadn't been paid for, a confusing situation that is occurring too often on tour these days.

Still, the great thing about being in the UK is that it quickly gets your enthusiasm back for playing and being a part of the game. I know from speaking to Warney today he has the same feelings as me — just being here in England makes you feel as if you are back in the home of cricket. You have an extra 10 per cent of energy and an edge that can sometimes disappear in other parts of the cricket world. I noticed this at practice this morning, which was clearly really enjoyable for all the guys, the best for a long time. You could see the increased energy and excitement.

I'm fired up, and looking forward to the Cup. I believe I'm going to have a big series, not least because the publicity on myself has quietened down, with players such as Gilchrist, Bevan, Warne and McGrath, our high-profile one-day stars, expected to be the team's most prolific performers. I'm much more low-profile and I like it that way. I believe it's time I put my hand up, score consistently and set the standard and tone for the team.

# MAY 4   London to Cardiff

THE CAPTAINS' MEETING at Lord's took place this morning. Before concentrating on more serious matters, the skippers posed together for a photo, exchanged pleasantries, then sat down to go through the ICC Rules and Regulations of the tournament with the ICC World Cup committee. We learned, to our great surprise, that a lot of things are not yet set in stone, and some rules that I believe should be strictly enforced are still open to a variety of flimsy interpretations.

A number of things England captain Alec Stewart and I brought up, including the 12th man being named before the game and being the automatic first-choice replacement fieldsman, were skated over. I also brought up the point that players should not go off the field unless they are genuinely injured, but once again I only got support from Alec. One comment I do remember came from an official from the Pakistani team, who said, in relation to my request that rules be adhered to, that, 'You should always play cricket to the spirit of the game.'

I'm not quite sure what he meant by that.

Eventually, too many things were left up in the air, to be discussed further at an umpires' meeting in two or three days' time.

Perhaps the major rule change from previous tournaments that we have been involved in is the 'carry-over' rule — if a game is not completed on the day, then play will continue on the following day. This, in my view, is a good thing. It would be a great shame if the English weather has too great an influence on the outcome of this event.

Meeting over, I had a photo shoot for the BBC, followed by an appearance at a cricket competition involving handicapped children. They played on a table tennis table, with a miniature bat, and a ball rolled down a ramp. I noticed that a lot of the kids were very badly disabled, but were having a fabulous time. It's situations such as this that make you realise how lucky you are to be able to enjoy life to the fullest. However, at the same time I was reminded how great the human spirit can be and how uplifting a positive approach to life is. Too soon, it was back on the train to return to Cardiff and the team, most of whom had been playing golf in my absence, after yet another request from a sponsor.

In the evening I went out to dinner with Tom Moody. Moods has been in the game for just about as long as I have, and his experience, allied to his all-round skills, make him a very valuable member of the team. He, like me, thought our training since arriving in the UK had been excellent, but he also raised one or two concerns. It seems one or two of the guys aren't as keen on the curfew and drink ban as I am, and Moods is of the view that it could lead to possible dissension in the ranks.

The last thing I want to do is damage team spirit, so clearly I need to discuss this situation, first with Geoff Marsh and Warney, and then, perhaps, at our next team meeting.

# MAY 5  Cardiff

TODAY WILL PROBABLY go down as one of the toughest days on tour, at least in regard to functions and other requirements we have to juggle. We started at 8.30am, all in our yellows, at Cardiff Castle. It must have been quite a sight to see this vast yellow army marching in to take over this magnificent 12th-century venue. We had a function inside the Castle's cathedral, where we were introduced to the media, after which I gave a short speech, then we went outside for a team photo and individual photos, followed by some media 'one-on-ones'.

'We expect to win,' was how I responded to a question as to how I rated Australia's chances. 'Anything less and we'll be disappointed. The World Cup is the Holy Grail in terms of one-day cricket, and we are treating it as the ultimate challenge. Our preparations have been excellent, and I think that we've got a pretty good chance of doing well.

'If people want to make us favourites, then that's fine. We know that it is down to us to do it on the day, and we are shaping up well.'

All up, the press took up about an hour, and then I had just enough time left to head off with Adam Dale and Shane Lee to find a hairdresser, which was quite relaxing after the morning's events. And amusing, too, as it is not often a head of hair resembles a tennis ball in the way Chippen's did after half an hour and 20 quid's worth of work.

*Pigeon (above) and Warney (below), in their bright yellows, keeping the Pommy press core enthralled at Cardiff Castle during our opening media conference.*

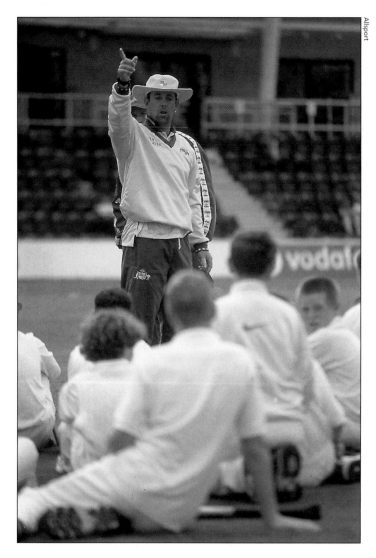

*Darren Lehmann does his bit at the ECB-organised coaching clinic.*

Then it was off to training, where we enjoyed a three-hour session. Not a bad hit-out, but the ball was moving about too much. I, for one, had a very poor net session. The ball was doing plenty and against guys such as Tom Moody it was as if I was batting on a trampoline. So I settled for some 'throw-downs', and by the time the three hours was up I was already making plans to organise a long indoor net the first chance I could, to get my confidence and timing back. Perhaps I'm a little impatient, because it is always going to take some time to adjust from the harder Caribbean tracks, with their greater bounce, to the soft, spongy wickets of England.

This said, from a team point of view the practice session was outstanding, especially the fielding. The guys' attitude so far on this leg of the tour has been fantastic and augurs well for the journey ahead.

The late afternoon was occupied by a three-hour coaching clinic, involving about 300 local kids, and although the children were fantastic I have to rate the event as one of the worst-organised such clinics I have ever been involved in. There were no local coaches and no equipment; just the children and an apparent obligation on our part to run the whole show. This was one of two such coaching clinics the ECB had compelled us to do, which I find quite ridiculous during the World Cup, when our time is so much at a premium. I just can't understand how we have to give up our preparation time for the ECB, who, after all, stand to make millions of pounds from this World Cup. I guess there must be reason in this somewhere, but to me it seems that we, the players, are merely satisfying an agreement made between the cricket boards of the world that we had no say in.

We finished after 6pm. After a quick Indian meal, I settled in to watch Manchester United and Liverpool finish 2-all in a thrilling Premier League game. Meanwhile, downstairs in the bar, a rumour was circulating that reporters from *News of the World* and the *Daily Mirror* were pursuing a Shane Warne story. There was a photo in the *Mirror* this morning of Shane smoking a cigarette in the Caribbean, which no doubt will cause huge news back home, given his commercial deals. I guess this exposure demonstrates once again just how big he is across the cricket world, and the resultant pressures he constantly finds himself under.

# MAY 6 Cardiff

GEOFF MARSH gave the guys the day off from on-field training. We've been training pretty hard, which you can't do every day, and Swamp wisely recognised that we needed a break from the day-to-day regime. But this didn't mean we got things all our own way, as it was away from the paddock and into the gym and pool.

This was an hour and a half of sweat, a really tough session led by our fitness adviser Dave Misson. Swimming, bike riding, with an emphasis on the explosive stuff, then a little bit of rest in between, then back to it to get the heart rate going again and to burn off even more calories.

After that, it was off to another function, this one at the Cardiff Cricket Centre, where they officially opened their new indoor arena. The great New Zealander, Sir Richard Hadlee, was the guest speaker. Shane, Steve Bernard and I were on the top table, which gave us a chance to have a long conversation with Sir Richard. He's a pretty good fella off the field and obviously extremely knowledgeable about the game he dominated through the late '70s and '80s.

From there, it was back to the hotel, where Swamp, Warney and I had a chat as to how the tour is going and what lies ahead. I have prepared individual reports on each of the players, and with Geoff will be having individual chats with each of the players tomorrow afternoon. That is when I'll be outlining how I see the role of each player and what I expect of each player. In the past, these 'one-on-ones' have worked particularly well. We also have a team meeting scheduled for tomorrow night, which I'm busily planning for at the moment.

I decided a couple of weeks ago that we needed to try to build some real tradition into the Australian one-day cricket team. So I gave our cricket analyst Mike Walsh the job of working out what 'number' each member of this current squad is in the roll call of all Australia's one-day cricketers, from the first XI who represented Australia back in January 1971 through to today. For example, I'm No. 90 — the 90th player to play for Australia at one-day cricket. Moods is No. 98, the only other member of the squad in the first 100. We'll be putting the appropriate number on each guy's yellow Australian cap, to constantly remind each player that he is part of a proud and exclusive club, and in doing so hopefully develop a bit of a tradition in one-day cricket.

Number 91 is current coach Geoff Marsh, who made his one-day international debut two games after me, back in January 1986. I've made sure a couple of times already, since Mike produced his list, to remind Swamp who's the more senior.

Unfortunately, the hats have come back tonight and the printing job looks a bit cheap and nasty. Tom's really disappointed as I'd left it to him to get the job done, but we've had a bit of a laugh now. Tomorrow we'll be going out to locate a professional embroiderer and get the job done properly.

Pics: Steve Waugh

*Above: A lovestruck Geoff Marsh seems mesmerised by the Australian swimming great Sam Riley as she applies some patriotic zinc cream to his face during the swimming events at the Commonwealth Games. Somehow we managed to regularly wrangle our way into the area that was off limits to all but team and support staff — thankfully, we were warmly welcomed by the Aussie competitors.*

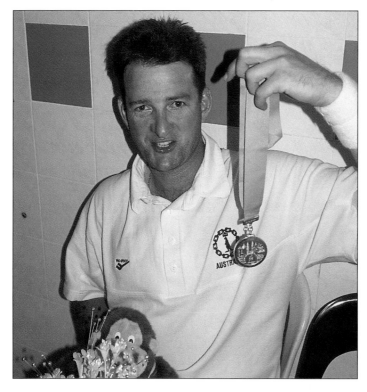

*Left: It was not exactly the colour we were looking for but, having seen what any medal meant to the other athletes, our Silvers will hold a special significance for us all. More importantly, our medals will always remind us of the great time we had at the KL Commonwealth Games.*

Left: One of the reasons why we are one of the top cricket nations is because we train with an intensity as close to match conditions as we can reach, even to the extent of bouncing each other in the nets. However, in Karachi, much to the misfortune of Brad Young, a fired-up Ricky Ponting let rip a quickish bouncer which our left-arm spinner, normally a proficient hooker of the ball, missed. Doubly unlucky was the fact it also dodged the grill of his helmet and smashed into his nose, breaking it quite badly. Hence the 'Hannibal Lecter' look.

Below: On a rare day off during the Pakistan tour, a few of the lads travelled to the hills surrounding Islamabad, near Rawalpindi, to a place called Murree, where Pigeon bravely mounted this decorated horse, always hoping that it wouldn't gallop off down the steep, narrow alleyway.

Pics: Steve Waugh

*Above left: Colin Miller, who made his Test debut in Rawalpindi and then played in his first Ashes Test eight weeks later, in Perth. Above right: Tubby and Lang savour the moment after enjoying milestones they'll never forget. For Justin it was his long-awaited first Test century, while Mark had scored that amazing triple century.*

*Below: When in 'Rome' you do as the 'Romans' do. Some people have been critical of us (in this instance, Robbo and Lang) holding guns, but to have not been available for this photo would have been considered an insult by our hosts and an affront to their culture.*

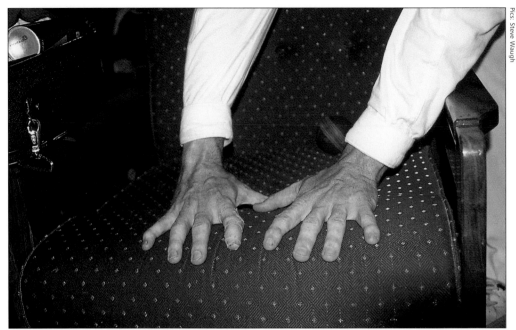

Pics: Steve Waugh

*Above: The craggy and crooked hands of the world's greatest wicketkeeper, which, as you can see, have taken enormous punishment over the years, It is further power to Heals that he has only ever missed one Test match due to injury. This photograph was taken in Rawalpindi on the evening of the day Ian broke Rod Marsh's world record.*

*Below: Darren Lehmann joins our much-admired stand-in physio, Patrick Farhart, in a head shape comparison, while behind them a sign lurks ominously. This shot was taken at Peshawar Fort in Pakistan, shortly before our team photo was snapped.*

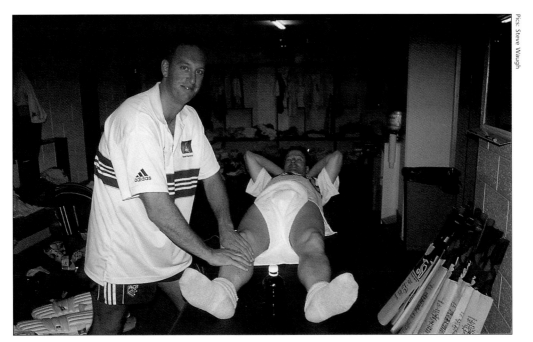

*Above: Fitness and massage man Dave Misson gives my long-suffering 'compartment syndrome' affected legs a going over in the hope that they'll settle down for the next day's play. Nearby, against a wall, lies the curse of the players — an endless stream of bats waiting to be autographed.*

*Below: Nothing puts off our legendary physio Errol Alcott in his quest for excellence. I'm just glad he's got his protective gloves on as he goes to work on the gluteus maximus of Darren Lehmann. This angle also shows just how proud Boof is about South Australia's Shield victory a couple of years ago — afterwards he decided to decorate himself with the team's Redback logo.*

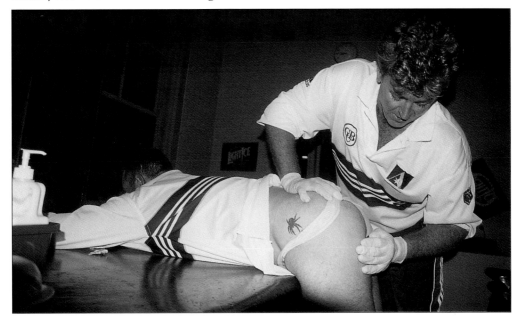

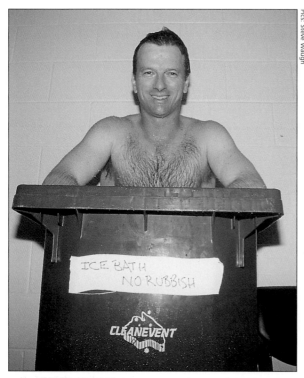

Pics: Steve Waugh

*Left: This new method of recovery — sitting in a rubbish bin, full of ice and water — takes some getting used to. But the benefits are noticeable and have helped the quicker bowlers in particular overcome little niggles and strains much quicker than had been the case in the past.*

*Below: Huge underdogs, the 'Steady Eddies', mount the rostrum to collect the spoils during the World Cup team's go-karting day out. Rank outsiders, Geoff Marsh and Errol Alcott, slot into the runners-up spot while the highly-fancied Paul Reiffel and Glenn McGrath took third place.*

Pics: Steve Waugh

*Above: These are 'The Nerds', posing for a team photo before our unexpected loss to the Julios in Leeds before our quarter-final match against South Africa. Flem and I had been shopping during the previous week and came up with the sunglasses — discounted from £9.99 to £1.99 — and the shirts, which just happened to be on sale at a motorway service stopover from £3.99 each. Being the fashion-conscious cricketers that we are, we opted for five different colours, each colour signifying our doubles combinations. Swamp and I took on the orange strip, but sadly our outfit was the highlight of our performance.*

*Below: Here are 'The Julios' in their unique team strip. The key component, of course, are the Phantom of the Opera masks that had been picked up by fitness guru Dave Misson during the interval of the world-famous theatrical show at Her Majesty's Theatre in London a couple of days before. The would-be Phantom at the far right is our answer to Placido Domingo — big Tom Moody — a man with very impressive vocal cords.*

*Above: All the hard work and sacrifices are worthwhile. For a team it doesn't get any better — arm in arm, singing 'True Blue' with an army of Aussie supporters at Lord's in the background, after claiming the World Cup. The missing team member in this photo is Tom Moody, but he had a good reason: he took the photo.*

*Below: Sitting next to Warney for the Melbourne ticker tape parade was a spine-tingling experience. The support and fanatical backing the home crowd gave Shane was one thing, I'm sure, that convinced him that it wasn't the right time to call it quits from the international arena.*

It goes without saying that the World Cup never left our hands for too long, even though it weighed 11kg and was, in fact, a replica. The original stays in England, which I can't quite understand, because I would have imagined that as the champions we had every right to bring home the real thing.

# MAY 8   Cardiff to Worcester

**Warm-up match**
At Cardiff, Glamorgan 2-21 (10 overs) v Australians. Match abandoned

WE'VE REACHED THE END of the first week, and what a hectic, if often humdrum in terms of the number of functions, week it's been. We began yesterday with an excellent training session and ended with a productive team meeting. Also completed were the one-on-ones, and Sandy Gordon, our sports psychologist, conducted a series of meeting with the players, with beneficial results for all.

We've eased off the alcohol ban. Now the grog is just going to be off limits on the day before each game; in other situations the players will be able to drink up until the end of their meal. After games, it will be as it has always been, although we might still place a limit on how late the revelry goes. Midnight, to me, seems a reasonable time to call a halt. When we won the Cup back in 1987, we all swore off the grog for the entire campaign — an approach which I believe helped instill a discipline that helped in our victory.

Sadly, our first practice match, against Glamorgan here at Cardiff, was washed out today after only 10 overs. But at least the 10 overs were excellent. And we weren't the only team to fall victim to the British autumn, as only two of the six scheduled Cup warm-ups were completed. Cup favourites South Africa didn't even get on the park at Sussex.

All indications are that Adam Dale and Damien Fleming are going to form an opening partnership that will be crucial to our chances. If they get us off to a good start, then the opposition will have to handle all of McGrath and Warne in the middle overs, which will be a tough ask for anyone. Unfortunately, though, we never had the chance to see Pigeon and Warney strut their stuff, but we still had to wait around the usual three or four hours before the game was abandoned. Then it was on to the afternoon bus to Worcester.

During the journey, I sat back and observed what the guys were doing. The usual suspects were playing cards — up the front was the quartet of Bevo, Pigeon, Chippen and Misso, with the Queenslander copping a verbal hiding during every hand, while down the back, Warney, Punter, Boof and Moods carried on like good sorts. Shane Lee was strummin' on his guitar, while a couple of guys up the front were watching movies. This mixture created a lively atmosphere, good for bonding, which made our bus a great place to be.

On arrival at Worcester, we checked into the hotel and then went straight out for a feed, and then a few of the guys went out for a bit of a night on the town, which was just what we needed. We have survived a week where we worked under pretty strict guidelines, so it was nice to let the hair down and enjoy a good night and some laughs.

*While we were in Worcester, some of the lads had the opportunity to catch up with a group of blind cricketers, who were eager to show off their game and the tools of their trade. Here Shane Lee is at the batting crease, hemmed in by as keen a slip cordon as you could ever meet.*

# MAY 9 Worcester

BACK TO THE GRIND of touring life. It was wet again, which meant the scheduled morning training was put back until the afternoon. But when we did get on the park we had a great session. We had an hour and a half, featuring soccer and touch rugby — all of it 'Nerds v Julios' stuff and all closely contested. Battles won, we headed out for a solid centre-wicket practice. I, for one, needed a good hit and although I started off a bit shakily, by the end I was feeling comfortable, particularly after some morale-boosting throwdowns. The adrenalin is starting to flow now and I can't wait to get really involved and stuck into the opposition.

We've decided, not surprisingly, that our XI for the upcoming practice game against Worcestershire will be the same as it was for the washed-out game in Glamorgan. We're still trying to get Tom Moody a game for Worcestershire as well, but apparently the Worcestershire coach doesn't want Tom to play, even though he'll be captaining the county once the World Cup is completed. Seems a bit crazy to me. We can only conclude that this is a situation where the English are trying to make things that little bit harder for us. Such pettiness is annoying, but we must keep our cool and concentrate only on the things we can control.

Disappointingly, the weather forecast for tomorrow isn't promising, but there isn't anything we can do about that. So long as we stay focused for what lies ahead, that's all that counts. Personally, I feel good about my cricket. I just want to get out into the middle and spend a bit of time out there, to get a feel for the slower surfaces that lie ahead.

But I'm missing home. It's been upwards of 11 weeks now since I last saw my wife and daughter. It's very difficult to be away from home for that length of time. I know Shane Warne for one is suffering as much as I am. To make matters even more difficult for him, his wife, Simone, is expecting a baby shortly. But this is life as an international cricketer. You have to sacrifice things if you want the rewards.

# MAY 10   Worcester to Taunton

**Warm-up match**
At Worcester, Worcestershire 7-162 (44 overs; WPC Weston 44, DW Fleming 2-28, SK Warne 2-27, S Lee 2-42) lost to Australians 4-181 (34.1 overs; AC Gilchrist 86, ME Waugh 64) by six wickets

WE MANAGED TO GET a result out of today's game against Worcestershire, and Shane Warne took the first wickets in what we hope will be a productive World Cup campaign for him.

Warney took two of the first three wickets to fall, and finished with two wickets from 10 overs as the English county made 7-162 (later upgraded to 178 under the new method of calculation that will be used during the World Cup because of interruptions for rain) in a game that had to be reduced to 44 overs a side because of the weather. Glenn McGrath was also in good form, taking 1-19 off eight.

These performances were heartening, especially as neither had got a bowl in our first practice game, against Glamorgan last weekend, which was abandoned after 10 overs. The one downside for our performance was the 34 extras conceded, the second-highest scorer in the Worcestershire innings. This is an area that must be tightened up.

When we batted, Adam Gilchrist began living up to his pre-World Cup billing as a man to watch out for. Gilly smashed 86 as we reached the target with six wickets and almost 10 overs to spare. He added 127 with Mark Waugh for the first wicket, before Junior was dismissed for 64, and looked set to end the innings unbeaten until he was out near the end, part of a slide that saw us lose three wickets for three runs. Unfortunately, I was one of those three dismissals, caught behind for 2, which wasn't really surprising given that 10 minutes before I was preparing my bag, in readiness for our departure for Taunton, the next venue on our Road to Lord's. On the way out to bat, I was at least half-asleep and, as you'd expect, I paid the price. This simply wasn't professional enough, and I must ensure that it doesn't happen again.

# MAY 11 Taunton

THE WICKET we practised on in Taunton this morning was the best we've seen so far in England, and it led to an encouraging session. The key for most of the players, myself included, was to have a solid workout and build confidence.

In the afternoon, quite a few of the guys played golf, while Flem and I went out to buy some Nerds outfits. We've pencilled a Nerds v Julios tenpin bowling match into our diaries for later in the tour, hopefully as soon as Worcester on the weekend. Unfortunately, all we ended up buying were 10 pairs of tortoise-shell, round-rimmed, nerd-looking glasses, which had, conveniently but for no apparent reason, been marked down from 10 pounds to two pounds. But we just couldn't find any shirts of sufficient quality, so we'll have to go shopping when we get to Worcester to finish off the outfit. If that expedition proves unsuccessful, we may have to put a call into Tubby back in Oz to send over some of his kit.

One pleasant little surprise today came when Brad 'Buzzard' McNamara and Simon Cook, both familiar to followers of Australian cricket, came down for the day. We had a good meal and a great laugh, which was just what I needed. Buzzard actually ending up sleeping on the lounge in my hotel room. It was good to catch up with an old friend and relax with someone who's removed from the hype of the tournament and is outside the team, as it gets you away from the stress that can start to affect players if they don't relax.

The first 10 days have been pretty much spot on from our point of view. The pressure seems to be more on the favourites, South Africa, although Warney has copped a little bit of heat because of the smoking thing back in Australia. For me, Shane's situation confirms once more how times have certainly changed, illustrates how much we have become public property, and demonstrates how careful we need to be even outside of cricket hours.

These pressures can be a tough call on him, on all of us. However, the other side of the argument is that we make good money from the game and the endorsements that come with it. We've become public property, whether we like it or not.

*My fellow Nerd, Damien Fleming.*

# MAY 12  Taunton to Worcester

**Warm-up match**
At Taunton, Australians 5-243 (50 overs; ME Waugh 46, SR Waugh 44, MG Bevan 68*, S Lee 30*)
defeated Somerset 208 (45.2 overs; PCL Holloway 40, DW Fleming 3-43, SK Warne 3-35)

OUR TWO-DAY SOJOURN in Taunton is over, and now we find ourselves back in Worcester to begin final preparations for our Cup opener. The game today went pretty well and all in all was a satisfactory final warm-up for the Cup. We played some good cricket in patches, although some other parts were not so good. I was certainly happy with the way I batted — I hit 44 off 54 balls, but more importantly had some precious time in the middle — while Michael Bevan was also very impressive. I see both Bevo and I being crucial to our chances in this World Cup, because, as I've said, the middle orders of all teams will be called upon to shoulder more responsibility due to the favourable bowling conditions.

The wickets over here are definitely a bit slower than what we've been facing in the Caribbean, so getting the chance to experience them pre-tournament was crucial. Today, I was reminded that you need to bat in a slightly more conservative way over here, compared, say, to the manner in which you might approach things in a one-dayer in India or Pakistan. You've got to leave a few more balls and find your feet a bit more. It's not as if you can just go and blaze from ball one, as the white Dukes are seaming around a bit more than on the sub-continent. In my view, this Cup will feature a more traditional way of playing than the last World Cup, where there were so many innovations. Because of this, the technically strong teams will do well, more so than the 'cavalier' sides.

Also confusing many teams' Cup preparations has been the lousy weather, which has restricted some teams more than others. Pakistan has been unable to complete any of their three warm-up games, while West Indies captain Brian Lara, hampered by an injured wrist, has not appeared on the field as yet.

Apart from ourselves, the Lara-less West Indies and New Zealand beat the weather and managed to complete wins against county opposition. Strangely, Courtney Walsh has not played for the Windies, although he is reportedly fit, while the Kiwis' No. 3, Craig McMillan, has been in splendid form, especially in their most recent seven-wicket victory over Sussex. If you're a punter and looking for value for money, the Kiwis are, in my opinion, a good bet. They're ideally suited to the conditions over here, which aren't too dissimilar to what they play in at home.

Less encouragingly, the Cup outsiders, Scotland, were defeated today by Yorkshire, while Bangladesh went down to Northamptonshire.

Back to us, though. From the bowling side of things, Shane Warne has continued to bowl very well, taking three of the first four wickets to fall today. In fact, all of the bowlers seem to be in good touch — Adam Dale has been bowling very well, as has Damien Fleming, who in recent times has often led our pace attack with consistency and a high level of skill.

*Cold and windswept on the away-team balcony at Taunton, but grateful that the weather has cleared sufficiently for our Cup preparations to finally move up a gear or two.*

During the match, a few of us strolled around to the Ladbroke's tent to check out the World Cup odds. Now I don't pretend for one moment to be an expert on these kinds of things, but I thought the 33-1 they were quoting about me being the leading run-scorer in the tournament were pretty generous odds. The 33s about Damien Fleming being the leading wicket-taker were enticing, too. Shane was 20s, so was Adam Dale — all of which seems good value, but as we all know, you can look but you don't touch.

The team has a good feeling about it, similar to what happened in 1987. I just get the feeling we're building up the right way. Allan Border, who will be commentating on the Cup for BSkyB over here, has been to see us and share some thoughts. It's always good to see him in and around the guys and having his usual positive influence.

Tomorrow shapes up as being a day off, left to do what you want to do. For me, that means a hit of golf and a 'Footy Show' interview along with Shane Warne that we have to do as part of our commitments with Channel Nine. There's never really a complete day off on tour, but tomorrow is probably as easy as it's going to get.

After that it will be full on with the World Cup, and all the lads can't wait.

# MAY 13  Worcester

AS I MENTIONED YESTERDAY, at 12.30pm Warney and I had to participate in a live cross from the Worcester ground back to the rugby league version of 'The Footy Show' in Australia. We successfully deflected a couple of questions from Ian Healy, a guest on the show, and one or two from the regular Footy Show panelists. It was an inconvenience really, because this was meant to be a morning off for us, but instead we had to wait an hour and a half for the satellite feed to come through. However, as we are both part of the Nine team, it was expected of us that we would comply with their request. In the end, we got it done, and then we headed off to the world-famous The Belfry golf course, former English home of the Ryder Cup. A round cost 60 quid, but such was the high quality of the course that it was money well spent.

Swamp and I teamed up, but couldn't get our act together, meekly surrendering to Mark Waugh and Glenn McGrath. Three holes was the margin in the end, but the victory was hardly mentioned during the post-mortems in the clubhouse afterwards. Instead, all we could talk about was the carnage that occurred at one particular par three.

The group in front of us was made up of Darren Lehmann, Ricky Ponting, Shane Warne and Adam Gilchrist, and they had just completed the shortish-in-length hole. Junior was first to tee off, and he underclubbed, landing on a footpath short of the green. From there, his ball bounced wickedly, eventually ending up bang, smack on the roof of a cart carrying two members of the group in front. This stunned them, to say the least, and for a moment it seemed a major traffic accident was a possibility. We'd just recovered from that when Pigeon strode onto the tee. But just as he went to tee off, we all broke up again, which caused a huge divot to hurtle through the air, almost as far as the ball, as a result of a dreadful swing. Then, mysteriously, the iron slipped out of Pigeon's hands in his follow through, went about 30 metres in the air and three times as far as his ball, and landed on the concrete path. And this was no ordinary blade, but a brand new Titleist hired from the club.

Swamp was in no condition to play next, but he tried and managed to shift his tee shot a couple of metres off the tee. Then I scuffled a ball into some thick under-growth, via McGrath's pathway. One of the great holes of golf, and a good day had by all.

After retrieving the twisted, mangled seven iron, Pigeon took one look at it and disposed of it thoughtfully into the adjacent swampland, never to be seen again. This ingenious piece of work created a fine alibi, as Glenn explained to the club pro later on that he had inadvertently misplaced one of his clubs during the round.

'Don't worry,' he assured the pro, 'it'll probably turn up.'

During the round, I completed a live cross to the 'Today' show in Sydney. Besides that, this was an afternoon away from cricket.

# MAY 14  Worcester

GROUP A
At Lord's, Sri Lanka 204 (50 overs; RS Kaluwitharana 57, AD Mullally 4-37) lost to England 2-207 (46.5 overs; AJ Stewart 88, GA Hick 73*) by eight wickets

WHILE THE WORLD CUP began in earnest at Lord's, where the home team disposed of the defending champions, we were settling on our combination for our first match of the tournament. We'll be starting with the same side that has taken the field for all three warm-up games. The fact that four guys — Tom Moody, Damien Martyn, Paul Reiffel and Brendon Julian — haven't had a hit is desperately unfortunate for them, and a reflection of our limited, rain-ruined build-up. However, I'm particularly impressed by the way those four guys are getting stuck in, and revving up the guys who are keeping them out of the starting line-up.

The quality of a starting XI can often be judged by the players who have been left out, and for us, having such cricketers on the subs' bench is a very promising sign.

Our training session today, another centre-wicket hit-out, occurred this afternoon, after a fitness session with Misso in the morning, which involves skipping, running, boxing and a gym circuit. This workout left all the boys absolutely knackered, but better for the experience. At least that's what Misso told us!

# MAY 15  Worcester

GROUP A
At Hove, India 5-253 (50 overs; SC Ganguly 97, RS Dravid 54. L Klusener 3-66) lost to South Africa 6-254 (47.2 overs; JH Kallis 96, JN Rhodes 39*) by four wickets
At Taunton, Kenya 7-229 (50 overs; A Vadher 54, NC Johnson 4-42) lost to Zimbabwe 5-231 (41 overs; NC Johnson 59) by five wickets

MUCH DEBATE has been going on about comments by Warney in *The Times*, published yesterday, in which he teed off on Sri Lanka's captain Arjuna Ranatunga. However much something might be true, I don't believe it's wise to get too personal, as it only creates problems for everyone involved. As has been said many times, sleeping dogs should be left to lie. In this instance, Warney probably crossed that line in his condemnation of Ranatunga. Whatever the arguments, it's been done and this afternoon Shane was handed a fine of 50 per cent of his match fee and a two-match suspended sentence for the next six months.

After practice, we had a bit of time off and most of us watched the conclusion of the India v South Africa match. I was impressed by both sides. Afterwards we had a brief team meeting to discuss the Scotland game — we'll be concentrating on our game and how we're going to play, rather than worrying about the Scots. We don't

*The controversial Sri Lankan captain Arjuna Ranatunga, the subject of a much-debated article by Shane Warne, pictured here with England skipper Alec Stewart during the opening match of the World Cup, played yesterday at Lord's.*

know many of their guys, but we do know that if we play to our potential then it really should be no contest.

Then it was on to the team dinner. It was good for the boys to get together the night before the first big game. I sat with BJ, Moods, Marto, Gilly and Punter and had a good laugh. The West Australian boys were telling a few stories about their team-mate, Joey Angel, who's quite a character.

And a huge eater. One night, we were told, he even eyed off the decorative carrot that the chef had prepared to make the meal even more aesthetically pleasing. Joey was so peckish he couldn't resist any longer, and began munching away ... to the absolute horror of a female staff member. She sadly informed all in attendance that this particular piece of artwork that was now being introduced to Jo's digestive juices was indeed entered in a contest the next day, having been the result of many hours' work.

I'm looking forward to tomorrow's game, which should result in a comfortable win if we play well. I'm hoping we'll set a high standard, particularly in the field, which will set us up for the future, tougher games. At this stage, we're feeling and looking good.

# MAY 16 Australia v Scotland, at Worcester

**GROUP B**

At Worcester, Scotland 7-181 (50 overs; GM Hamilton 34, SK Warne 3-39) lost to Australia 4-182 (44.5 overs; ME Waugh 67, SR Waugh 49*) by six wickets

At Bristol, Pakistan 8-229 (50 overs; Wasim Akram 43, CA Walsh 3-28, M Dillon 3-29) defeated West Indies 202 (48.5 overs; S Chanderpaul 77, Azhar Mahmood 3-48, Abdur 3-32) by 27 runs

We have all seen Braveheart and applauded the courage
But today it is our turn to play with shit and be savage.
For there's no doubt they will come at us with the ferocity of William Wallace,
But we must stand firm, be tough if we want to hoist the chalice.

Our other foes will be watching to study for cracks
Let's show them nothing but a team that's as sharp as tacks
Because I'm sick of hearing about the professionalism of others
   (and how hard they work)
Let's set our standards today and not waiver or shirk

Because we all know the importance of a first-game win
Today, let's flash our kilts at the other teams in this competition.

**Dave Misson**

MISSO SET THE SCENE at warm-ups this morning, leading us into the match with a clever poem he'd crafted in the days leading into the game. This idea originated in the West Indies, when I suggested to Dave that he might come up with a quote or a poem that would provide some inspiration for the day. Not needing a second invitation, Misso had delivered without fail, motivating us in his own thought-out way. I'm hoping this concept will now filter through to all the guys, who I'd like to see get involved by writing their own inspirational stanzas or finding some appropriately inspiring quotations.

I guess the Scotland match went according to plan, in that we got the two points, but I was very disappointed with the way we fielded and our general attitude in the field. A lot of guys had their heads down and, to be perfectly frank, our effort just wasn't up to scratch. Scotland ended up getting past 180 on a wicket we should have bowled them out for a 100. I thought Damien Fleming bowled very well and was a stand out, and the other guys were reasonably consistent. But we had 39 extras — including 22 wides and eight no-balls — which is not acceptable. And we dropped three easy catches. Our general attitude was poor, and I let the team know what I thought after the first 50 overs.

It seemed to me that there were too many guys who were carried away with looking good and consequently were not actually doing the job. Then the whingeing started. Clearly, there are some things we need to address for the future.

From my point of view, I was happy with the fact that I bowled six overs. I thought I bowled okay, too, took one wicket. My goal for this tournament is to try to take at least one wicket in every game and to score 50 runs per match. I think this is one area where I have let myself down in one-day cricket in the past — by not setting my own goals and instead worrying too much about the team I've probably not given myself enough chances to succeed on a personal level. In this World Cup, I'm determined to do well.

Batting-wise, it seemed we were a team who needed a hit-out. But there were some encouraging signs. Mark played pretty well for his 67, and Ricky Ponting hit some nice shots during his 33. But Gilly missed out, and so did Darren Lehmann. I was happy with my own form — 49 not out off 69 balls — which was pleasing. Like some others, I felt I needed a decent hit, because I haven't had a lot of practice over the past month. Overall, I am comfortable with the win, but disappointed with our commitment and the team effort.

And I didn't mind the world knowing. At the post-match press conference, I described our out-cricket as 'atrocious'. Sitting next to me, Geoff Marsh said, 'Our fielding was disappointing. I don't think it could get any worse than it did. Let's hope it was one of those days that's come and gone but we do need to improve. In practice, we need to make sure we don't become casual.'

I then added, 'I would give us four out of 10 for the way we played. I thought our fielding was very poor. The bowling was not too bad, but I thought our batting looked like it needed a run.

*Mark Waugh got off to an encouraging start against Scotland, top-scoring with 67.*

*The Tartan Army at Worcester, very loud and very Scottish.*

'All aspects of our game have to improve but the fielding in particular — you cannot afford to drop three chances against really good teams.'

One issue that I raised again was the question of security for players when the fans swarm onto the field. Today, just as they did in the Caribbean, people were able to run onto the ground and hassle us after the game, and for three or four minutes there was no sign of security people or the police. I don't see that as top-notch security, which is something World Cup organisers promised would be provided for us.

'How many times do we have to say it?' I complained to anyone who would listen afterwards. 'At the captains' meeting the World Cup organisers assured all the players that security would be the highest priority. After today, I don't think it was their No. 1 priority. In fact, there didn't appear to be any security there. It was not so much threatening behaviour, but people got access to you. I got jostled out there. If the crowd have had a few drinks anything can happen.'

The evening was taken up first with a half-hour function in the clubroom and then, later on into the night, seven or eight of the boys went out for a drink and mixed with some lively Scots. Their chants filled the pub, and were good fun to listen to, although they did give Warney a bit of stick. But this seems to be par for the course in England. He has a genuine 'love-hate' relationship with the Poms.

During the game today, the Scots' loudest group of supporters, the self-named 'Tartan Army', never left Warney alone. They arrived complete with a brass band and a huge inflatable whale, which was apparently an image of our champion leg-spinner, and hurled abuse every time Shane looked their way. Is it really fair that anyone has to put up with all of this? Inevitably, Warney's patience ran out when their taunts continued incessantly, and he gestured their way. My guess is that response is what will make the papers tomorrow, under a big anti-Warne headline, which to me will be a total distortion of what actually went on.

# MAY 17  Worcester to Cardiff

**GROUP B**
At Chelmsford, Bangladesh 116 (37.4 overs; GI Allott 3-30, CL Cairns 3-19, GR Larsen 3-19) lost to New Zealand 4-117 (33 overs; MJ Horne 35, RG Twose 30*) by six wickets

WE WERE SUPPOSED to have the morning off, but Swamp and I decided we should have a fielding session — a reaction to our poor performance the day before. We also had a chat to Pigeon, who I believe is five or 10 per cent away from where he should be. Yesterday, he wasn't concentrating as well as usual. He seemed distracted, a situation he needs to address straight away. As professional as he is, he'd already recognised his problems, and assured us he'd be okay.

There were a couple of other minor incidents coming from the game that also needed clearing up, which is what occurred. It seems at the moment that we are all a little bit on edge and not enjoying our cricket enough — perhaps the hype of this tournament being the be all and end all of international one-day cricket has worn us down a little.

It was freezing cold for the session, but the guys put in a good performance. The commitment was there, which was excellent after the disappointment of the Scotland game.

One issue that is receiving plenty of coverage here is the fact that South African captain Hansie Cronje wore an earpiece linked to coach Bob Woolmer while in the field during their Cup opener against India on May 15. The South Africans are pointing out that the ploy breaks no rules, but the authorities are arguing that while this may be the case, there is the question of whether they have acted contrary to the 'spirit of the game'. I believe a captain should be thinking for himself — that's why he's in charge. To have someone yelling instructions in your ear would to me not only be unnecessary, it would be distracting. From the moment I heard about it, I thought the practice should be stopped and it seems that it either has been, or is about to be, outlawed. Let's not Americanise our sport too much!

The afternoon was spent on the bus down to Cardiff. I can tell you, that bus can be an extremely uncomfortable place when you're looking for a sleep. I ended up on the floor in the aisle, with a couple of the other guys. Meanwhile, the usual card games were on in earnest, while on the video screen Arnie Schwarzenegger was taking people out left, right and centre. Some of the guys had their headphones on,

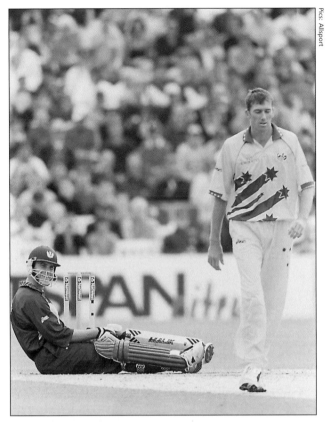

*Left: Glenn McGrath did manage to put Scotland's No. 9 James Brinkley on his backside during our Cup opener, but in the main I thought our performance lacked a little fire.*

*Below left: As I did during the Windies campaign (see Justin Langer caption on page 80), before the World Cup began I met with each squad member and discussed on a one-to-one basis how they were going to approach the tournament. This is what I had put to Michael Bevan ...*

- Continue to set the standards — make this your personal stage to show off your skills.
- Keep working on the other guys' strategies and game plans if you think it will help them.
- Stay involved on the field with ideas and look to get into the ring if you think it will lift the team.
- Prepare yourself to bowl in the game, the best way you see fit.
- Get involved in team meetings and discussions. Your input is rarely off the mark and guys listen.
- Keep crossing the T's and dotting the I's in everything you do.

Be the man!

Every sacrifice we make is a down payment on the acquisition of the World Cup.

Play well!

most notably Flem, who loves his music, a couple were reading books, while BJ was scouring all the trendy male magazines.

After we reached Cardiff, I spent some time walking around the shops, doing a bit of shopping with a couple of the lads. Then in the evening I ventured to a Thai restaurant with most of the single guys, while the guys with partners headed off in a different direction. In a way this situation is a bit disappointing, because we're always trying to get all the guys out together. What we're going to have to do is arrange more team functions.

I had a good chat with Michael Bevan tonight. In his view, we're putting too much pressure on ourselves, which is why our fielding wasn't good yesterday. He wants us to seek more enjoyment and relax more when we're playing. He is certainly a good thinker about the game and his views tonight made so much sense.

In time, Bevo will go down as the greatest one-day player of his generation, maybe of all time. He is capable of inventing strokes, while at the same time being consistent and totally in control of his game and the needs of the side. It is a captain's dream to have a player of this calibre in his line-up and I know I can relax knowing that he can look after himself and be relied upon in any tough situation. This Australian team has many matchwinners, but this tournament will be won by the unit that has the most people putting their hands up and contributing to the team performance. I know Bevo will be doing his part.

Bevo is also known as a guy who can come up with the occasional piece of wisdom that makes you sit up and take notice. His latest one, oh so true, was along the lines of, 'Fielding is a real guide to a team's togetherness, because it is the only facet of the game that you truly do for the team and don't get statistically rewarded for, as a consequence of good play.'

# MAY 18 Cardiff

**GROUP A**
At Canterbury, Kenya 203 (49.4 overs; Ravindu Shah 46, SO Tikolo 71, D Gough 4-34) lost to England 1-204 (39 overs; N Hussain 88*, GA Hick 61*) by nine wickets

TWO DAYS OUT from the New Zealand game, and we had a day off. We were supposed to train, but the wet weather put a stop to that and instead all the guys relaxed. I went shopping with Brendon Julian and Adam Dale, settling on the 'Next' store as our favourite. BJ watched while Chippen tried on every pair of pants in the store but bought nothing. Meanwhile, I was walking out with two pairs of strides I'd purchased. The afternoon was spent at the movies with Dave Misson, BJ, Marto and Moods, where we saw *Best Laid Plans*, which for mine is a bit overrated, despite Misso's recommendation.

Feeling a bit let down by our fitness guru's judgement, Marto and I decided to stay on to see another flick, *True Crime* with Clint Eastwood, which was excellent. From there, we had a bite to eat at an Italian restaurant and the rest of the evening was spent watching World Cup cricket on the TV. England has managed another victory and the whole country seems to be carried away with their performances. Suddenly, they're hot favourites to win it all.

Now, late into the evening, I'm just waiting for a call from Triple M in Australia. The phone sure has been busy. As captain, you have many more commitments and much more on your plate. You always have people ringing up, or seeking some of your time, and these are often people who see things from a different perspective to you and the team. In the end, you must make decisions for yourself and the team, which can sometimes alienate people.

I spoke to Lynette and Rosie this morning. It's been 12 weeks now since I've seen them — far too long — and I wonder how much Rosie has grown up while I've been away, and what she'll look like when I get back. And what's she's learnt and whether she'll remember me when I get home. One thing's for sure, Rosie's grammar and ability to hold a conversation have improved enormously in recent months. She seems to have grown up now, and I miss her dearly.

# MAY 19 Cardiff

**GROUP A**
At Leicester, Zimbabwe 9-252 (50 overs; GW Flower 45, A Flower 68*) defeated India 249 (45 overs; S Ramesh 55, A Jadeja 43, HH Streak 3-36, HK Olonga 3-22) by three runs

At Northampton, South Africa 9-199 (50 overs; DJ Cullinan 49, L Klusener 52*, WPUJC Vaas 3-46, M Muralitharan 3-25) defeated Sri Lanka 110 (35.2 overs; RS Mahanama 36, JH Kallis 3-26, L Klusener 3-21) by 89 runs

ONE THING I HAVEN'T ruled a line through on this tour is S. Waugh making some sort of contribution at the bowling crease. I have had my eye on bowling in this World Cup for at least the last six months, and have been gradually building up in the nets and in games. In this regard, the six overs, 1-22, against Scotland was a nice start. This is the sort of role I see myself playing — not bowling 10 overs, but maybe five or six if they're coming out okay. I've got no injury worries and feel very good, so there is no reason why I can't contribute.

On another matter, we have received a message from the Australian Cricket Board that, following the controversy over Warney's comments on Arjuna Ranatunga, the players in the squad who are writing for newspapers — and I am one, contributing a column for the *Sunday Times* — will have their contributions to the literary world vetted from now on.

ACB boss Malcolm Speed said, 'Shane and the other players who are writing columns have been directed to provide a hard copy of any proposed article to the team manager, and if he's not happy with it it will be rejected.'

At our team meeting tonight, the prelude to our important game against New Zealand in Cardiff, we acknowledged that the game is going to be a lot tougher than many observers think. New Zealand always seem to play well against us and the wicket in Cardiff is one that is very similar to Kiwi wickets, in that it will be low and slow.

The dangermen we have singled out are Chris Cairns and Chris Harris, but we know that New Zealand are a team without any real stars. Instead, they are a group of individuals of around the same ability, so you have to respect them as a team, particularly as they also have an excellent coach in the former NSW and Australian wicketkeeper, and NSW coach, Steve Rixon.

# MAY 20 Australia v New Zealand, at Cardiff

**GROUP B**

At Cardiff (Wales), Australia 8-213 (50 overs; DS Lehmann 76, RT Ponting 47, GI Allott 4-37) lost to New Zealand 5-214 (45.2 overs; RG Twose 80*, CL Cairns 60) by five wickets

At Chester-le-Street, Pakistan 6-261 (50 overs; Yousuf Youhana 81*, Moin Khan 47) defeated Scotland 167 (38.5 overs; GM Hamilton 76, Wasim Akram 3-23, Shoaib Akhtar 3-11, Abdur Razzaq 3-38) by 94 runs

Every wicket we take, every run we score
Is never enough, we must want more
And if we do, we will be kings
Then all of us, can have a sing

We'll sing about whatever we please
'Cause the rest of the world will be at our knees
And if we win for our great land, we then will sing
'Underneath the Southern Cross' I stand.

**Ricky Ponting**

THE RESPECT for the New Zealanders as a team that we talked about during our pre-match meeting was certainly justified, because they ended up beating us quite comfortably.

We had our chances, but we didn't take them. First, we recovered from a pretty poor start — both Mark Waugh and Adam Gilchrist failed — as Ricky Ponting and Darren Lehmann put on an excellent partnership. Unfortunately, however, neither of these two went on to post a really big score, and then I was very disappointed to play the shot that I got out to, for 7. The sweep shot is a shot I have been playing well lately, but this time, facing Chris Harris, I didn't quite get on to it, probably because I knew instinctively that it wasn't the right shot to play against him. As we all know, indecision is nearly always a recipe for failure. I was dismissed at 4-149 in the 36th over, but after Lehmann's fall at 5-172 six overs

*Warney on the balcony at Cardiff, proudly letting the world know about the birth of his son and heir.*

later, we went downhill. We should have made around 240 or 250; instead, we were all out for just 213.

Then we had New Zealand in big trouble at 4-49 after 15-and-a-half overs, with Glenn McGrath and Shane Warne bowling against Roger Twose and Chris Cairns. But from this point the script certainly didn't go the way we expected it to. McGrath had Twose caught off a no-ball. Then we had him dropped when he was on 0. To top our misfortune off, we missed a run out chance when he was still 0. Then he was half-volleyed at second slip by Mark when he was still 0. After that, Twose didn't look back, playing an outstanding innings, and showing that these guys always have a point to prove when they play Australia. Like most sides, they really want to beat Australia, which always makes our task a bit more difficult.

It certainly was a disappointing day, and not made any easier by the fact that the crowd was clearly behind the New Zealanders. This, apparently, is something we are going to have to get used to.

Afterwards, we went out for a team dinner to celebrate the arrival of Warney's son, Jackson, who had been born the previous evening. We all had a cigar, a laugh and a good drink at our favourite local Italian. It was a good night. Nearby was a table full of priests, who had come in for the evening, and we had a singing competition against them. They clearly fancied themselves, while Tom Moody was our star performer, and many neutral observers thought we took the cash. After that we had a few more drinks downstairs. We tried to relax and forget about the cricket, and get together as a group, which is even more important when you lose. Such camaraderie allows you to regroup and get things moving in the right direction.

# MAY 21 Cardiff to Leeds

**GROUP B**
At Dublin (Ireland), Bangladesh 182 (49.2 overs; Mehrab Hossain 64, Naimur Rahman 45, CA Walsh 4-25, RD King 3-30) lost to West Indies 3-183 (46.3 overs; RD Jacobs 51, JC Adams 53*) by seven wickets

TONIGHT I SET OFF into the heart of Leeds with Adam Dale, who is a good fella. We had earlier survived a six-hour bus trip to get up to Leeds, after which we had a bite to eat at a Chinese restaurant. This was followed by a game of tenpin bowling and some video games, and capped off by a trip to the cinema to see a movie called *Existence*, which wasn't that great. Still, this was a nice relaxing evening away from cricket life and closer to normal life, which is something all the guys crave.

Of course I couldn't help but reflect on our loss to New Zealand. We knew beforehand that the match was going to be a closely-fought and scrappy affair. They have a well-balanced side with innovative batsmen and an attack well suited to the Sophia Gardens wicket at Cardiff, which played like most tracks in New Zealand.

The Kiwis are a team who have worked enormously on their fielding and in players such as Chris Harris and Nathan Astle they have men who, given the right conditions, can be match winners.

And, inevitably, the New Zealanders were motivated to do well against us. I heard Roger Twose comment that they felt we were like bullies to them, always trying to intimidate and pressure them. Their determination to prove themselves on this big stage, plus their skill, made this, for us, a game that was always going to be a difficult test. Zimbabwe, I am sure, had pretty much the same attitude and feelings going into their game against India two days back, even though Sachin Tendulkar was not playing.

We had plenty of opportunities to win the game, but our batting was not as effective as we had planned it to be.

There were some soft dismissals, causing us to lose momentum and fall about 30 runs short of the total we should have achieved. Totals beneath 220 are not enough in this tournament, as indeed is the case in all 50-overs cricket, be it at domestic or international level.

In such situations, quick wickets are required, and we did not gain enough of them. Shane Warne and Glenn McGrath bowled well, but a few missed half-chances cost us dearly. Both Twose and Cairns played intelligently and forcefully enough to guide their team to within sight of the finishing line. Their eventual victory was well deserved.

And for us a wake-up call. We need to be hungrier and more focused if we want to proceed to the Super Six.

# MAY 22 Leeds

**GROUP A**
At The Oval, South Africa 7-225 (50 overs; G Kirsten 45, HH Gibbs 60, L Klusener 48*) defeated England 103 (41 overs; AA Donald 4-17) by 122 runs
At Worcester, Zimbabwe 9-197 (50 overs; GW Flower 42, A Flower 41; GP Wickramasinghe 3-30) lost to Sri Lanka 6-198 (46 overs; MS Atapattu 54, GJ Whittall 3-35) by four wickets

ALTHOUGH TODAY'S MATCHES went pretty much as I expected them to, a couple of quite unexpected victories in this World Cup have illustrated what many of us have known for a while — that we have reached the point where every major one-day nation is sufficiently well equipped to beat just about any opponent they come up against. This closing of the gap between the teams is much more apparent in the shortened form of the game, for many reasons. The most obvious is the increased exposure of the so-called cricketing minnows, such as Zimbabwe and Kenya, to a more extensive international program, instead of the previous bits-and-pieces schedule that didn't allow them to move forward.

This commitment from the cricketing authorities has enabled these countries to make their players full-time professionals, playing against tougher opposition week after week, which has led to an overall improvement in standards and attitudes. In addition, each one-day team now has a back-up support group made up of a coach, manager, physiotherapist and fitness adviser. Many also delve into what was the 'taboo' area of sports psychology, in order to give the players every opportunity to advance their game and be looked after in a professional way. Many teams also have a computer system that can provide detailed information, such as a player's susceptibility to a certain type of bowler, when a bowler may try to bowl an in-swinger following a number of out-swingers, and perhaps an analysis of how somebody bowls a slower ball — all of this can be seen in a matter of minutes. Some people might say you should know this already, without the aid of technology, but what the computer does is confirm or disprove what you had previously believed.

Teams are also more knowledgeable. They are constantly playing against each other, which takes away the element of surprise and doubt often used to affect certain individuals. By its very nature, the one-day game is also restrictive, thus evening up the contest. For example, you cannot bowl a bouncer in the limited-overs game. This takes away the fear factor for many batsmen, and their need to have a complete and competent technique. This rule, together with the strict interpretation of the wide, means the batsman generally knows which areas a delivery will land in, so it makes sense to work on your front-foot driving. Bowlers are restricted to 10 overs each and subject to fielding restrictions. Hence, if you see off their most dangerous individuals, the task will inevitably become easier. You still need enormous skill and technique to do well, but the window of opportunity for the traditionally powerful nations to stand out and dominate is much smaller than it once was.

Our performance against New Zealand lacked an edge and this indefinable quality must be found against Pakistan at Headingley tomorrow, for this is a match we must win. In major competitions there are always crunch moments when everything is on the line. If we are to make an impact, we must give our all against the likes of Shoaib Ahktar, one of the quickest bowlers, if not the quickest speedster, in the world, and Wasim Akram, whose pace and ability to swing the ball has not been affected by the passing years.

This morning at training at Headingley it was freezing cold, and all the guys were able to try out their new longjohns, which had just been freighted over by the Australian Cricket Board. They go from bottom to toe, and come in a variety of colours, which look appalling with our bright yellow outfits. Nevertheless, they did the trick, keeping us nice and warm.

After what for me was a satisfying training session, we had an open team discussion, where everything was laid on the line. Basically, what came out of that was that we need to support each other more and be a bit more patient in our cricket. I think, too, that we need to enjoy our sport a bit more, something that has been suggested to me by more than one team-mate. It's important and beneficial to occasionally have these open sessions, to give players the chance to get things off their chests and work on what has been going wrong. As long as everyone can see such discussions as being constructive, and not take any criticisms personally, then such exercises are usually of substantial benefit. In this case, I feel our chat was something of a breakthrough session for us all, and that things will be on the up from here.

The time has come for us to translate our practice form onto the field. Tomorrow is a big game. I think if we lose to Pakistan, more than likely we're going to miss out on making the next stage. But if we win, I believe it will be the catalyst for us to go all the way. This could be the crunch game of the tour.

For us, Shane Lee is injured, out with a knee ligament injury and replaced by Damien Martyn, but to be honest, the change might have been made anyway. And Paul Reiffel will come in for Adam Dale. Chippen is a little unlucky; he's bowled well, but we need a bowler with a little more bounce and whose 'length ball' pitches a fraction shorter, and that's Pistol. He took six wickets in our last Test appearance up here at Headingley, in 1997, and eight in 1993, so we know he'll be comfortable in the surroundings.

As I sit here tonight in my hotel room, watching a bit of TV, I can't help reflecting on some points we have to prove tomorrow. The press has started to write us off, and it will be nice to show them up. But, as even our kinder critics have observed, things are going to have to change real soon.

Today, England were hammered by South Africa, which to me was predictable, but the local press didn't see it coming. They thought that because they beat Kenya they were going to win the World Cup. They can be so fickle, the media, yet sometimes I believe they don't think enough about the game.

Tomorrow's game is what I have to think about. Here's hoping we play well.

# MAY 23 Australia v Pakistan, at Leeds

**GROUP A**

At Bristol, India 2-329 (50 overs; S Ramesh 44, RS Dravid 104*, SR Tendulkar 140*) defeated Kenya 7-235 (50 overs; K Otieno 56, SO Tikolo 58, DS Mohanty 4-56) by 94 runs

**GROUP B**

At Leeds, Pakistan 8-275 (50 overs; Abdur Razzaq 60, Inzamam-ul-Haq 81, Moin Khan 31*) defeated Australia 265 (49.5 overs; ME Waugh 41, RT Ponting 47, SR Waugh 49, MG Bevan 61, Wasim Akram 4-40, Saqlain Mushtaq 3-51) by 10 runs

> Every great work, every big accomplishment,
> has been brought into being through holding to the vision.
> And often, just before the big achievement,
> comes apparent failure and disappointment.
>
> For the greatest accomplishment is not in never falling,
> but in rising again after you fall.
>
> **Muhammad Ali**

THE GAME DIDN'T GO as we would have liked, although we did play some excellent cricket, and the final result went Pakistan's way, by 10 runs.

I won the toss, which makes 13 out of 14 on this international tour. Quite amazing! However, we haven't used winning the toss to our advantage all that often. Today, we looked to be in reasonable shape in the morning session, having them 3-46 in the 13th over; even after Abdur Razzaq was dismissed near the 40-over point they were only 4-164. At this point, all the bowlers were going well. Unfortunately for us, our opponents went berserk in the last 15 overs, scoring 145 runs. Every bowler went for big runs, even Glenn McGrath, who conceded 40 runs from his final three overs.

A target of 276 represented a massive chase, especially on such an overcast day with the ball zipping around a bit and Pakistan having two world-class quick bowlers in Wasim Akram and Shoaib Akhtar. It was always going to take a massive effort to get the runs against those guys, even before we lost Adam Gilchrist from the innings' third ball, 1-0. Mark Waugh and Ricky Ponting put on a great counter-punching partnership of 91, but for the second straight game no-one went on to post a big score. Michael Bevan got 61, I managed 49, and for a long time we were in with a real chance. In fact, we needed 38 off the last five overs, 67 off the last 10 with six wickets in hand, but we weren't quite good enough. Near the end, with the light fading, it was almost impossible to hit fours against the Pakistanis, who for some reason seem to get more reverse swing than anyone else.

Getting so close was a fine effort, but also extremely frustrating. We now must win our next two games to have any chance of qualifying for the Super Six, and probably win seven in a row to win the Cup. We're going to have to be pretty good, and better than we've been in the last week, to do that.

Pics: Allsport

*Above: Pakistan's captain Wasim Akram*

*Right: Shoaib Akhtar seems reasonably pleased to have knocked me over, as Pakistan surge to a 10-run victory at Headingley.*

*Ricky Ponting on the balcony at Headingley, watching the chaotic scenes at the end of our match against Pakistan, and, at the same time, pondering our second loss of the tournament in three matches.*

However, the mood in the dressing room was more upbeat than after the New Zealand game. We know we're getting a little closer to our best, but we're also aware that we're leaving our run very late.

I still believe we can go all the way, although it is going to take a major effort from all the players to make this happen. Even though most people are writing us off, the vibe in the team is immensely better now than it was just a couple of days ago.

Trying to find a place to assess our performance and down a few beers at the same time wasn't easy on this, a Sunday night. However, Adam Dale, Damien Fleming and I managed to squeeze in half an hour before closing time at a pub not too far from our hotel. During our brief debate we all agreed that our bowling simply wasn't up to scratch today, especially when the Pakistanis starting swinging, and that perhaps it was time to develop a broader bowling plan that covers all scenarios. Basically, we were talking common sense, but if it's down on paper then everyone is heading in the same direction and there can be no excuses if things go awry.

I left the pub feeling even more positive about the rest of the World Cup than I had been after leaving the Headingley dressing room a couple of hours earlier. And as captain, I was grateful that Chippen and Flem are willing to put a plan together in a couple of days, to be presented to the lads before our next game.

# MAY 24 Leeds to Durham

GROUP B

At Edinburgh (Scotland), Bangladesh 9-185 (50 overs; Minhajul Abedin 68*, JAR Blain 4-37) defeated Scotland 163 (46.2 overs; GM Hamilton 63) by 22 runs

At Southampton, New Zealand 156 (48.1 overs; M Dillon 4-46) lost to West Indies 3-158 (44.2 overs; RD Jacobs 80*) by seven wickets

ONE ISSUE that received some press this morning was the behaviour of the young Pakistani quick Shoaib Akhtar, who was given an 'unofficial rocket' from match referee Raman Subba Row after being involved in several incidents, including a couple of chats with myself and Ricky Ponting during our innings.

Shoaib did seem to lose his cool at one point, but I thought Wasim Akram, Pakistan's captain, handled it very well on the field. This is certainly not the sort of thing I'm going to worry about, then or now. I play the game as hard as anyone out in the middle, so I'll leave these things to whoever has to pass judgement. I do remember, though, my parting comment to Shoaib after he tried to give me a nudge with his boot …

'Every dog has its day.'

Yesterday was his. Hopefully before this competition is over, I might have mine.

We began today with a 9am pool session, to get the stiffness and soreness out. I know myself that I'm feeling a bit stiff after the bowling, fielding and running between the wickets I enjoyed yesterday. This post-match recovery session is part

*Shoaib Akhtar and I exchange pleasantries at Headingley.*

of our strategy to reduce injuries and is going to be a regular part of our routine, like stretching before each game. The rehabilitation complete, we set off on a two-hour bus trip north to Durham.

In the afternoon I had an excellent game of golf. Moods and I took down Pigeon and Junior by five holes, in a huge upset. It was good to get out and have a walk around and take the other lads' cash. Tonight we went to a Pizza Hut, where Moods, Punter, Warney, Allan Border and I joined in for an enlightening evening full of anecdotes, memories, ham and pineapples.

Earlier, I'd had a lengthy discussion with my old mate, Tim May, now President of the Australian Cricketers' Association, on the burning issue of player security during and after matches. Maysie is planning to issue a statement saying that the team is so upset by the lax security at the end of matches that we are considering taking sterner action if the situation doesn't improve.

Hopefully, that might make an impact. I think the whole situation is ridiculous, yet it seems the chaos won't be corrected until we see a disastrous incident.

# MAY 25   Durham

**GROUP A**
**At Nottingham, Zimbabwe 8-167 (50 overs; GW Flower 35) lost to England 3-168 (38.3 overs; N Hussain 57\*, GP Thorpe 62) by seven wickets**

FOR SOME REASON, over here we haven't quite gelled over the past week or so. Guys have gone their separate ways a bit and I think some players are becoming a bit distracted, thinking that if they do well in this World Cup it's going to set them up afterwards. Unfortunately, it seems to me that the team aspect has been lost a bit. This is an issue that must be addressed, and I'm sure it can be — all the guys are great fellows and we all want the same thing.

This was brought home in Leeds, where a press report had Warney and I feuding, based on 'a source close to the side'. I couldn't understand this, as I certainly haven't got a problem with Shane. I don't know where it's come from, but to have this sort of thing aired in the media, raised by an Australian commentator, too, is very disappointing. Inevitably, I've started thinking there are some rumblings about, even though I haven't heard them. I brought the issue up at the team meeting tonight — if anyone has any problems, I asked, bring them into the open in a team atmosphere, rather than outside of the team. But although some minor concerns were raised, there was nothing sinister, or major, to substantiate the allegations in the media. In fact, I now feel totally reassured that everyone is 100 per cent behind me. Many members of the squad admitted they had been quite shocked when they read the allegations. If we were as divided as the reports had suggested, our chances in this World Cup would be less than zero.

Anyone who writes us off now is a bad judge. I reckon we're going to win these next two games, get through to the next round and then play some good cricket after that.

And I know at least one bloke back in Australia agrees with me. I read today that our two losses had not prevented one punter putting $10,000 on us to win it all. A spokesman for Darwin Allsports, who took the wager, explained that his staff were amazed at the bet, which was made after our odds blew out to 10-1 following the loss to Pakistan.

'He stands to win $100,000 dollars, but boy we reckon it's a pretty brave bet,' the spokesman said, before adding that after the bet was placed Australia's odds shortened to 8-1. South Africa are favourites at 13-10, ahead of Pakistan at 23-10.

The bowling plan Flem and Chippen have worked on is now in place, after we convened a meeting to discuss it fully. The strategy covers the different phases of the innings, the first phase being 0 to 15 overs, then 16 to 25, 25 to 40 and finally the last 10. All the things we could expect to see in those 50 overs were covered, including the condition of the wicket, the opposition's tactics and our own strengths.

Specifically, we see the last 10 overs as being probably the most crucial when we're in the field. This is the part of the game where we have been punished in recent times. We've decided we need to get back to bowling the yorker length, to try to stop the boundaries that have been hurting us. More generally, we've come to the conclusion that we need to be more patient, particularly in the middle overs, although we'll keep attacking if we can at the start. Of course, these tactics can be modified if certain situations arise. The bottom line for all of us is to put our full concentration into the next ball and execute what we need to do to the best of our ability, and for the benefit of the team.

# MAY 26 Durham

**GROUP A**
At Amstelveen (Holland), Kenya 152 (44.3 overs; Ravindu Shah 50, L Klusener 5-21) lost to South Africa 3-153 (41 overs; JH Kallis 44*) by seven wickets
At Taunton, India 6-373 (50 overs; SC Ganguly 183, R Dravid 145, GP Wickramasinghe 3-65) defeated Sri Lanka 216 (42.3 overs; PA de Silva 56, A Ranatunga 42; RR Singh 5-31) by 157 runs

FIRST THING, we set off for a go-kart adventure, an activity that has in the past proved to be a highly enjoyable break away from the routine of touring life. It also managed to get all the guys together, which is something we need to do more often. Afterwards, miraculously considering the number of near misses and scant regard for safety shown by the likes of Martyn and McGrath, there were no serious injuries to report.

The winning pair was Mark Waugh and Michael Bevan in a bit of an upset. They called themselves the 'Steady Eddies', which was exactly what they were. No mistakes, no crashes, stayed out of trouble and won the day. I paired up with Chippen, and we won pole position during the warm-up laps. But unfortunately when it came to the actual race, Chippen was pushed off early and spent two laps on the off-field grass, which cost us any chance of glory and him a good deal of grief from his co-driver.

Watching TV tonight proved to be not only entertaining but also highly inspirational. I was enthralled by the never-say-die attitude displayed by Manchester United in the Champions Leagues Final against Germany's Bayern Munich in Amsterdam. Two minutes to go in injury time, United were down 1-0 to the German club, but they came back to score twice and complete a historic treble, as they have already won the English Premier League and the FA Cup. As I watched this stunning fightback I couldn't help thinking that anything is possible in sport and in life, if you want it badly enough and have enough faith in yourself and those around you. What we have to do in the World Cup suddenly seems quite simple — go out there, give it a 'red-hot go', and trust ourselves.

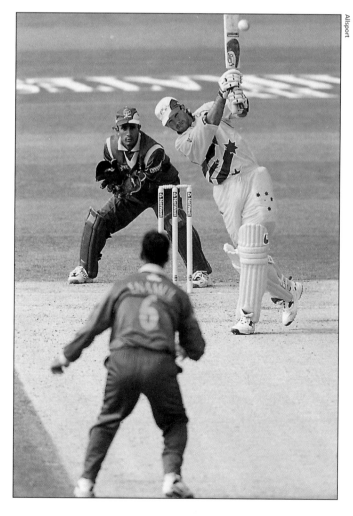

*Ricky Ponting at Chester-le-Street, during our top-order's tremendous assault on the Bangladesh bowlers.*

# MAY 27 Australia v Bangladesh, at Chester-le-Street

GROUP B

At Chester-le-Street, Bangladesh 7-178 (50 overs; Mehrab Hossain 42, Minhaz-ul-Abedin 53*, TM Moody 3-25) lost to Australia 3-181 (19.5 overs; AC Gilchrist 63, TM Moody 56*) by seven wickets

At Leicester, Scotland 68 (31.3 overs; GM Hamilton 24*, CEL Ambrose 2-8, CA Walsh 3-7) lost to West Indies 2-70 (10.1 overs) by eight wickets

Opening the innings is Junior,
Who has no equal when it comes to class.
Gilly is explosive — that day at the MCG,
Who can forget what he did to Sri Lanka and Vaas.

Punter, with his exciting fielding and reliable batting,
Behaves like the rudder of our ship.
And at four is Boofa with his clever placement and innovative shots,
Let's not forget he also hits them long and crisp.

Tugga is our boss and a true leader of men.
Then there is Bevo, who has been rated the best one-day batsman ever,
With an average of 60 plus.
Marto is as good as any of the lads that have been mentioned,
And, of course, we have wonderful allrounders in BJ, Pistol and Moods,
Who are in the the eyes of the team, very much true legends.

Warney is the best spinner in the world,
Without a single doubt.
With Flemo and Chippen bowling into the wind,
Trying to swing the ball both in and out.

Pigeon is our spearhead, and what a wonderful bowler he is,
And we can't forget Swamp, Misso, Brute, Walshie,
And our true friend we call the Phys.
The names I've listed are true champions indeed,
All we have to do is believe in ourselves and, yes, we will succeed.

So, thank you, my mates, for listening to this poem,
I know none of you want to leave the World Cup early,
And watch the Super Sixes from home.
So lastly, don't forget the numbers that sit proudly on our hats,
For we all very much did earn them,
By doing what everyone here does best ...
Speaking with the ball and speaking with our bats.

**Adam Dale**

YESTERDAY'S GO-KARTING set the mood for today's match, which turned out to be our best day's cricket so far during the tour. Because of the possible importance of run-rates in calculating who will go through to the Super Six, the agenda before the game was simple — we needed to bowl Bangladesh out cheaply, and then score quickly ourselves, or we needed to score as many as we possibly could, and then bowl our opponents out for as little as possible.

We managed to restrict them to 178, more than we'd planned the night before but in fact not a bad effort considering how good the Chester-le-Street track is. However, besides Shane Warne, who I thought bowled really well, and Tom Moody, who came back into the side and took 3-25, our bowlers were not overly impressive. They lacked the edge we've been looking for. But Ricky Ponting was his usual superb self in the field, lifting all around him.

With the West Indies having completed an easy win over New Zealand, it was imperative we boosted our run rate, and we smashed 180 runs off just 19.5 overs. Adam Gilchrist hit 63 off 39 balls, Mark Waugh also batted well, Ricky Ponting had a good knock, and the big bonus was Moody, who was sent in early and smashed 56 off 29 balls, the fastest-ever World Cup half-century. Tom's effort today has given him a huge boost and nailed the No. 7 all-rounder spot in this Australian World Cup team.

Afterwards, all the boys went out for a drink together. I sense that the mood in the camp, which had improved somewhat after the Pakistan game, has now changed dramatically. The style of the win over Bangladesh has reminded us that we're capable of achieving anything if we set our minds to it, and that winning is so much more enjoyable than being in a losing dressing room full of rueful post-mortems.

# MAY 28  Durham to Manchester

**GROUP B**
**At Derby, Pakistan 8-269 (50 overs; Ijaz Ahmed 51, Inzamam-ul-Haq 73*, GI Allott 4-64) defeated New Zealand 8-207 (50 overs; SP Fleming 69, CZ Harris 42, Azhar Mahmood 3-38) by 62 runs**

WE SET OFF MID-MORNING for Manchester, which is a favourite cricket spot of ours as we have put in some excellent performances on Ashes tours past. This was where we won the Ashes in 1989, and for me there is the memory of my two Test hundreds in the Third Test of the 1997 series. We settled in nicely at the Copthorne Hotel, where we have stayed previously. This was our day off, and some of the guys took to the golf course, while I decided to chill out and plan for the days ahead.

I did have a good look at the papers, though, and one story caught my eye, and made me realise that I'm not going to get very far on the questions of crowd control and player safety. I read today that the World Cup organisers have released a statement which said that the 'carnival of cricket' they are eager to promote must carry on. After a meeting in Birmingham to discuss, among other things, the issue of crowd invasions at the end of matches, the organisers decided that the existing security arrangements were satisfactory.

'I think people want to feel part of it,' a Mr Michael Browning, the event manager, said, 'which is why we promoted this World Cup as a carnival. There is a tradition in England that people are allowed on the field at the end but I would appeal to members of the crowd to come on a little bit more slowly, and in a more orderly way.'

Mr Browning was quoted as saying that he understood the concerns expressed by Steve Waugh, but apparently added that there had been only one 'nasty' incident involving a player, at Leicester, where India's captain Mohammad Azharuddin had been jostled by a spectator but declined to press charges. He must have been looking elsewhere during our game against Pakistan at Headingley, because I clearly saw a Pakistani player scuffle with a spectator, in an incident that appeared to end with a punch being thrown.

I would have thought that was one too many, but I've made my last comments on the issue. Thankfully, though, the ACB and the ACA are both supporters of my views.

# MAY 29 Manchester

**GROUP A**
At Birmingham, India 8-232 (50 overs; SC Ganguly 40, RS Dravid 53) v England 3-73 (after 20.3 overs) — play abandoned for the day, match to be completed tomorrow
At Chelmsford, Zimbabwe 6-233 (50 overs; NC Johnson 76, AA Donald 3-41) defeated South Africa 185 (47.2 overs; SM Pollock 52, L Klusener 52*, NC Johnson 3-27, HH Streak 3-35) by 48 runs

I AM CONVINCED Glenn McGrath will put his hand up tomorrow and be the man to do the damage to the West Indies, in the same manner as he did during our recent Test series in the Caribbean. It is, of course, a must-win game for us, but in a way this will suit us, as we generally perform at our best when the stakes are at their highest.

There are many scenarios as to who is going to go through to the Super Six stage from Group B, but in one sense our requirement is simple — for us to progress, with either two points or no points, we must get past the class and gathering momentum of the Windies.

For both ourselves and Brian Lara's men, the first couple of weeks have been a period where they have had to acclimatise to the colder weather and, more significantly, manage to cope with the white balls. As I've said before, the English white Dukes are harder than normal, swing much further through the air, and are deviating considerably off the favourable bowling surfaces that we have encountered.

This is why, as I predicted before the tournament, many of the top-order players have struggled to make an impression while the middle-to-late order have prospered. The two form teams of the World Cup — Pakistan and South Africa — have great depth in their batting, with players such as Lance Klusener, Shaun Pollock, Azhar Mahmood and Moin Khan coming in at eight and nine. In their matches to date, these guys have either consolidated the good work of those who batted before them or have rebuilt the innings and made the final total respectable enough for their teams to compete.

These two sides, South Africa in particular, have backed up their quality batting with some tremendous fielding. To cap it off, their strike bowlers have consistently done early damage, which enables the rest of the attack to settle into a rhythm without too much pressure.

While it is always encouraging to get off to a flyer and begin your campaign in grand style, the team to lift the World Cup will be the one to peak at the right time, which generally means gathering momentum as each game passes by. But we cannot afford to wait any longer to slip into top gear, so the increase in intensity and improvement in our general all-round cricket that has seen us get better with every game to date has been most encouraging.

The clash with the West Indies at Old Trafford will be the decider in many ways, not only for Group B, but also to establish who has had the better of the previous two months of tough, exciting and uncompromising cricket. The one-day series in the Caribbean ended in unsatisfactory circumstances, with the crowd's intervention leading to a reduced game in Barbados that left us with an empty feeling after our

## Team Meeting — the Captain's Notes

### Group B, Australia v the West Indies, at Old Trafford

- Thanks for the input, which was excellent.
- Our training has been very good, and now things appear to be going our way. The results and momentum are in our favour.
- Getting 265 v Pakistan was a big effort, then a great result v Bangladesh.
- We play our best cricket when we hustle — let's play with a bit of purpose in our game, and do it with the bat and ball.
- Let's play aggressively — together as a unit.
- Let's save every run, and push them hard in the field.
- Get through the tough periods in the game, and identify when the going is tough.
- Make them feel unwanted — it's 11 v 2 where we're in the field.

Pics: Steve Waugh

*Above: We're on our way to meet the Queen, as we pass Hyde Park on route to Buckingham Palace, and, of course, there was enough time to squeeze in a quick game of 500. Our sojourn to the palace provided us with some of the best moment of humour for the trip, such as when Mike Walsh tripped and stumbled on a carpet edge just as he was being introduced to the Queen. Thankfully for Walshy, he regained his balance and avoided falling and head-butting the Monarch, who was clearly amused by our scorer's unusual style of greeting.*

*Below: This stumble against New Zealand typified our early World Cup performances. I made my ground on this occasion, but losses to the Kiwis and to Pakistan put us in a difficult position if we wanted to win the tournament.*

*Above: The Cup captains at Lord's on May 4, photographed with the ultimate prize.*

*Below: The initial team press conference at Cardiff Castle had a pretty relaxed atmosphere — so much so that all the journalists couldn't believe how much access they had to the players. They complained that all the other teams were so uptight about the media that they made it hard to communicate with them. Here, Mark Waugh is being interviewed for an 'exclusive', while a photographer takes a candid shot and a bemused peacock looks on.*

Allsport

*Left: Shane Warne at the Cardiff Cricket Centre, passing on some secrets (but not too many!) to some budding English champions.*

*Below: One of the pitfalls of playing cricket in England can be the unpredictability of the weather and in Worcester during a warm-up match we fell victim. As you can see, the guys all have ways to fill in time, with some reading, while others wait in a pensive mood for play to resume. Glenn McGrath, as is customary for fast bowlers, enjoys the luxury position of the bench, taking it easy as he reads a story on the controversial former English opener Geoffrey Boycott.*

Steve Waugh

Pics: Allsport

*Above: My World Cup cap, featuring the number '90' to proudly signify that I was the 90th Aussie to play for my country in international one-day cricket.*

*Below: Pakistan's many fans sought every available vantage point, in and outside Headingley, for their Group B encounter with Australia.*

Pics: Allsport

*Australians on the attack —
Ricky Ponting (above), the
acrobat, against Scotland;
Adam Gilchrist (left) on the
charge against Bangladesh.*

*Above: Damien Martyn (right) offers some last-minute instructions, as the drivers await final starter's orders during our go-kart day out near Durham.*

*Below: The Waughs on the run against Zimbabwe at Lord's.*

*Left: Shane Warne celebrates at Headingley. This was the start of a brilliant fightback by our champion, who in our final three games in the World Cup proved that, rather than being washed up as many people had suggested, he was still very much the most important spin bowler of his generation.*

*Below: This could be the best shot I have ever played in limited-overs cricket. As we accelerated the scoring rate during our thrilling run chase, I half-swept/half-pulled the South African quick Steve Elworthy into the crowd beyond the mid-wicket boundary.*

Allsport

*Left: The winning run, a snick just wide of the keeper. The single off the ball before had got us through to the semis, but this was the time to truly celebrate.*

*Below: Tom Moody and I take time out from the euphoria of our win at Headingley. In what is a relatively recent innovation in the quest for a speedy recovery, Dave Misson has the players alternate between an ice-laden bath and a steaming hot bath — the idea being to stimulate blood flow and then slow it down. After our dramatic win, neither Moods nor I seemed to bother with the temperature extremes. All we wanted to do was relive the final few overs and talk about what lay ahead of us.*

chances had been diminished to a point where there was only one possible winner (which, of course, was not Australia!).

To be fair, the West Indies would have felt a little unlucky after the crowd invasion at the end of the previous encounter in Guyana led to a tie being declared after Warney and I tried to scramble a match-saving three off the last ball. It was during that third run that I was cleaned up by a souvenir stump hunter, which resulted in whiplash that is even now still troubling me.

The West Indies, as always, are a dangerous unit with world-class match winners in Lara, Courtney Walsh and Curtly Ambrose — all capable of changing the mood and tempo of the game with acts of brilliance. Lara is obviously their key batsman, but he has yet to play a significant innings in the tournament. Here's hoping he doesn't awake from his slumber tomorrow.

Many have said that Ambrose and Walsh are past their best, but I can assure you, after dealing with them in the recent series, that this is a fallacy. They may not be as consistently quick these days, but both have a great feel for the game, knowing when to bowl the odd ball a metre quicker, when to tighten things up, and when to go for the ascendancy. For us to win, we must handle these champions with care and authority.

I'm expecting this to be one of the matches of the tournament. I believe we'll see a quality contest, with the winner going on to make a big impact on the overall outcome. I, for one, can't wait to lock horns with the likes of Ambrose and Walsh. As a cricketer, you love to test yourself out against the best opposition in the toughest and most crucial games to see whether or not all that hard work in the nets and off the field has been worthwhile.

We had a good team dinner tonight, where many of us again commented on how the feeling in the camp has changed noticeably for the better. We tried something a bit different for this match. Each member of our team was given one opposition player to focus on in the lead-up to the match, and was then invited to provide an analysis of that opponent during a team meeting. I think this worked well. We collated all the information these studies gave us, and the result was a much more extensive scrutiny of our rivals than what we would usually have. And, as a bonus, because all the players came armed with notes, we have our analysis down on paper, to be referred to whenever we need it. No longer do we need to try to memorise everything that's been said.

On a sad note, Mark and I learned today that our grandfather has been taken seriously ill with cancer. The prognosis isn't encouraging, which is desperately hard to take, especially as we are so far from home.

**GROUP A**

At Birmingham, India 8-232 (50 overs; SC Ganguly 40, RS Dravid 53) defeated England 169
(45.2 overs; GP Thorpe 36, SC Ganguly 3-27) by 63 runs

At Southampton, Sri Lanka 8-275 (50 overs; MS Atapattu 52, A Ranatunga 50, T Odoyo 3-56) defeated
Kenya 6-230 (50 overs; MO Odumbe 82, A Vadher 73*) by 45 runs

**GROUP B**

At Manchester, West Indies 110 (46.4 overs; RD Jacobs 49*, GD McGrath 5-14, SK Warne 3-11)
lost to Australia 4-111 (40.4 overs; AC Gilchrist 21, RT Ponting 20, SR Waugh 19*, MG Bevan 20*,
CEL Ambrose 3-31) by six wickets

Two-all in the Tests, three-each in the one-dayers.
It's ironic that it's us and them to see who keeps playing
They ain't got bottles to save them now,
They can't rely on the crowd to run on the ground.

We've started slow, but we're coming home big
We just need to keep nailing the basics to win
There will be times in this game, the turning points of the day
These are the moments we must make go our way.

Don't wait for your mate to seize these times,
Be the man yourself, stand up, take it to the line
The time for talking has long since passed
Let's make our actions talk, sit these blokes on their arse.

**Dave Misson**

THIS WAS THE BEST we've played for a long, long while. The boys
were committed, and our spearhead, Glenn McGrath, just as I said he would,
came through with 5-14 from 8.4 overs of dangerous skill. Shane Warne was superb,
too, as was Tom Moody. To bowl the West Indies out for 110 was an exceptional
effort, especially as we had to win or we were out of the competition. To me, this
performance showed our true character.

The all-round fielding was much better than it has been in our previous matches.
A key factor here was the inclusion of Brendon Julian, who helped give the team
the spark and life it's been lacking in the field. Even though his bowling has been a
bit wayward, BJ is a luxury we can afford because of the other tangibles he brings
to our line-up, including his energy and positive talk.

In reply, we ran into Ambrose and company putting in one final big World Cup
effort, and our top-order batting found itself in a bit of trouble again. When Michael
Bevan came out to join me in the 20th over we were 4-62, and there were some
tense moments before we managed to guide the team through to the Super Six. I'm
glad we weren't chasing 180 to 200, as these guys are still as good as anyone with
a new ball in their hands.

*A moment of concern during my controversial innings against the West Indies at Old Trafford. Did the catch carry? I didn't think it had and fortunately the TV replay proved me right.*

It seems controversy wants to follow us everywhere, and it was no different here. The night before, I had pondered the fact that, if we did beat the Windies, it would be to our advantage to make it as difficult as possible for New Zealand to get through to the next round. Why? The Super Six has been structured so that the six teams involved will play a 'round-robin' format, with the top four going through to the semi-finals. But rather than the teams from the first-round groups playing each other again, their first-round matches against each other will be taken into account when calculating the Super Six table. Consequently, if the West Indies were to come through with us to the Super Six, we'd take two points through with us, from our defeat of Brian Lara's team. But if New Zealand came through we wouldn't take any points on to the next round, because we would have lost to the two other teams from Group B, Pakistan and the Kiwis, who made it through. And it must also be considered that, at the conclusion of the Super Six stage, if two sides are on equal points and fighting for the final semi-final spot, the calculations will revert back to the first stage to see who beat who. Thus, if New Zealand and Australia finish equal fourth in the Super Six table, they would go through while we would go home.

You have to agree that having two points is so much better than none, when you consider how the semi-finalists will be determined. So, when Bevo and I reached 4-90, we stonewalled to our target, taking nearly 20 overs to get the final 20 runs needed for victory. This didn't change the fact that we were through to the Super Six, but it made the Windies' net run-rate higher. And a higher West Indies net run-rate meant that New Zealand needed a bigger victory against Scotland in their final group match tomorrow to send the Windies home.

Complicated, for sure, but I think we were well within our rights. We had played some excellent cricket to get ourselves in a position to determine our destiny to some extent. So long as we made sure we won the game, I reckon it was permissible to play in whatever manner we saw fit.

'We're not here to win friends, mate,' I remember saying a little testily at the press conference afterwards. 'Our job is, if we can, to win the World Cup. I am not

*The match against the Windies, sensational early as Glenn McGrath cut through their batting line-up and dramatic when Walsh and Ambrose reduced us to 4-62 chasing 111 in reply, ended amid a series of taunts from the crowd as we took 13 overs to score the final 19 runs for victory. At game's end, spectators, as usual, streamed onto the field, while I was left to walk, happy with the result but apprehensive about the fans around me, to the safety of the Old Trafford pavilion.*

bothered by anything else at this moment. If this tactic helps us do that, then I am satisfied we have done the right thing.'

I can still remember my early experiences in international cricket. I was a loser for quite a few years and I didn't much care for it. Inevitably, though, there were some questions asked after the game, about 'morality', the crowd's interests and other issues. There was even a suggestion that the two teams might have colluded to slow the game down, which was complete rubbish. I appreciate that what we did wasn't dramatic or entertaining — though the cricket leading up to the slow conclusion certainly was — but what these critics tend to forget is that if we get booted out of the World Cup they're going to put the boot straight in. It's a no-win situation for us. It seems to me that, more and more these days, the media is desperate for headlines and they'll take any chance they get to work up or ignite a controversy. From my point of view, our effort was a professional performance. As captain, I did what I had to do. I thought the situation through and came up with a strategy that was best for the team. As I said, I'd thought about what we would do in such a situation the night before, so in this sense I was one step ahead of most critics. And I was definitely happy with how things worked out.

Now, we have to wait for the result of tomorrow's game. If New Zealand get through against Scotland, we'll join them in the Super Six, but with no points. Obviously, we really want the Scots to put up a good performance, but if they don't we'll know exactly where we stand.

Win all our remaining games, or we won't be playing at Lord's on June 20.

# MAY 31 Manchester

**GROUP B**
At Northampton, Bangladesh 9-223 (50 overs; Akram Khan 42, Saqlain Mushtaq 5-35) defeated Pakistan 161 (44.3 overs; Khaled Mahmud 3-31) by 62 runs
At Edinburgh (Scotland), Scotland 121 (42.1 overs; GI Allott 3-15, CZ Harris 4-7) lost to New Zealand 4-123 (17.5 overs; RG Twose 54*, JAR Blain 3-53) by six wickets

UNFORTUNATELY FOR US, Scotland didn't live up to the early promise they showed in their debut Cup game against us, and New Zealand have won through to the Super Six through their superior net run rate to the West Indies. In fact, the Kiwis finished third in Group B, with Australia second, but they go through with two points, us with none, Pakistan with four (even though they lost to Bangladesh).

From Group A, India, having knocked the Englishmen out of the World Cup, go through with no points, South Africa with two, Zimbabwe with four, even though the Zimbabweans didn't finish top of their group (they beat India, without Tendulkar, who flew back to India for his father's funeral, and South Africa, but lost to England and Sri Lanka). The point-scoring method used to calculate second-round qualifications has proved to be a little complicated and controversial, and doesn't appear to reward the sides with the best overall performance.

However, we knew about the points system when we started, so we can't really complain now.

In regard to the controversial finish to yesterday's match, I can tell you that the press certainly haven't missed us. The *Daily Mail* reckons we reduced the tournament to a 'farce', and told how the Old Trafford crowd 'booed its contempt'. *The Independent* suggested that the match 'degenerated into the cricketing equivalent of a slow bicycle race'.

The London *Daily Telegraph* commented that the game's final overs were 'a poor advertisement for the World Cup spoiled by the complicated points system which actually encouraged Australia to adopt go-slow tactics'.

I did see, in contrast, that New Zealand skipper Stephen Fleming said he understood why we had played as we did, and even added that he would have done the same thing.

Apart from dodging a few media bullets, today was a day off from the cricket, and it was nice to get away. Quite a few of us went to this massive shopping complex, where we enjoyed a morning of tenpin bowling with a few of the Channel Nine crew, with whom we've become good friends. The highlight of this session came in the warm-ups, when BJ slipped during his follow-through and ended up sprawled on all fours, a couple of metres down the lane. I had my money's worth before a ball was delivered.

The afternoon was spent at the flicks, watching *The Waterboy*, which was just what the doctor ordered, because you don't require any grey matter to appreciate the plot.

An important man, Sandy Gordon, our sports psych guy, has rejoined us for the rest of the World Cup tour. He will play an invaluable role, asking questions of the players that no-one else would ask, seeing things from a different perspective. In Manchester, he went around to all the guys and gained important feedback.

In my view, Sandy is vital to our chances, as he provides the players with an 'escape valve' — someone outside the traditional team framework who the players can trust, can use to get things off their chests, or to air their doubts and fears. Sandy, in return, can offer suggestions as to how they might overcome such problems.

Swamp and I have been keen for Sandy to play a big part in the team's preparations, especially on overseas tours, where many potentially provocative things — such as homesickness, staleness, personal problems, whatever — can come into play. Cricket, many observers tell us with some justification, is 90 per cent mental and 10 per cent talent, yet practice and fitness take up 90 per cent of our training regime. My belief is that if we can get a better balance in the way we go about our pre-game routines, we'll be much better equipped to handle moments of adversity and times of self-doubt.

# JUNE 2  London

WE HAVE BEEN ASTOUNDED by the way the criticism of our slow scoring against West Indies has continued over the past two days, considering what was at stake and the importance of us carrying through two points to the Super Six stage, if at all possible. In one sense, in this era where the headline is so important, I can understand the reaction from a journalistic point of view, as our strategy was newsworthy and the cricket, aesthetically, was not good viewing. But to be vehemently criticised by some former players is quite dumbfounding. I'm sure they'd have done the same thing if they had thought about it.

Another subject of much comment in the press here is the question of who will succeed David Lloyd as England's coach. My only advice to the Poms is to appoint an Englishman. Australia has got its own team song, and I can't imagine someone from England or anywhere else singing that song with us after we'd won a Test match. When it comes to crunch time, desperation time, if you're not born with that inner passion, you can't make it up.

Today, all the teams came down to London for a Royal occasion. It was good of the Queen to organise this function to coincide with the 34th birthday of the Waugh twins. First, we were greeted by the Queen formally and then she came around later on and had a bit of a chat with the boys. At this point, I introduced her to a few of the lads who were keen to meet her, including Adam Dale, who is clearly something of a monarchist. When the Queen came our way, Chippen was totally tongue-tied, complete with sweaty palms, standing there unable to utter a syllable. It was quite funny to see a grown man freeze on the spot in this way.

The Queen made comment on our blazers, saying how 'noticeable' they were. Thinking back now, I don't know whether she liked them or not. We talked about her horses for a while, then she apologised for the British weather not being too good for cricket, and then she moved on to meet some of the other 4000 guests (actually there were only 300 people there, but she must get sick of meeting people at functions all the time, and it must seem that there is an endless stream of people waiting to be introduced to her).

Later into the event, all the players were asked to assemble with their respective teams, to be formally introduced to the Queen and Prince Philip. However, Murray Goodwin, who plays for Zimbabwe, somehow found himself lined up with the West Indies squad. When Prince Philip reached Murray, he remarked, 'You don't look too much like a West Indian.' To which Murray replied, 'No, but I wish I was hung like one.' Fortunately, the crack went down well with Prince Philip, who had a good chuckle about it.

So much for protocol! It was suggested to me beforehand that what is really needed from people who are being introduced to the Royal family is for them to be as normal as possible, and say whatever they would usually say. But maybe this wasn't quite what they meant.

London at the moment is very overcast, the wickets have been wet, and it seems there's more rain ahead. I reckon this will suit us more than the Indians, our first opponents in the Super Six, whom we face at The Oval on Friday. I'm very confident about this big match, especially if the wicket is seaming around and bouncing, as the lads from the sub-continent rarely see such conditions and only Dravid and Tendulkar, in my opinion, have the techniques to counter our quicks in these circumstances.

After the Royal function, to celebrate my birthday, I went out to see *The Buddy Holly Story* with Shane Lee. This was a night that I really enjoyed, and it was rewarding to alter the 'movies-restaurants-movies-restaurants' routine that I've found myself in lately. I think I'll pop along to the theatre more often in future. It's great to broaden your interests and experience a 'bit of culture' along the way.

But the World Cup is what we're here for and it all really starts in earnest on Friday, with the game against the Indians. It's time to slip into top gear and put it all together.

# JUNE 3  London

I RECKON WE'RE IMPROVING with every match, and gradually reaching our peak. But there's still room for improvement. We demonstrated against the West Indies what we can do once the chips are down. Those chips are still down, and will be for a while, because any loss is death. We've got to win our next five matches to win the Cup, but we know we can do it.

So what about the Indian trump card, the mighty Sachin Tendulkar?

'We are not focusing on Sachin alone and, anyway, he's capable of nicking the ball like anyone else,' I told a reporter earlier today.

Besides this, he's due to miss out against us. His last nine one-day digs versus Australia have included four centuries and three half-centuries, including an 80 and then three hundreds in his last four innings. Hopefully, he'll open the innings, as he did in Bangladesh last October when he smashed 141, but this time be exposed to our pace attack while the ball is doing a bit.

At that same conference, where I shared a table with Mohammad Azharuddin, I listened while the Indian captain remarked, 'We are playing good cricket now. There has been a big improvement in the manner in which we played the last two matches and I am sure the boys will be able to take the Australians in their stride.'

Azharuddin was in a happy mood. 'We respect the Australians and hope to beat them in this crucial match,' he said.

Who did he fear the most?

'Mark Waugh, Steve Waugh ... everybody!' he responded.

I liked that.

Later in the day, we enjoyed another productive team meeting, where we again asked every player to hone in on an opposition player's strengths and weaknesses. We also had a long group discussion where we identified their key players. On the bowling side there was the quick leg-spinner, Anil Kumble, whom we want to play down the ground.

There's no point risking too many crossbat shots against Kumble, who comes onto the bat and gives little away. Their paceman, Javagal Srinath, was nominated as their most attacking bowler and we stressed the need to see him off. But we are also aware that you can hit fours off him, because there are times when he can lose control.

We've targeted their swing bowler, Debashish Mohanty, as someone we can take runs off. He does swing the ball, but also bowls a lot of four balls. Venkat Prasad is a steady bowler whom we will try to work around. We stressed, too, the opportunity to score a lot of runs from their fifth bowler, who'll either be Robin Singh, Ajay Jadeja or a combination of the two.

Batting-wise, we knew that only their top three batsmen have had a lot of time in the middle, so if we can break through early we have a real chance. There is a lot of pressure on the Indians, given the number of cricket fanatics they represent back home and the fact that they, like us, cannot afford to lose another game. If we go out and play our natural game, we might overwhelm them.

## Team Meeting — the Captain's Notes

### Super Six, Australia v India, at The Oval

Our effort v the West Indies was great. Don't forget why! Let's reproduce again what we did then.

- We had urgency, aggression, hustle, intimidation, desire — must do the same, even if things aren't going our way.
- Let's put them under pressure — particularly in the field.
- Don't forget, the pressure is on them — they've got one billion people supporting them.
- During the game, the crowd will be on their side — let's take our time if they get on a roll. Especially if Tendulkar or Azhar gets going.
- Kumble is a key bowler —play him 'in the V'.
- Attack their fifth bowler.
- Try to take early wickets, to put them under the hammer. Remember, only three of their players have batted a lot in the middle.

# JUNE 4 Australia v India, at The Oval

SUPER SIX
At The Oval, Australia 6-282 (50 overs; ME Waugh 83, SR Waugh 36) defeated India 205 (48.2 overs; A Jadeja 100, RR Singh 75, GD McGrath 3-34) by 77 runs

With our backs against the wall and the Cup on the line,
We played the way we know in the nick of time.
We were up for the Windies and now we're in the Sixes,
And pretty soon there'll be five other teams playing for the riches.

We need to stick to plan and play from the heart,
For we all know that our Cup is just about to start.
Because we've done the hard work,

We'll get our rewards for everyone to see.
And that's why we'll beat India here today
Then we'll celebrate at the Café de Paris.

**Brendon Julian**


OUR TUSSLE WITH the much-heralded Indian batting line-up today at The Oval turned out to be a one-sided affair, after Glenn McGrath again stamped his authority and class on proceedings with a decisive opening spell that ruthlessly disposed of Sachin Tendulkar, Rahul Dravid and Mohammad Azharuddin.

However, although the period when Pigeon was dismantling the Indians' top order was a joyous time for all the Australian supporters and players, I believe we took control of the game in the first 15 overs of *our* innings.

I say this because at the start of play the pitch was helping the bowler-friendly Duke ball dart around off the seam which, in addition to the steepling bounce, made surviving at the crease an art in itself.

The fact that we had not lost a wicket after the opening 15 overs of the day psychologically affected the Indians. You could see this in their body language, as they desperately tried to take early wickets through the highly underrated pace and guile of Javagal Srinath.

The usual manner in which you judge whether a player looks in good form is by how he is timing the ball or piercing the field. Not so at The Oval yesterday. The key was the tightness of the defensive strokes …

My brother Mark played a perfect front-foot defensive shot in the third over of the match, at a time when it was difficult even to contemplate pushing forward at the steepling bounce. This one shot, which to most people would have gone unnoticed, instantly filled me with confidence that it would be Mark's day. There was more than survival at stake here — it was the way in which he was sending out positive signals through his body language. This refusal to be intimidated or dictated

*Right: Noted bird-lover Paul Reiffel is first on the scene after one of London's pigeons made the mistake of trying to intercept a cricket ball during our match against India. Incredibly, this was not the only bird to suffer such a fate during the day.*

*Below: An on-drive during my innings of 36 against India at The Oval.*

to set the pattern for our batting throughout the innings, which from a team perspective was as close as it gets to being perfect.

This was a pitch on which I thought 220 or 230 would be a very good score. To reach the heights of 282 we all had to contribute and back our abilities to the full, which, of course, is easier said than done. Ricky Ponting's straight six off Saurav Ganguly to get off the mark was a brave shot and a sign of what was to come. This was team batting at its best, with each new player carrying on the momentum that had been gathering with each passing over until we finally wore the Indians' spirit down and exposed them in the last four overs.

I thought our batting performance today was our best effort in a one-day game for a number of years. We lost the toss, were sent in, and every single batsman backed himself, playing shots from his very first ball. I rated 280 as a genuinely great score.

The batting talents of Ganguly, Dravid and Tendulkar had been on show regularly in this tournament. But it also presented them with a problem we had identified … their lower-order batsmen had not been out in the middle for any length of time. We felt if we could take early wickets we could dominate the rest of their order or at least control what they would be trying to accomplish.

To this end I was pleased to see Tendulkar coming out to take on McGrath and the new ball on a pitch that was always going to be difficult to negotiate early on. As usual, McGrath rose to the challenge, in concert with the gifted Damien Fleming, and victory was ours after the opening 10 overs of the Indians' innings had been completed.

Following on from our potent opening attack, Tom Moody bowled well, as did Paul Reiffel, but unfortunately Shane Warne was hammered by Robin Singh and Ajay Jadeja — his 6.2 overs going for 49 runs. The sting had gone out of the game by the time Warney came on to bowl, but the Indian batsmen certainly liked his bowling today. I can understand, after what happened today, why some people are suggesting that Shane's merely a very good bowler now, but not the great bowler he used to be. I can sense that some teams are treating him like that, too. I think, however, that both the critics and our opponents might get burnt if they continue taking this attitude.

I've learnt that you should never, ever underrate a true champion. If people want to start writing off the greatest spin bowler in the history of the game, I think they're going to be eating their words and ruining their batting averages before this World Cup is through.

Personally, I was very happy with my score of 36 from 40 balls. I thought it was a good innings, which kept the momentum that had been created by the top-order guys going. Bowling-wise, I took 2-8 from two overs and I snared a catch as well. Unfortunately, though, I hurt my groin bowling again, although I think it was a severe spasm rather than a tear, which means I should be right for our next assignment. But it is a worry and not something I wanted so near to the end of our World Cup tour. Fingers crossed, it will pull up okay in the morning.

Because of some treatment I received for that injury, I was a little late for the post-game press conference. By the time I arrived, Glenn McGrath and Mark Waugh had already satisfied many of our inquisitors' questions. My main point was to stress that we are feeling good about ourselves.

'It was a great team performance,' I told the throng. 'The guys are relaxed, they played their shots today and backed themselves, like Ricky Ponting going down the wicket and getting off the mark with a six. Our team meetings are good, all the guys are making an input. It's working well.'

Anything is possible in one-day cricket, and while we will be confident of victory in our remaining matches, we mustn't get too carried away with our form of the past week. Cricket is a great game and throws up many scenarios you would not expect. Take today's encounter — who would have thought at the start that Tendulkar would have made a duck *and* Shane Warne would be taken for 21 runs off a single over?

And have you ever seen two pigeons killed by a cricket ball on the same day?

# JUNE 5  London

**SUPER SIX**
At Nottingham, Pakistan 7-220 (50 overs; Moin Khan 63) lost to South Africa 7-221 (49 overs; JH Kallis 54, L Klusener 46*, Azhar Mahmood 3-24) by three wickets

IT SEEMS THAT the hourly ice treatment from last evening has helped my groin injury considerably and the prognosis was much more promising this morning. Even tonight, it does feel tender in general and sore in one specific spot, and the spasm still has a good hold, but with the expert treatment from the best hands in the business, Errol Alcott, I'm confident I'll be on deck against Zimbabwe.

The draw for the Super Six has been kind to us, in the sense that we have been in London since my birthday last Wednesday, and will be remaining in London until after our match against Zimbabwe at Lord's. Not only has this given us the chance to enjoy a day off in the UK capital today, as we recuperate after our big win over India, but it also gives me a chance to further my newfound interest in the theatre. I followed up my night at *The Buddy Holly Story* last week with a look at *The Phantom of the Opera* tonight, courtesy of Ray Phillips, our Emirates Air liaison officer, who kindly organised tickets for the team and paid my bill as a belated but much appreciated birthday present.

All the 'heavies' from the Australian Cricket Board have arrived in England, including Chairman Denis Rogers and Chief Executive Malcolm Speed. In fact, it seems as if everyone's in town. Despite the demise of the home team, the World Cup is hotting up, and it seems we're coming good at the right end of the

*Tom Moody smashing the quickest World Cup 50 ever against Bangladesh.*

competition. I really feel we have the momentum to go all the way now. All the guys are confident and we're firing on all cylinders.

Cynical commentators who a week ago were dismissing our chances and ridiculing the omission of some Test players from the Australian one-day squad are now admitting we're a real chance to win it all. It has been very pleasant being able to put the criticism back into the faces of the journalists who wrote us off. They had no faith in us, whereas I knew we'd come good. It was only a matter of time.

Warney is a concern to all of us at the moment. He's been a bit quiet, as if the pressures and hassles of the past fortnight have worn him down. Besides that, everything is going well. Tom Moody is playing some good cricket, and the inclusion of Paul Reiffel in the side has given us more stability and experience. I can rely on both of them to handle the pressure and be consistent. I'm particularly pleased at their good form because Moods and Pistol are guys I've been keen to see in the side, as they are both highly experienced and reliable, two crucial assets.

I can't tell you how much I'm missing home. It's been a long, long time since we left for the Caribbean, a long, long time to be away from the people you love. I'm not sure how much Rosie has changed since I last saw her or what she's doing, but I do know she is talking in full sentences and conversing very clearly compared to when I left home in February. Back then she knew individual words, but couldn't put more than three or four together. And Lynette is well and truly pregnant now — the size of her belly will be a surprise that I can't wait to see.

Home is always the best place to be, but there is still a job to do, which must remain my No. 1 goal at the moment.

Being away from home is getting harder every year, as the amount of time we're required to be away and the amount of things I miss as a consequence increase all the time. But I guess it will all be worth the sacrifice if we can hold that trophy aloft at Lord's 15 days from now — and I believe, because of the way we're playing and the way our momentum is building, that we can do it.

# JUNE 8 London

**June 6 & 7**
SUPER SIX
At Leeds, Zimbabwe 175 (49.3 overs; MW Goodwin 57, ADR Campbell 40, GI Allott 3-24, CL Cairns 3-24) v New Zealand 3-70 (15 overs; MJ Horne 35) — no play possible on extra day, match abandoned, both teams receive one point on Super Six table

**June 8**
SUPER SIX
At Manchester, India 6-227 (50 overs; SR Tendulkar 45, RS Dravid 61, M Azharuddin 59) defeated Pakistan 180 (45.3 overs; Inzamam-ul-Haq 41, J Srinath 3-37, BKV Prasad 5-27) by 47 runs

IT'S BEEN A COUPLE of days since I last put pen to paper. In that time, the Super Six puzzle has been complicated still further by the washed out Zimbabwe-New Zealand contest and India's stunning defeat today of Pakistan. My calculator is a bit confused by all the permutations and possibilities, but it seems that if we defeat Zimbabwe tomorrow, and South Africa then beat New Zealand the following day, and India then beat New Zealand in their final Super Six match, that we could go through to the semi-finals even if we lose to South Africa in our final Super Six match.

But to consider such a situation means that we would be placing our destiny in the hands of other teams, which is something we don't want to do. And, anyway, such hypothesising goes against our much-repeated strategy of taking each game as it comes. Better for us to worry only about the Zimbabwe match, and then, if we win, move forward from there. If we want to think long-term, we have to believe we need to win *every* game if we want to get to Lord's for the Cup final.

I recall, back in my schooldays, how stunned I was when Australia lost to Zimbabwe in the 1983 World Cup. That was the first time Australia had ever met Zimbabwe in a one-day international, and the defeat is a poignant reminder for us to keep focused against the improved 1999 version. We know that these guys are not 'minnows' any more. They work well as a team, never give in and are always at you.

This was stressed at our team meeting tonight. When it was my turn to talk to the lads I began by underlining what a satisfying win it was against India and then emphasising a couple of things that stood out for me in that victory — the manner in which we summed up the conditions so well, our intensity, the way we backed ourselves, the hustle in the field, the control of our bowlers.

But we can't afford to be complacent for one delivery. After all, Zimbabwe are three points ahead of us on the Super Six ladder, and will give us nothing. We must respect them.

But if we keep the same intensity and desire, put the pressure right on them, and work as a team, then I think we'll be okay.

# JUNE 9 Australia v Zimbabwe, at Lord's

SUPER SIX
At Lord's, Australia 4-303 (50 overs; ME Waugh 104, SR Waugh 62, MG Bevan 37*) defeated Zimbabwe 6-259 (50 overs; NC Johnson 132*, MW Goodwin 47, PR Reiffel 3-55) by 44 runs

Five years ago it was Zimbabway, who are they?
Today it is Zimbabwee, on top of the tree
They play with fire and they play with guts
If we give them a sniff, they'll drive us nuts.

We all need to put our hands up and heed the shout
To stay focused and intense and keep complacency out
Today is a chance to keep showing we are contenders
But we must beat these guys well and let 'em know they are pretenders.

**Dave Misson**

ANOTHER EXCELLENT GAME for us. As the Lord's scoreboard showed, our batting has really come good. This time we scored 303, with Mark Waugh crafting a superb century and Ricky Ponting also in magical touch. I scored 62 off 61 balls, and was extremely happy with the way I hit the ball. I was also extremely pleased that I wore my helmet, because if I hadn't I might well have perished or at best copped a broken jaw after Mark launched a straight drive of such ferocity that I had no chance of escaping. All I could do was flinch as it crashed into the grill of my 'lid' at enormous speed.

The only downside of our innings was the injury suffered by Darren Lehmann, who split his finger when hit while batting, needed a couple of stitches and will in all likelihood have to miss our next match, against South Africa.

The most pleasing aspect of our effort was the manner in which each batsman came in and immediately backed himself. This allowed us, as a team, to keep the momentum going and put the pressure back on the bowlers and fieldsmen. This was the sort of batting we've talked about. With our talent and this approach, it will be really tough for our opponents to contain us.

Bowling-wise, our initial 10-over spell was fairly ordinary. I felt we needed to change the tempo of the game, which meant there was only option … Warney. In this situation, there are only two outcomes — either Shane turns it around or the opposition counterattacks. On this occasion, Zimbabwe's opener, Neil Johnson, threw caution to the wind, won the battle, and put his team within striking distance of an unlikely triumph. Fortunately, Reiffel and McGrath came back well and won us a reasonably comfortable victory, but, overall, we need to improve to go all the way. We are still to combine all the facets of our game into one dominant performance, which is very frustrating.

Shane has pulled up with a bit of a sore shoulder, but he'll be good enough to overcome that. I know he would like to have bowled better today, but the whole game wasn't hanging on his 10 overs. I think he'll bowl at his best if a situation comes up for him where his overs are critical.

All in all, despite our occasional struggles today in the field, everything seems to be going pretty well. We've got a trip up to Headingley now, to play South Africa, and I'm looking forward to the occasion. We're playing near our best and have got ourselves on a roll. I think we can win this competition, but we've got to get through our next game, which is going to be our toughest test yet, against the team most critics believe will lift the World Cup on June 20.

*Right: Mark Waugh hitting his fourth World Cup century, against Zimbabwe.*

*Below: Michael Bevan at Lord's, crafting another significant one-day innings.*

Pics: Allsport

# JUNE 11  Leeds

**June 10** — SUPER SIX
At Birmingham, South Africa 5-287 (50 overs; G Kirsten 82, HH Gibbs 91, JH Kallis 53*) defeated
New Zealand 8-213 (50 overs; SP Fleming 42) by 74 runs
**June 11** — SUPER SIX
At The Oval, Pakistan 9-271 (50 overs; Saeed Anwar 103) defeated Zimbabwe 123 (40.3 overs;
NC Johnson 54, Abdur Razzaq 3-25, Saqlain Mushtaq 3-16, including hat-trick) by 148 runs

THE MOST SIGNIFICANT event of the last 48 hours was a three-hour discussion I had today with the head of the Australian selection committee, Trevor Hohns, during which we went through all the candidates for Australian Cricket Board contracts and, more generally, how the Australian team is going at present. It wasn't a case of me making decisions, or even pushing for certain players, more the selectors searching for the captain's view on how everyone is progressing.

It was a frank and open debate. I found the conversation fascinating, as Trevor, an old team-mate from the 1989 Ashes tour, outlined the selectors' perspectives, explained why they prefer certain players in different conditions, and what their ambitions are beyond this World Cup campaign.

Once again, I put myself on the line for the one-day captaincy. If, I told Trevor, the selectors believe someone else is more qualified, or that I'm no longer worth my place in the side, then make the change. Trevor intimated that if we had been eliminated early in the World Cup, my tenure as one-day captain might well have been over, which made me stop for one second and recall how close we came to not reaching the Super Six. However, I'd like to think I'm still one of the better one-day players in the Australian game, and that I'm doing a good job as captain. I want to continue with both captaincy jobs — the Test side and the one-day team — for a bit longer yet. Trevor's honesty — the way he was totally up front with me — was much appreciated, as communication is vital to a team's success. The bold strategies and courageous decisions of Trevor and his selection committee have been a significant part of the Test and one-day team's recent successes.

When we take on South Africa at Headingley on Sunday, we'll know exactly how close they are to the World Cup semi-finals. The chances are that we will already be safely through, given that many people seem to favour India to beat New Zealand, but whatever our needs there is no way we'll be changing the level of our intensity. Keeping the intensity up is just about the main thing in one-day cricket. If you hustle out there and you're hungry, if the intensity is in your cricket, then you're going to play well. I know that's when we're at our best.

We like playing big games in pressure situations. South Africa play cricket similar to us, so not surprisingly we really enjoy the way they play the game. It's a tough contest out in the field. They certainly don't give you anything and we're not going to give them anything.

We wouldn't want it any other way.

# JUNE 12  Leeds

**SUPER SIX**
At Nottingham, India 6-251 (50 overs; A Jadeja 76) lost to New Zealand 5-253 (48.2 overs; MJ Horne 74, RG Twose 60*) by five wickets

WITH NEW ZEALAND having surprised India today, our match tomorrow is now sudden death for us, as we need to win to ensure a semi-final place. Not easy, sure, but if we want to win the Cup we have to beat everyone, so it's no big deal, it just means the pressure of a knockout situation has returned a little earlier than we wanted it. Pressure seems to bring out the best in this Australian side anyway, and if we do win at Headingley we'll have gained a huge psychological advantage over the South Africans, particularly if we are to meet them again in our next match.

South Africa have a highly motivated bunch of cricketers, well-drilled, with an emphasis on team harmony. There's no obvious weak link. They have won an amazingly high percentage of their one-day games in the past two years and are widely regarded as the premier side in this shortened form of the game.

But they can be beaten, and they have been in important games, which is something we will try to exploit, by keeping the pressure on. Of course, we have to play excellent cricket, which I believe we will, especially as our batting has started to fire. On a personal note, I can't wait to tangle with the likes of Donald, Pollock, Elworthy, Kallis and Klusener. These guys are top-class opponents who will exploit any weakness, but it is our job to expose their Achilles heel, if we are good enough and can create enough pressure.

Lance Klusener is the form player of the tournament, complementing his 'in your face' cricket with skill and poise. He is a huge asset for his team, particularly as he never backs down and always believes he is going to come out on top. His enormous strength is aided by a bat weighing more than 3lb. I have seen him strike balls over the boundary ropes that shouldn't have gone that far; our game plan for him will have to be well thought out.

Shaun Pollock is widely regarded as the premier all-rounder in the world, but he is yet to display his talents to the full in this World Cup. If he does, he can win a game with his tremendous clean-hitting and his ability as a bowler to hit the seam regularly. And Allan Donald, as so many batsmen have discovered over the years, is a class act, combining stamina and speed with a high level of skill, which gives batsmen few liberties. Scoring quickly against him invariably involves taking a risk.

Yet in a strange way South Africa's strength in bowling may also be their weakness, for there is a certain uniformity about it. There's no spinner, no left-hander.

But you must always respect opponents, and you also have to look at your own game and make sure all is in order. From our viewpoint, the vibes are good. We have improved with each outing. Confidence goes hand in hand with winning.

One player who has not made a huge impact yet with the bat for us is Adam Gilchrist. Gilly destroyed the South Africans in Sydney 18 months ago, and we'll be looking for a repeat performance here. It is a huge bonus to have him in the team, because he gives us more options. He is a specialist batsman as well as a quality wicketkeeper, and it lets us include another all-rounder or bowler.

Another of our key men is due to shine again on the big occasion. Two weeks after everyone was writing off Glenn McGrath as a threat in this World Cup, some are saying it is all over for Shane Warne. Well, anyone promoting this line of thinking is going to be proved wrong. As I keep saying to anyone who'll listen, the longer I am involved in sport at the highest level, the greater my belief that a champion must never be written off.

But Warney has had a rough couple of days. He's copped a lot of stick in the press over his bowling effort against Zimbabwe and the next day informed the boys he was going to retire. He was so disheartened then, but there were signs at practice today that he might be getting back on track. I do think he's been talked out of retirement, at least in the immediate term, but it appeared for a while as if everything had overwhelmed him. The 'bribery' affair that broke last Australian summer, the controversy over that one cigarette in Barbados, the debate over the captaincy after Mark Taylor retired, his dry run in the Test series in the Caribbean, which ended with him being dropped for that last Test, the controversy that followed his comments in the paper about Ranatunga, being away from home for so long, especially when his son, Jackson, was born, the rumours of a blue between he and I, the incredibly tenacious attention he gets from the tabloid media over here, the many negative, sometimes obscene chants he hears from sections of the crowds, the pressure he puts on himself to always be at his imposing best, the worries over his shoulder — these have all combined to gradually but relentlessly wear him down. Forget the cricket, as friends of many years Shane and I went for a long walk in the park, and had a good discussion. As for his sporting future, I suggested he play through the tournament, then go home, talk everything over with his family and make his decision then.

To be honest, I really don't know which way Warney's going to go. It might depend on how he bowls tomorrow against South Africa and then, if we get through, how he goes for the rest of our tournament.

Such is the nature of one-day cricket that statistics don't always reveal the truth. Only a short time ago, after our convincing win against West Indies, everyone was saying how superlative Shane's bowling was. Suddenly, after a couple of overs of brilliant strokeplay from India's Robin Singh and Zimbabwe's Neil Johnson, many reckon the magic is gone. Don't believe it.

Knowing Shane, he is priming himself for a match-winning performance tomorrow, against a side he respects, in a match he sees as a challenge. Added to the importance of the occasion is the mouthwatering thought of Warne tangling again with one of his great rivals, Daryll Cullinan. Shane seems to raise his game for this confrontation and it should be a stimulating contest.

*Adam Gilchrist, a key member of the Australian line-up, but a little out of sorts with the bat for much of the World Cup. His time in the sun would come in the final.*

Allsport

Playing against South Africa is my favourite type of cricket. They are tough, uncompromising and unforgiving on the field, but, once the game is over, you can have a chat and a beer and look forward to the next time — and the way things are shaping up, that could be as soon as a few days later.

But only if we win.

We've had a good build-up to the game, a nice and relaxing couple of days. Geoff Marsh has ensured that we haven't overdone our training, and from my vantage point it seems the guys are ready to go. The only real downside I can see is that Darren Lehmann won't be playing because of his damaged finger, while, like every time, I imagine, there are a couple of other guys with niggles — the sort of 'injury' you know is there but would never prevent you from playing. Punter has a slight hamstring strain, my groin remains a bit sore, Pigeon has admitted he has a bit of a thigh injury, and Junior's calf is playing up a little. These are things that are part of the game these days and you just have to play through them. I bet, for instance, that there are some players in the South African squad with similar injuries; in fact we've just heard there is very little chance of Jacques Kallis playing tomorrow, which could be a huge setback for our opponents.

Luckily for us, we have the best support crew in the business, with Dave Misson and Errol Alcott working together to keep the guys on the park. A key is the way in which they seek to rehabilitate injured players as quickly as possible. To date on this arduous adventure they have done a brilliant job, getting guys back on the park faster than would have occurred in days gone by.

We know we have to be at least close to our best to beat South Africa. But for the past week we've been the form team of the tournament, so we must be a chance. I firmly believe that if we play well here, and win the game, we will go on to win the tournament.

# JUNE 13 Australia v South Africa, at Leeds

SUPER SIX
At Leeds, South Africa 7-271 (50 overs; HH Gibbs 101, DJ Cullinan 50, JN Rhodes 39, DW Fleming 3-57, SK Warne 2-33) lost to Australia 5-272 (49.4 overs; RT Ponting 69, SR Waugh 120*, MG Bevan 27) by five wickets

> Believe in yourself, and in your plan
> Say not I cannot, but I can
> The prizes in life we fail to win
> Only if we doubt the power within.
>
> **Anon** (read by Adam Gilchrist)

FOR STEPHEN RODGER WAUGH, this has been a dream come true. Not just because we won and therefore reached the World Cup semi-finals, but the way we did it and my contribution to the victory.

After playing international one-day cricket for all these years, and throwing my wicket away so many times and not really achieving what I wanted to do as a batsman, everything finally came together for me … today, on one of the biggest stages of all. To make a big hundred in a crunch situation — coming in at 3-48, chasing 272, on a wicket that was up and down, up against four outstanding quick bowlers — I don't think it gets much tougher than that. To come through in that situation was immensely satisfying.

Bowling-wise, however, we didn't go all that well. The South Africans batted exceptionally to score 271 on a wicket that was doing a little bit. Unfortunately, we bowled on both sides of the wicket, and our length wasn't consistent. The only exception was Warney, who was absorbed by the big occasion and took 2-33. I felt this morning that he might be fired up for a big one, as if the prospect of a clash with his old mate Daryll Cullinan was going to bring the best out in him.

Glenn McGrath wasn't too bad, but the rest of our attack was a mixed bunch at best. We know we must bowl much better when we play these guys again on Thursday. Our fielding was just okay as well; we have to pick up in this area. We're not taking the half-chances — the crucial run out or the spectacular catch — that can turn a game.

The batting in the main, though, was excellent. We did lose the early wicket of Adam Gilchrist, who is struggling, playing from the crease. Geoff Marsh and I have spoken to him about it and we'll be working hard on this area of his technique for the next week. I believe Gilly can still win a game for us. Mark Waugh was the victim of a stupid running-between-the-wickets mix-up with Ricky Ponting, and Damien Martyn tried to pull one from Steve Elworthy, who's much quicker than he looks, but lobbed it to mid-on. It was a tough ask for Marto to come into the team at this point in the World Cup, but I thought he, like Mark, was shaping well until his dismissal.

*Right: Shane Warne has just dismissed Hansie Cronje, lbw for 0. While our other bowlers were relatively expensive, Warney was superb, taking 2-33 and reaffirming his status as the best spin bowler in the game.*

*Below: Ricky Ponting at Headingley, during one of the most important innings of his international career.*

Walking out to bat in a highly-charged pressure situation such as the one that confronted me was, to say the least, challenging. It was time for deep breaths and clear thinking. I'd be lying if I didn't admit that I had my doubts about our chances at this point. The key in such a situation is to only think about the positives and what you can control, and to rely on your experiences to guide you through the crucial moments. As I took guard, ready to face Elworthy's first ball, I said to myself, 'Come on, watch the ball … Now! … Concentrate!!'

And then I added quietly, 'You've played one-day cricket for 14 years and this is not the time to end it. There's some unfinished business to be done.'

The thought of playing in another World Cup final, and the conflicting image of us going home straight after this game as failures, were the spurs that fired me. First, cautiously, Ricky and I established a partnership, at the same time halting the South Africans' momentum.

We scored just 22 in our first 10 overs together. At this point we had a critical mid-wicket chat in which we acknowledged that we had stopped the flow of wickets but conceded, too, that if we didn't up the scoring rate immediately the semi-finals would be beyond reach. Cronje had just brought their left-arm spinner, Nicky Boje, in for the injured Jacques Kallis, on and he became our first target. We hit 82 off the next 10 overs, as we attacked their bowlers and put pressure on their fieldsmen, something we'd emphasised during our pre-game meeting. And the South Africans cracked, as we thought they might. They are a regimented side — when things are going well they look ultra-intimidating, but when you put it back in their face, give them a bit of stick and go at them hard, they can unravel like any other side.

The most obvious sign of their distress came from their captain, who normally doesn't say much on the field. But here he was quite animated and agitated as the game began to turn in our favour.

Not long after I had reached my 50, with the score at 3-152, came an incident that had a huge bearing on the eventual result. I tried to place a ball through the leg-field, but only managed to chip a simple catch straight to one of the best fieldsmen in world cricket, Herschelle Gibbs. However, in his haste to throw the ball in the air in celebration, Gibbs put the chance down. I was furious at my lack of concentration, but thankful for the break, and with Ricky got back to working away at our big target.

Ricky hit some spectacular shots, including one six that crashed into an advertising hoarding above the old Headingley dressing room. By the time of his dismissal we needed 98 from 95 balls, and Michael Bevan, as dependable and classy as ever, came in to keep the mood bubbling in our favour. The manner in which Bevo adapted to the required run-rate was magnificent, as he pushed for ones, raced for twos and fashioned the occasional boundary to keep us on track. I, meanwhile, set my sights on seeing the innings through to its conclusion, as we pushed towards a famous victory.

We did not come to the World Cup to lose. I remember, out in the middle when

*Tom Moody was born on October 2, 1965, so he's exactly four months younger than me. We both went to the 1987 World Cup as fresh-faced 22-year-olds and enjoyed the tremendous thrill of being part of a World Cup success. Now 12 long years later, we'd got Australia over the line together in another crucial World Cup game and the satisfaction we both felt at having done this in tandem was immense.*

I was around 50 not out, I found myself thinking about all of those who had written us off. That gave me some inspiration, because I wanted to make liars of those critics. I also thought of all of the people back home in Australia whom we would have had to explain our failure to if we did not qualify for the semi-finals. But most of all, we wanted to win for ourselves.

Bevo was dismissed for 27 in the 46th over, with the score at 247. Out to the middle strode the 98th man to play one-day international cricket for Australia, my old comrade, Tom Moody, determined to help take Australia to the semi-finals. After a brilliant Pollock over which cost only three runs, we needed 15 from the last two.

Seven precious runs came from Donald's final six balls, then two from the first ball of the last, then Moods went 'inside out' to the backward point boundary and we needed just one to tie, two to win. The image I saw later on the TV news of Swamp on the balcony, willing the ball to the boundary rope, will stay with me for a very long time. It meant a great deal to him, to all of us. The tie would be enough to get us through to the final four, and when we scampered through of the third ball of the over I couldn't help but give a little 'victory' jab. And then I knicked a Pollock yorker past keeper Mark Boucher and we were home.

It was particularly pleasing to score the winning runs with Moods. When we were chasing victory over the final four-and-a-bit overs, our mid-pitch discussions revolved around the fact that we had both played first-class cricket for many years for this moment, so let's just go and do it. Don't rely on each other, do it yourself.

In the dressing room, there was, inevitably, pandemonium. It was fantastic to win in this way and the boys were ecstatic. The celebrations were amazing, though I missed some of it because of the hour-long media conference I had to attend. By the time I returned, the guys had settled down, realising that this World Cup adventure is still in full swing. But nothing could dull my sense of satisfaction.

I know that one-day international hundreds don't come along too often when you are batting five or six. As I said, making one under the kind of pressure I was under today is something I have dreamt of doing. I always thought I could play that sort of innings in one-day cricket — it's something you work for your entire career. But it's only when you put yourself on the line and then come out on top, that you truly know you are good enough.

It seems all of Australia stayed up to follow the win. Tonight I received a mountain of phone calls, including congratulatory calls from my parents, and from Justin Langer and Ian Healy. It's wonderful that so many people are right behind us.

Now we must prepare for the semi-finals. We've finished second on the Super Six table, with six points — same as Pakistan and South Africa, but behind Wasim Akram's team because of our loss to them in that Group B match and in front of Cronje's team because of today's result. The fourth team through are the Kiwis, who finished level with Zimbabwe but go through because of their higher run rate.

So Pakistan meet New Zealand on Wednesday at Old Trafford, while we await another clash with the South Africans 24 hours later.


# JUNE 14  Leeds to Birmingham

EVERYONE IS STILL on a high after yesterday, and I reckon it's this adrenalin that was the reason I couldn't go to sleep last night. I was wide awake at 2am, so I decided to watch the highlights show on the television and relive the whole saga once again. I don't mind admitting I enjoy watching the replays when things have gone well, although I can't recommended them when fate hasn't been so kind. The lasting impression for me on this occasion is that we're now very firmly on a roll and are going to be very hard to beat from this point.

Despite the lack of sleep, it was straight into the pool this morning for another team recovery session. These inevitably get the lads whingeing, but in fact this method of recuperation brings us closer together and adds that little bit of extra discipline which might prove vital down the road.

We had a three-hour bus trip down from Leeds to Birmingham. After we checked into the hotel, some of the guys headed into town to have a look around. Nine of us went to the golf course, where I played in a threesome with Warney and Moods, against two other groups, and while we finished a less-than-respectable third it was still an enjoyable day. The course was good, our golf wasn't, and by the halfway stage my legs were beginning to stiffen up a little. So Shane and I detoured to the pro shop and drove back to the 10th tee in a heaven-sent golf cart.

This was a nice way to wind down after the excitement of yesterday, and a chance to get away from the press and all the people not linked directly to the team but associated with the cricket. We appreciate that these people want their little piece of the action, understandably so, but as a player — and even more so as a captain — you need to escape at some stages of a tour to keep your sanity.

Tonight, Darren Lehmann (who remains in doubt for the semi-final), Geoff Marsh, Dave Misson and I enjoyed dinner at an Indian restaurant. We had a really good night, a bit of fun, and then back for an early night and a chance to contemplate the job ahead.

# JUNE 15  Birmingham

THE STORY IS DOING the rounds that after Herschelle Gibbs put down that catch at Headingley, I waited until he was nearby and quietly asked, 'Mate, how does it feel to have just dropped the World Cup?'

In fact, that's not quite what I said, but it's a nice story which the press are beating up over here.

What I actually put to him was, 'I hope you realise that you've just lost the game for your team.' This in itself was a pretty bold and potentially stupid comment, but it was brought on by the lead-up conversations we'd been having. All day long, Herschelle and I had been engaged in friendly banter, chipping away at each other, with each of us being as vocal as the other. Words and phrases such as 'pressure', 'gas take', 'let's see how you go now', and others were being bandied around and I guess, with an impressive hundred under his belt, Herschelle was in the box seat until his premature celebration changed the game. I'm sure he'll never do it again, but thankfully he did at Headingley, or else we might have been on our way home.

Herschelle's chance of redemption will come in a couple of days' time and we must be ready, because he's a fine player. However, I honestly believe the psychological damage may be hard to turn around, not only for him but also for the entire South African team.

It was soon apparent at practice today that Darren Lehmann is back to match fitness, which means we will have a decision to make as to whether he or Damien Martyn will play in the semi. I was impressed with the way Marto performed against South Africa — he handled the pressure well and looked good until he was dismissed. It will be a tough choice, almost a toss of the coin, but I lean to Boof, as I'd like to show some loyalty to and faith in a guy who has been very consistent over the past 18 months.

Crucially, Warney is starting to feel much better about things. The guys have really rallied around him in the last week, and have managed to get him back on track. I would say Shane is now pretty pumped about the rest of this competition. And, obviously, his performance is going to be crucial to our chances against the South Africans. This type of team commitment is what the best sides are made of and is the extra five per cent that makes you pull through in the tight games.

I'm looking forward to another clash with these guys. I have a handy track record against them, and I definitely enjoy the challenge of playing them. I also get plenty of satisfaction from the fact that they don't respond too well to our style of cricket, especially the way we get in their faces. This is especially true of Hansie Cronje, whom I have great respect for. However, I also believe I have a bit of an edge over him, similar to the advantage I have over the West Indies' Carl Hooper. As a player, there are opponents you enjoy locking horns with and others who sense they have it over you; the key to it is to try to exploit the former and suppress the latter.

This afternoon was spent relaxing, then in the evening we went to a restaurant called 'Shimla Pinks' which my former team-mate, now head of the Australian Cricketers Association, Tim May, rates as the No. 1 Indian dining establishment in the world. Maysie would know, having sweated many beads of perspiration and endured countless swollen lips in the quest for the perfect curry.

# JUNE 16 Birmingham

**FIRST SEMI-FINAL**
At Manchester, New Zealand 7-241 (50 overs; SP Fleming 41, RG Twose 46, CL Cairns 44*, Shoaib Akhtar 3-55) lost to Pakistan 1-242 (47.3 overs; Saeed Anwar 113, Wajahatullah Wasti 84) by nine wickets

OUR PRACTICE SESSION today was in the afternoon, so we didn't see a lot of the first semi-final. Having to wait until after lunch can be a little off-putting when you're used to having a hit-out in the morning. However, the late practice did give me a chance to sleep in, a nice change as I've been waking up pretty early for the past couple of weeks, always thinking about the cricket ahead. This, I've found, is one of the prices you pay for being captain; there's always some tactical ploy to be considered, a problem to fix, a potential hiccup to be averted.

When I finally woke, I went down for a spa and a pool, and enjoyed a massage. There is still some lactic acid in the legs, a legacy of my full day at Headingley — I've found that, as I get older, it takes longer to recover, but this is a pain I love to get and hope to continue getting for a while to come.

**The Semi-final, Australia v South Africa, at Edgbaston**

- Treat every ball as if it's the most important of the match — such as Warney's catch to get rid of Klusener off the last ball of their innings at Headingley, which saved two runs.
- Believe you can achieve anything.
- Put pressure on them — they will crack. Especially put pressure on their fielders, such as Cronje, Gibbs and Cullinan.
- Play at our pace — if we're doing well, up the ante. If they are, slow the pace down.
- Keep wearing them down — they'll crack before us!
- Bowling — dot balls.
- Batting — wickets in hand.

TRUST YOURSELF — BODY LANGUAGE — PRESSURE — PARTNERSHIPS

Finally, be decisive.

The pre-semi-final press conference went for about half an hour and was pretty intense. The journos were clearly trying to get me to say that the South Africans take the gas, and are no good under pressure. In all honesty, I think we are better than they are in stressful situations —a psychological thing that has evolved over a time. I know they think about how they should respond in such situations, and the more I can reinforce that on the field the more I believe they might crack under pressure. But I tried to play this down when the media focused on it today.

This evening we had another excellent team meeting. I think one of the features of this World Cup tour has been the way the team meetings have developed, as everyone looks to contribute and think about what lies ahead. As usual, Swamp led the meeting, we all contributed to a general discussion, then we went through the South African line-up, and I finished things off. I could sense that the guys are all excited about what lies ahead and realise what a tragedy it would be to waste the opportunity we've earned.

The team dinner was held at an Italian restaurant. I'm not aware of any other team that gets together, as we do, in this way. We talk a bit of cricket, have a bit of fun, and relax. When the conversation turned to the upcoming clash, we all agreed that the semi-final is going to be a tough and close game, another difficult but irresistible challenge. We've handled everything that's been put in front of us since the West Indies game, and hopefully we can handle the two more to come.

# JUNE 17 Australia v South Africa, at Birmingham

**SECOND SEMI-FINAL**
At Birmingham, Australia 213 (49.2 overs; RT Ponting 37, SR Waugh 56, MG Bevan 65, SM Pollock 5-36, AA Donald 4-32) tied with South Africa 213 (49.4 overs; JH Kallis 53, JN Rhodes 43, SK Warne 4-29) — Australia proceeds to final because of their higher position on Super Six table

We come to Birmingham with our momentum strong,
but to think it will just happen would be terribly wrong.
They will come at us hard, like the good team they are,
so we must focus on our job in order to dim their star.

The road to Lord's is nearing its end
We are one step away from the final bend,
But we cannot afford to dwell on the Sunday just gone
... or the Sunday ahead

We must focus on our task, our role,
in today's game to the death.
Pressure is the key, it will win us the day.
Because we embrace it, they'll crumble under its weight

As we contemplate our day
and how our fortunes may fare
Let me pose you these questions,
when you look in the mirror and stare ...

If not you, then who? If not now, then when?

**Dave Misson**

'YOU SEEMED pretty calm out there,' I was informed by a bloke at the post-match press conference. 'Geez,' I replied, 'is that what it looked like?'

'Actually, we were shitting ourselves.'

This was another amazing game. I'm now sitting here in my hotel room, about three hours after the final, extraordinary play in this extraordinary semi-final. After the post-match celebrations, I did go out for one drink, but there were too many people in town for me to savour the moment as I wanted to, so I quietly returned to my room. It was an incredible 'win'. We had thought the previous game was something of an escape; this was even more miraculous.

The game ebbed and flowed all day, although South Africa probably had the momentum for most of the play. In my view, the only time we had our noses in front was when we had them nine down, with 16 runs needed by them to win, but then Lance Klusener smashed them back in front and it seemed they'd won the day. Then there was that crazy run out to create the tie. Maybe we held our nerve marginally better than they did, although we missed four or five chances towards the end — a couple of dropped catches, a couple of run outs.

It was just a remarkable game, featuring another tremendous Australian come-back. After another shaky start, 4-68 after 17 overs, Michael Bevan and I forged a vital partnership. I was really happy with the way I played under pressure. Bevo and I took it to the South Africans and put it back in their faces once again. Bevo was outstanding, hitting an excellent, highly-intelligent and highly-principled 65, and Shane Warne contributed as well, in a crucial seventh-wicket partnership of 49 near the end of our innings.

We finally put 213 on the board, which was respectable but not great. Before the toss, I rated the Trent Bridge track as a 250 wicket, although at four wickets down we set ourselves to reach 220, and did a reasonable job to get close.

Then Gary Kirsten and Herschelle Gibbs, the South African openers, came out smokin'. They were 0-45 from nine overs, and in desperation I threw the ball to Warney. In a crisis always go to your great players. Shane responded magnificently. First he buzzed through Gibbs with a delivery not dissimilar to his famous 'Gatting' ball from 1993, and in the process, as Gibbs' team-mates saw how far the ball turned, sent a streak of panic through the South African dressing room. They

Allsport

*Warney in the middle of one of the greatest bowling spells in international one-day cricket history. First he'd spun a beauty through Herschelle Gibbs. Now, he's bowled Gary Kirsten, with a big-spinning delivery that fizzed past the left-hander's attempted swing to mid-wicket.*

certainly appeared to go right into their shells against the great legspinner.

Spin played a key part in our revival. Not only did Warney take three wickets in his first three overs — Gibbs, Kirsten and Cronje — brother Mark bowled eight good overs of off-breaks. And Michael Bevan deserves special praise for his outstanding fielding. He really set the standard and got the boys going.

When Cullinan was run out to make it 4-61, meaning four wickets had fallen for just 15 runs, I didn't think we were favourites, rather that the game was back on an even keel. Kallis and Rhodes batted very intelligently, adding 84 until Paul Reiffel dismissed Jonty in the 41st over. Then Pollock and Kallis edged their team closer, to the 45th over, Warney's 10th and last of the day. The score was 5-162.

The first ball went for two, then Pollock slammed a big six over long on, then a four through extra cover. 'My eyes started spinning,' Shane confessed later, 'I was so fired up I had to calm myself down.' Another single, a dot ball, and then Kallis was done, deceived by our great leg-spinner into lobbing a catch in my direction.

In came Klusener, who straightaway hit Flem to deep mid-wicket. But late in the over our man had some revenge, bowling Pollock off the inside edge. At the other end, McGrath emerged for his final spell and in his first over we might have had a run out, but Junior's throw collided with umpire David Shepherd instead of the stumps. But while Boucher struggled for any runs at all, Klusener was such a threat — wherever Pigeon or Flem pitched it might go for four or more. Snicks raced like mortars to the fence. One colossal 'nine-iron' might have been caught, might have been four, but was eventually palmed back into play on the first bounce by Moody at wide long-on, saving two runs and keeping Boucher on strike for the first ball of the 49th over.

McGrath's final over was dramatic and superb. The first ball cost nothing, the second took Boucher's middle stump. The third, a nervous edge by Elworthy, conceded a single. Seventeen were needed, from nine deliveries. We'd talked often of the need to keep the ball and Glenn, going for the yorker, bowled a full toss, which Klusener clubbed to Paul Reiffel at long on. He wanted two, needed two to retain the strike, but it appeared that Pistol's throw had beaten Elworthy at the bowler's end. Umpire Shepherd called for the replay, and it took Steve Bucknor up in the booth an eternity to rule that, yes, the ball had deflected off Pigeon's hand onto the stumps, with Elworthy far from home. We learned later that only the camera behind Pistol's throw confirmed beyond doubt what had transpired. Without that angle, the batsman would have got the benefit of the doubt.

Nine for 198. Eight balls to go. It was now, as I said, that I thought we were in front. McGrath pitched full again, Klusener swung hard again, and the ball, like a tracer bullet, shot out to 1-1. Pistol's first reaction was to run in at the ball, but this was no ordinary hit. Never far off the ground, it kept coming, kept coming, and our man was in trouble. It reached him half-a-metre above his head, and all he could do was palm it away like a goalkeeper keeping a blasted volley from close range out of the net. Where did it go? For six, the replay told us, after another delay. We were stunned. Everything had changed so quickly. But later, when asked

Pics: Allsport

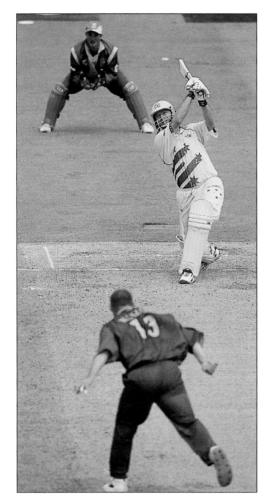

*At 4-68 in the 17th over of the semi, we were in trouble, but fortunately Michael Bevan (above) and I (left) were able to turn things around. Batting first, we'd decided, after a shaky start, that 220 would be our target, and Bevo was magnificent in steering us towards that score.*

*Above: Paul Reiffel's throw from long-off deflects off Glenn McGrath's wrist and Steve Elworthy is run out late in the semi-final at Edgbaston. At this point, I thought we had our noses in front. But Klusener remained. Much drama was still to be seen.*

No Regrets **201**

*Above: A moment frozen in time. Poor Allan Donald can't believe it, I'm ecstatic, and Gilly and Pigeon are looking for team-mates to hug.*

*Below: The end of the semi-final, with all 11 Australians plus Allan Donald and umpire Venkat in the frame.*

*Above left: The once new, now tattered and torn 'Road to Lord's'. This was the mountain that we had to climb, starting off in Pakistan and ending at Lord's, with Swampy ticking each target off as we successfully negotiated it. It was a long, hard road, with many obstacles, but in getting from start to finish both the Test and one-day teams showed why they are the best cricket squads in the world, through a series of courageous wins and come-from-behind performances.*

*Above right: Manager Steve Bernard (obscured) introduces the Duke of Edinburgh to me before the World Cup final. Soon after we were walking out through the Long Room and onto Lord's (below) for the biggest day of our one-day cricket lives.*

*Above: The catch that set the mood for our brilliant fielding effort in the final. Mark Waugh has launched himself to his right to snare the Pakistani opener Wajahatullah Wasti.*

*Right: Adam Gilchrist during his thrilling half-century.*

*Below: Tom Moody catches Azhar Mahmood off his own bowling, and Pakistan are reeling at 8-129.*

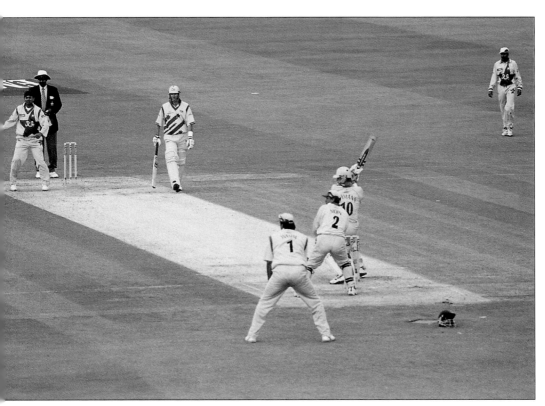

*Above: Darren Lehmann hits the World Cup-winning boundary, and sets off an Australian party that lasted long into the night.*

*Below: The Aussie balcony, the moment Boof's square cut got through the infield.*

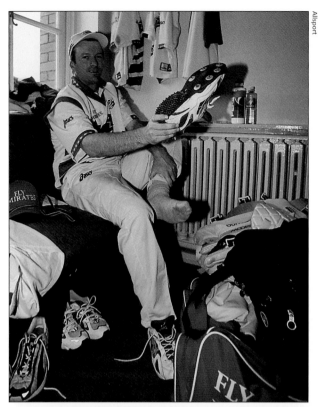

Allsport

*Left: This has always been my special corner of the away dressing room at Lord's. Now, as I took the pads off having not been required to bat, its place in my cricket life was even more treasured.*

*Below: A World Cup winner's view of Warney receiving his man-of-the-match award on the balcony at Lord's, as the boys look on and wait to be handed one-day cricket's greatest prize.*

Steve Waugh

*Above: With Gilly, Marto, Punter, Flem, Warney and the World Cup.*

*Below: Time to take in our achievements after the pandemonium had died down in the change rooms. The cup was now ours and we could hardly believe it.*

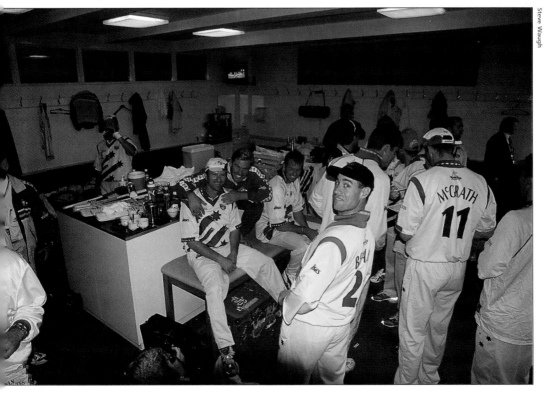

Allsport

*Above: Any regrets? Not now, not one!*

*Below: A career highlight were the street parades through Melbourne and here in Sydney that followed our World Cup triumph. The passion and genuine delight the people expressed about our win was a humbling experience and made all the players proud to be able to bring so much joy to all the supporters around Australia.*

Stev

*Klusener attacks McGrath late in the semi-final. With Glenn bowling superbly but the South African juggernaut smashing fours almost at will, every ball meant so much.*

about what was happening on the field at this time, Shepherd told a reporter, 'There was a hell of a lot of tension out there.' Then he added, 'And a lot of encouragement going on between the fielders.'

That last line meant a lot to me. All the emphasis we had placed on team spirit, staying positive and backing each other would prove crucial in these final few deliveries.

A single off the last ball kept Klusener the strike. Nine to win, eight to tie, but because we'd finished higher in the Super Six table, the tie was useless to them. But precious for us …

Flem was reasonably happy with his first two balls of the 50th over, both well-pitched up aiming for the yorker, but Klusener smashed them away for fours. What to do? Flem went back over the wicket, looking for the out. I brought the field right in, hoping to force them into a mistake. There was no mid-wicket conference between the batsmen — Klusener, it seemed, wanted to finish it with one more monstrous strike. With everyone in so close, it appeared he didn't consider the sharp single to be an option. I was hoping he'd go for the big one, miss, and be bowled or lbw.

Flem bowled, Klusener swung, and the ball dribbled back to mid-on, not far from the stumps at the bowler's end. Darren Lehmann grabbed at the ball and shied at the stumps. Donald, instinctively, had set off for the run and was well out. But Boof missed. Donald smiled sheepishly. We couldn't believe it. Our one last chance was gone.

But in fact that incident had played a part in what was to follow. The tension was extraordinary. Klusener, we assumed, was still thinking four. Donald had a million conflicting thoughts going through his head. We were concentrating hard, hearts in our mouths, on none or out. Flem pitched right up again, Klusener miscued up the pitch ... AND RAN! ... Donald, the previous escape foremost in his mind, dived back for the safety of the bowler's end ... Mark Waugh, close in at mid-off, flicked the ball to the bowler's end ...

As Flem gathered Junior's flick, Klusener was arriving at the bowler's end. Donald had lost his bat, but was now forlornly running to the keeper. As we all cried, 'KEEPER'S END! KEEPER'S END!!' Flem turned and rolled the ball to Adam Gilchrist. Donald was mid-pitch, Gilly broke the stumps ... Australia was in the final!

# I Was There ...

## THE TIE
By Chris Ward

You know what it's like. Once you combine two or more men and try to get them to an event on time, it's virtually impossible. So as the eight of us strode into Edgbaston, the first words we heard were, 'The new batsman for Australia ... Ricky Ponting.' Mark Waugh gone, and we hadn't even found our seats, which turned out to be five seats left of the sightscreen at the City end, the most perfect spot.

There was a feeling among all of us that the best game of the World Cup had been played between the same two sides in the Super Six, and what we were about to witness would be an anticlimax. But it *was* the semi-final, and surely a time for great players to rise above average ones and show their worth. And so it proved, initially for South Africa. Shaun Pollock has looked mediocre for the entire tournament, pitching too short, and really troubling no-one. Here he bowled sharply, and with plenty of movement, while the previously impressive Elworthy looked ordinary and came in for some fearsome blows, from Ponting in particular.

The next great player to enter the game

was Donald, bowling with more venom than in any previous game. His first ball, though, was dross, but Ponting somehow lobbed it to Kirsten. The Tasmanian looked gutted, and so were we. We could have watched him all day. Then Lehmann got a beauty from Donald, Gilchrist was gone, too, and Australia were in some trouble. But again the stars shone.

Enter Steve Waugh, who no-one thought could do it again, and Michael Bevan. There is always discussion about Bevan — yes he's good, yes he plays it about well, but does he take enough risks, should he go big, or does he play the percentages too much? So the terrace arguments started ... he should get on with it; should he consolidate? In hindsight what he did was probably right. It was a struggle though, as Kallis and Pollock bowled superbly. Then Waugh clubbed some runs from Klusener. With the stand finally broken, Moody immediately got a good one from Pollock, and the rest froze in Donald's headlights. A target of 213, we thought, might be a stroll without early wickets. Proves how much we know.

I think this was Steve Waugh's defining moment as a captain. Everyone knows how inspired he can be with the bat, but no-one was sure about his skippering. Here, watching it unfold in the flesh, he was superb. He obviously knew the value of the early wickets, and tried at least everything. But McGrath

The feeling in the dressing room afterwards was incredible. Everyone was hugging each other, jumping on top of each other, screaming and shouting. We really could not believe that we had sneaked through to the final, that we'd got away with the game. It was a mixture of relief … ecstasy … all the emotions came out at once. I could feel the blood and adrenalin rushing through my system.

Now, back in the quiet of my hotel room, I can't help thinking of the similarities between our situation here and in 1996. I just hope we won't waste our opportunity for World Cup glory in the final this time. Like '96, we've had two fantastic wins to get to the decider. But last time, we didn't prepare well for the final; this time it's going to be different — we'll be ready for the Pakistanis.

At the post-match press conference where I let my guard slip for a second, Hansie Cronje bemoaned his side's misfortune but refused to blame any of his players.

---

was negated by a slow pitch, while Fleming moved the odd one around, and found some bounce, but no wicket. The ticket price of £65 suddenly looked a lot of money to watch a cakewalk.

Enter Shane Warne. I think he has bowled without confidence in the tournament so far and, it appeared to me, with a fear of re-injuring his shoulder. Here it was shit or bust. Suddenly the ball was fizzing again. Wickets fell, Warne punched the air, and South Africa had created an exact replica of Australia's innings. The perfect test of who would be the chokers. As Kallis and Rhodes set about the Waugh/Bevan repair role, the game became unbelievably tense. The fielding, from both sides, was superb. A big factor was that the pitch was turning, and what a test of nerve for Mark Waugh to send down eight overs. He got away with murder, but did cover the fifth bowler and that was crucial.

As the game entered its final stages everyone in the crowd had one name on their lips. Klusener. I don't think there have been many players in the history of the game who have struck fear into sides as Klusener has in this tournament. Captains, bowlers and fielders have trembled as Klusener has bludgeoned from the crease. I think Australia did it right, bowling as full as possible. At least it means four, not six, and the chance for a bottom of the bat shot to spoon into the

outfield. And so it did, straight down Paul Reiffel's throat in front of us. Unfortunately, Reiffel misread the missile's power and ran in too far. As the ball went for six, Australia's World Cup looked all over.

The first two balls of Fleming's (surely a last-over specialist?) final over also disappeared, and South Africa looked to be in the final. But Fleming held his nerve under unbelievable pressure, and the rest will go down in history. Hearts were in the mouths of neutrals, God only knows what it was like for supporters of the two teams.

The only way it could have been better for us would have been if England had triumphed in a similar manner. We may, though, have to wait a couple of generations for a side capable of playing like this. It was the immovable object against the irresistible force, Waugh against Cronje. The two most determined teams in the world. It was a privilege to be there, and to be given the opportunity to tell our grandchildren that we saw the best one-day international ever.

What a day! Let's hope for fine weather and a Sunday repeat.

As well as remaining a keen Oxford United supporter despite their plunge into the English second division, Chris Ward is a keen enough follower of English cricket to journey halfway around the world for the last two Ashes series in Australia.

*Above: Gilly's knocked over a stump, Allan Donald stands forlornly in mid-pitch, we're about to go crazy. We're in the final!!!*

*Below: While I stand on the Edgbaston balcony, waiting for the awards ceremony to begin, Hansie Cronje sits dejectedly, scarcely believing what has happened to him.*

'You experience a lot of highs and lows in your career,' he said. 'It doesn't get more exciting than this and it's unfortunate to be on the wrong side of it. At the moment it feels like a cruel game.

'We felt we had a real chance — and when Lance Klusener is batting you feel in control all the way through — and we're all very disappointed, but we'll pick ourselves up. If you look at the way things have been running for Lance, you almost thought it had to go for him, but unfortunately it didn't.

'I think with four balls to go, one run needed and Klusener on strike, 90 per cent of us thought we had a very real chance of winning the game. You can't blame Lance or Allan for what happened. These things happen and so many things happened in the game that you can't blame one person.

'It was very quiet in the dressing room afterwards and obviously we're down but I'm proud of the way we've played through the tournament.'

I'll confess that I almost felt sorry for the South Africans after the match. We were numb after we realised we'd made it through to the final. It was an unbelievable comeback. We never gave in but we were down and out three or four times.

It's not really for me to rank our achievement, if we do win the whole thing. But to get through seven games in a row, under the pressure we've been under, against the world's best, must compare pretty highly with other Australian sporting achievements of recent times. From my point of view, I was happy with the manner in which I captained the team. I went with my gut instinct a lot, when other people were saying different things. Fortunately, today, my instincts proved to be correct. And, again, I was happy with the way my batting held up under pressure.

The support we received after the game was wonderful. I've had so many phone calls from home. We've got one game to finish it off. And I know we can play better!

Now to Lord's! This is the culmination of a lot of cricket —remember, we have been on the road for nine months now — and we're now just one step from achieving a goal we set ourselves a long time ago. There has been some incredible cricket over the past few months, so many ups and downs, but we've hung in there and played tough, and now there's only one more game to go.


# JUNE 18  Birmingham to London

FIRST UP, some reflections on the semi-final …
The more I think about it, the more I keep coming to the conclusion that we should have won reasonably comfortably after South Africa went nine wickets down. But the pressure was always going to be on both teams in those final overs, and despite a couple of slip-ups, I think we showed just what a tough, professional side we are. But it was a shame one team had to lose. Or, more correctly, fall victim to a

countback. However, as we had beaten them at our only previous outing in this World Cup, I guess if one team had to go through it should have been us.

It's funny — after the previous game, which was, in effect, a quarter-final, one journalist had remarked to me, 'Well, you can't get any closer than that.' As we know now, he was very, very wrong.

If I had to pinpoint one moment that got us through, it would have to be THAT ball ... the one from Warney that rocked Herschelle Gibbs. And if there was a lesson for the team to come out of the victory it is that we should never, ever give up.

So now to the final. In 1996, we did very little homework before our game against Sri Lanka, but this time is different. There are a lot of similarities when you compare the tied semi-final and the previous Super Six game against South Africa with the sensational victory against the West Indies at Chandigarh in the 1996 World Cup semi-final and the win over New Zealand in the quarter-final at Chennai. I just hope we do better at Lord's than what we did in the '96 final in Lahore.

As much as I'm trying to learn from that defeat, I'm also thinking of our Cup triumph in 1987, which represented a great turnaround in Australian cricket. Our team spirit during that competition was magnificent, as was the way the team hierarchy developed a game plan and the way we, as a team, stuck to that plan.

Much of the press this time seems to be revolving around the Pakistani pace attack. The new star, Shoaib Akhtar, might well do for fast bowling around the world what Shane Warne has done for leg-spin bowling — create passion among youngsters. He's a wonderful spectacle to watch and enjoyable to play against. He has his say, too, and you can have a good contest with him. He's been good for the World Cup: people have come just to watch him, just as they have for so long with

Steve Waugh

*Swampy on the verge of a heart attack after our miraculous escape at Edgbaston. For a man who can't sit still, chews his nails incessantly and consumes a mountain of coffee while he watches his team play, the theatre of the semi-final was pure torture.*

*A very pumped Michael Bevan charges off the field with Paul Reiffel and Darren Lehmann after the semi-final. Bevo's fielding, always excellent but at Edgbaston sometimes breathtaking, was a key factor in our 'win'.*

Shane. The Pakistan paceman has a good, tight action but he is in a honeymoon period. The next 12 months will enable us all to make a more realistic assessment of just how good he can be. We won't be aiming just to see him off: you can score off him, as we did at Headingley. You can use his pace to hit boundaries.

Shoaib's velocity has captured the cricket world's attention, but to be honest we are not worried about his speed. It's the reverse swing Shoaib and Wasim Akram can generate that is the worry, especially when it happens during the last 10 to 15 overs of a run chase. And in a way, the press boys' infatuation with the 'Rawalpindi Express' breaking the 100mph barrier is in our favour. I believe that there are signs about that he is over-extending himself in quest of the magical mark and in doing so losing his focus. This must be to our advantage.

Pakistan loom as a difficult opponent simply because of their unpredictability. They have been world beaters one day, but less than convincing the next throughout the tournament, a fact reflected in their six wins/three losses record. This inconsistent trait makes them a difficult opponent to plan for, as does the fact that they are a young side, with some players we have not seen a lot of. This was a point Wasim Akram made today, during an interview in which he described this Pakistani team as 'one of the best sides I've ever played in'.

'Look who's brought us to the final,' Wasim remarked. 'It's been the younger players all the way.'

He then went on a different track.

'The Australians must be tired mentally and physically, because winning and winning like they have, it has been a lot of stress,' Wasim said. 'I think we are mentally tougher than them. The amount the whole Pakistan side have had to go through over the last couple of years has made us tougher than any opposition in the world. We have stuck together and qualified for the final and we are now just one match away from winning the trophy.'

From our point of view, we know we're well prepared for a tough day. I'd like to think we can play in a similar fashion to the manner in which South Africa attack the Pakistanis. Cronje's team have beaten Pakistan the last 13 times they've met. It figures that the way South Africa play Pakistan must be a good way, and, if we can put some of their strategies into practice, we'll have a good chance of winning.

In my view, many things are in our favour leading into this game. There are plenty of whispers doing the rounds that the result of the game may influence the outcome of the entire bribery/match-fixing inquiry, which must, of course, be a heavy burden for their players to carry. Also, the fact that quite a few of their finds of this competition — Razzaq, Mahmood, Wasti and, to a lesser extent, Shoaib Akhtar and Afridi — have very little experience of playing in a 'big occasion' match might work against them.

And there is the 'Warne factor'. While the Pakistanis tend to be bracketed with the Indians and the Sri Lankans as fine players of spin bowling, this is actually a bit of a myth. Sure, they'll destroy the average spinners, but the quality ones, such as Warney, have enjoyed good results and I made this point strongly at the press conference.

One thing that might become a factor is that Pakistan will enjoy an extra day to recover between their semi-final and the final than we will get. Having just two days of rest between such big games is not ideal. But we could argue that because we are on such a roll a breather might stop the momentum we have gathered.

# JUNE 19 London

IT'S BEEN INCREDIBLY hectic, with everyone wanting interviews. I've done as many as I could. A press conference went for half an hour, and I also did the press before and after training.

Now, I'm lying in bed watching the US Open golf, and thinking about tomorrow. I think everyone is a little bit apprehensive, but I know if we play good solid cricket we're going to win the World Cup. We can take great heart from South Africa's recent performances against Pakistan in international one-day cricket. If we stay similarly focused and disciplined, I believe Pakistan will crack under the pressure. I hope our discipline will be our trump card tomorrow.

The Final team meeting was very positive. Everyone is in such a good frame of mind. Our preparation has been a bit hurried, with only two days between matches, but that shouldn't matter.

We considered changing the team this afternoon at training — Damien Martyn nearly forced his way in ahead of Darren Lehmann — but decided that, as we've gone with this batting order for 18 months we needed to show faith with the guys who've done the job for us. So Darren retained his spot. Either way, I'd have had full confidence that the job would have been done and done well.

For me, two things stand out — we need to believe in ourselves and enjoy the occasion. If anyone doubts himself, then he is going to drag everyone down. I hope we all have that inner self-belief, which we should have, especially after our last two miraculous games. I know I do.

There is no way we'll be relying on fate to beat Pakistan today. Whoever bats best, and handles the pressure best, will triumph. So far, we have focused hard on each match and hung tough in pressured situations. But now, given the unique

## Team Meeting — the Captain's Notes

**The Final, Australia v Pakistan, at Lord's**

- Well done to everyone — bad luck to the guys missing out. Your commitment and attitude have been tremendous.
- The key to tomorrow is to enjoy the game — the result will look after itself. Back yourself, be decisive.
- Remember that we beat them 3-0 in Pakistan.
- Play like the South Africans — they've beaten Pakistan 13 times in a row. Why? Because they're ruthless, consistent, persistent. And they constantly apply pressure — let's really put it on their fielders — ones will unsettle them, boundaries will follow.
- Batting — get through the tough times, it will get easier. Change the ball if we can.
- Bowling — take early wickets, stop the fours. They will get themselves out.
- The pressure is on them, with the bribery scandal hanging over them.
- If the pressure is on us — enjoy it. Go forward, take on the challenge.
- Hype — forget it, as it is rubbish.
- Don't forget, it's okay to be nervous and apprehensive (but remember, so is your opposite number).
- Stay focused — come out on top.

pressures of the World Cup Final, the scenario is different. If we enjoy the game and don't fret about the opposition, I believe we will win. But if we think too much about holding that World Cup aloft, then we'll be in trouble.

Eight of us played against Sri Lanka in that 1996 final, which we lost by seven wickets. Our preparation was poor and we did not respect the Sri Lankans enough. If we are to beat Pakistan tomorrow, we must guard against feeling the work is done. Pakistan will not be intimidated easily. They are a pretty aggressive bunch of cricketers, much different from the more passive Indians. In my view, keeper/batsman Moin Khan is the key to their side, their heartbeat. They talk a lot, incessantly almost, and not always in English. For example, Saqlain Mushtaq never keeps quiet. It's not sledging — they're hyping each other up. They get very emotional and you know you're in a game of cricket. When they're good they're great, but put pressure on them and often they can go the other way.

As a side, though, Pakistan have not been together a long time and I said at the start of the competition that teams that have a togetherness and players who benefit from such camaraderie under pressure will win. That said, they have an excellent bowling attack, and an exciting one, but a couple of their guys are inexperienced and this is a big occasion.

I am not sure what I will do if I win the toss. All I know is it is hard to chase runs under pressure, as South Africa showed chasing 213 on a pretty flat deck. You would have expected them to get that score nine times out of 10. But pressure does funny things to batsmen. You tend to look at what lies at the end of the rainbow rather than what is immediately on the road ahead. If someone's going to crack it's generally the batsman rather than the bowler.

Our guys cannot reverse swing the ball as well as Pakistan, and we found to our cost at Headingley just how hard it can be to score runs quickly in the day's final overs. Another reason to bat first. But whoever goes in at the start, because the Pakistanis have that ability to swing it more than most in the last 15 overs, we have got to work out a way of countering this advantage — taking a shorter backlift and watching the ball really closely won't hurt. But if we can get 265 against them at Headingley we can definitely do it at Lord's, which is generally a pretty good batting pitch, with less movement than Headingley.

One factor in our favour is that Glenn McGrath loves bowling at the Home of Cricket. Who can forget his effort on the 1997 Ashes tour, when he took 8-38 in one of the finest Test bowling performances I have ever seen? One of Pigeon's chief responsibilities will be to get Saeed Anwar out, and the conditions will be perfectly suited to him as the ball moves away from the left-hander down the slope. It is his natural angle of attack and if Saeed has a weakness, it is his penchant to 'fish' outside his off stump.

We've had a couple of major escapes on our way to the final. There were moments in the last two games against South Africa when, if we'd lost those moments, we would have lost those games. To get out of these tough situations required some good management, but we know there was an element of luck involved, too. But we did hang tough in those situations, and were rewarded for our persistence, which is something we've talked about in our team meetings over the past few days.

Our resilience has been immensely satisfying on a personal level, too. I was written off as a one-day captain in some quarters at the start of the tournament. And, after the team took time to settle, so were we as a team. But even after we lost to New Zealand and Pakistan in the Group matches, I always felt that if I could do my best, and if we could do so as a team, we would prove the critics wrong. I couldn't quite believe a lot of the stuff that was being said and written. It appeared to me that many critics were writing for headlines, and looking for cheap shots, without looking at the facts or bothering to recall our record over the past 18 months.

I reckon I've done a pretty good job. I'm used to the criticism, because I was written off as a player in my early days and had to achieve more than others to get recognition. It seems I'll have to fight the same battles with the captaincy. Maybe it is just my personality, or the way I come across. You see, I'm not into talk. While I have loyal friends and once I make friends they will always be friends, I do not open myself up to people until I trust them and really know them. Perhaps some observers see that as arrogance and consequently find it harder to write good things about me, which I can accept. But the only way to prove something is to go out there and do it.

I'd like to think I have done a lot of work behind closed doors to establish my authority as captain, and it was nice get to public recognition for my century at Leeds last week. Not that I am not going to get carried away by all this new-found acclaim, because I know it can change quickly, but it was satisfying to play an innings like that, leading from the front and setting an example from which the other blokes can take a lead. It is good to have in the back of the team's mind the knowledge that you can win from any situation.

But am I now established as captain? I am not sure what it will take to bring me right out of Mark Taylor's shadow — if that is where I am now. My goals are simple: I am going to try to do well for the team, myself and all the people back home. That said, winning the World Cup would leave me with a legacy, hopefully set me firmly on my own path and, most importantly, establish Australia as the undisputed No. 1 cricket nation.

I will be taking my usual place in the visitors' dressing room at Lord's tomorrow. It is close to the balcony and my good mate Pigeon will be sitting next to me. We have had some exciting times there together. We asked for the away dressing room, which was fine with Pakistan because the home one is bigger. Most teams like that one but the away changing-room has always been our room and we feel comfortable there.

Our plan for tomorrow is to have breakfast 20 minutes before we leave the team hotel, have a bit of a chat, and then try to relax on the bus and just enjoy the day. We've had lots of messages of good luck from our Prime Minister, the Leader of the Opposition, and many sporting teams across Australia. If we win, we'll have a really good party to celebrate. Hopefully, we'll be lucky to get out of that favourite dressing room of ours before midnight.

Our lucky Italian restaurant, which we've frequented before each match in London, was again the setting for our pre-game get-together. Now the planning is over. We've certainly had an enormous amount of press over the past couple of days, which has created some difficulties, especially for me as captain. It's hard to concentrate on the cricket with so many distractions about, but I'm sure once we walk onto the hallowed turf we'll be switched on and ready to put on a show that we can be proud of.

# JUNE 20  Australia v Pakistan, at Lord's

**FINAL**
At Lord's, Pakistan 132 (39 overs; GD McGrath 2-13, TM Moody 2-17, SK Warne 4-33) lost to Australia 2-133 (20.1 overs; AC Gilchrist 54, ME Waugh 37*) by eight wickets

> Well here we are, at the home of WG Grace,
> it's taken something special for us to arrive at this place.
> We've watched Swampy Marsh tick off his tattered road to Lord's,
> it's our destiny, make no mistake, unlike his spelling on the blackboards.
>
> So let's make a pact to fight as only we can,
> to show the ANZAC spirit, where it all began.
> It'll be a time we'll never forget,
> and one where we can all say I've got no regret.
>
> I can't wait to get the goosebumps,
> from shoulder to hand
> As Punter stands aloft
> and sings ... 'Under the Southern Cross I stand'.
>
> **Steve Waugh**

WE'RE ALL AGREED — our effort in the final was our best all-round performance in one-day international cricket since we began the Road to Lord's a long 18 months ago. Over that year and a half, we often talked about getting the three aspects of our game — batting, bowling and fielding — together, and we finally came good on the biggest stage of all. It was a fine achievement, not just for the 15 players, but also for the coach, who has put in a tremendous effort without many accolades, the management, and for all the squad, too.

All the planning went perfectly on the day. Eighteen months to the day after we set our goals for winning the World Cup and how we wanted to play, we achieved our dream.

*Tom Moody, Ricky Ponting, Darren Lehmann and Shane Warne take to the card table, while we wait for the weather to clear so we can start the 1999 World Cup final.*

It was just magnificent, and suddenly made all the moments of self-doubt and heartaches seem so trivial.

We had woken to a morning still damp after overnight rain. A nervous peek out the hotel room window revealed cloudy skies. The game was delayed for half an hour, but even before the scheduled start we were ready to play. On previous occasions, we would have waited until the rain stopped before we went out for our pre-match preparation, but not this time. We rehearsed as the rain sprinkled about, keen to ensure we were totally prepared from the jump rather than caught short as can happen in this type of atmosphere.

We were introduced to Prince Philip before the game, in front of the Lord's pavilion. For a while it seemed this historic moment might take place elsewhere, as the authorities debated moving the presentation to the Long Room, because of the weather. First, we were to be introduced on the ground, then off it; finally, thankfully, it occurred as originally planned. Calm as I could, I introduced all the players, but we raced along the line so quickly that I missed Damien Fleming. I immediately thought that this might be a bad omen for him, but thankfully it turned out to be nothing of the sort. In fact, Flem took the crucial wicket of Saeed Anwar in his opening spell, a moment in time that signalled to me that it was going to be our day.

Once the formalities were over, I walked out to the middle of the ground, where I lost the toss to Wasim Akram. This, I thought at the time, was not necessarily a bad break, as I wasn't sure what was the right thing to do. I would have batted, as Wasim decided, but I wasn't unhappy about bowling. There was still some cloud about, moisture in the air, and a little greenish tinge to the wicket.

True to our game plan, which was built on discipline, patience and consistency, we wore the Pakistani batting order down. We also took some brilliant catches. Mark took a magnificent grab early on, which set the mood for the entire innings. In fact, we did nothing wrong at all, except for one dropped catch from Glenn McGrath, and bowled Pakistan out for 132. It was, as I said, our best performance on a one-day international cricket field in a long, long time — as close to perfection as I have ever seen.

The bowling was excellent, committed, exactly true to our plan, and the Pakistani innings withered. Warney was superb, taking four wickets, as was Glenn McGrath (2-13 off nine), while our other bowlers, Tom Moody, Paul Reiffel and Damien Fleming, all contributed. Mark's catch was the first of a number of excellent fielding efforts, Ricky Ponting's brilliant catch at third slip to end the innings was the last of them. Such was the pressure we put them under, from our bowling, fielding and passion, that when a Pakistani batsman made a mistake, he was gone. It was as if we strangled the life out of each of them, slowly but surely.

A small total is not always an easy target, but Adam Gilchrist was inspirational. All the hard work of the last week, trying to get his game back in order, paid off big time today. Swamp and I had discussed with him his lack of runs, and told him there was no escape — he simply needed to work extremely hard to get his batting going again. Now, here at Lord's, Gilly set the ground alight, slamming 54 off 36 balls and putting the World Cup Final right out of the reach of our opponents. Mark also batted really well, going right through to the end, while Ricky Ponting played superbly, too.

And Darren Lehmann finished it off, much to his delight and to our collective joy on the balcony. This was sheer bliss, with hugging, back-slapping and hand-shaking capturing the overwhelming emotions of all the guys. It was such a special time for all of us — we had overcome the doubters and doomsday prophets, growing in strength as a unit and following through on a dream we all had.

It was a monumental victory, well executed, thoroughly professional. The Pakistanis weren't in the game as we won in 20.1 overs, an outrageous end to a contest that most critics before the start had rated an even-money bet.

At the press conference, Wasim Akram was magnanimous in defeat. 'I have no disappointments really because we lost to a better side,' he said. 'They played their cricket better than us and we should give credit to Australia.

'I thought Warne bowled brilliantly,' Wasim continued. 'He is the best leg-spinner in the world.'

We just couldn't celebrate enough. As we raced towards victory, I sat on the balcony and experienced goosebumps all over my body every time we hit a four. I can tell you, it was a unique and wonderful feeling to be on that Lord's balcony as the victory unfolded. And to get the World Cup in our hands was something very special, a dream come true; for me, being captain, it was doubly special. Just to sit in that room in the Home of Cricket and see the trophy sitting atop the bench was

*Mark Waugh (left) and Darren Lehmann run towards their team-mates in the Lord's dressing room after securing a second World Cup triumph for Australia.*

*Left: Here's a sight that is sure to send the 'old guard' at Lord's into shock ... a female (Tracey Bevan) in the Pavilion! After capturing the World Cup trophy we decided to let the wives and partners enjoy the moment as well — after all, they make many sacrifices on our behalf to let us pursue our dreams. For the girls it was a moment they never thought possible and, I imagine, one many 'bacon and egg' men will never want to see again.*

*It's only just starting to sink in. Because of a press conference and a variety of TV interviews, it was an hour and a half after the Cup final ended before I had my first chance to sit down. The only problem with being captain is that you miss out on the priceless time immediately after the result, when the lads are on a real high and celebrating hard. Still, it was wonderful to see the likes of Michael Slater, Ian Healy and Mark Taylor come in and join our celebrations.*

a moment when you wish time would stand still. Looking around, you could feel the mixture of joy and relief felt by the eight guys who had played in the 1996 Cup final. Now it was ours. Losing that one made this win even more rewarding. I recall thinking after that game that I'd lost a one-and-only chance to win the World Cup again. This is why sport is so special — you never know what's around the corner.

But even for the guys not associated with that 1996 Cup campaign, this was still a time to savour. I'll never forget the togetherness of the team and the genuine delight we all felt because we'd done it for each other. I can clearly remember thinking … it doesn't get any better than this.

The celebrations went on for many hours in the Lord's dressing room. A singalong with the boys culminated in an experience that was more than just a highlight of our careers — it was one of the great experiences of our lives. Ricky Ponting took us all out onto the ground, we put the World Cup down on the middle of the centre wicket, Punter got up on top of Moods' shoulders, pulled out a poem that he had written a couple of weeks ago, read it slowly, with much feeling, and then led us in one of the most stirring renditions of 'Under the Southern Cross' I'll ever witness. We sang it once, then again, then we stopped, and then we sang it again. At 8.30pm, with no-one else about, our victory anthem echoed around this temple of our sport. A magic moment.

Back to the hotel, where one of the biggest cricket parties went on all night. Unfortunately for Mark and me, our revelry was ended by the news at 2am that our grandfather had passed away back in Australia not long after the winning run had been scored. It was very emotional, but in a way a relief for our family. We didn't want to see him go through any suffering. In this respect it was a mixed day — a huge high, followed by a massive low at the end of it.

Looking back now, I can rate our Cup triumph as, more than anything else, an experience we earned. It's always satisfying to get a big return for all the hard work you put in. I know our win was one we enjoyed thoroughly, as fantastic a victory as any I have had in this wonderful game. Hopefully, we can now all go home, have a rest, reacquaint ourselves with our families and contemplate all we've achieved here. It's been a remarkable experience, and I'm just grateful and proud to have been a part of it. It can honestly be said by all in the Australian squad …

We've got NO REGRETS!!

*It doesn't get any better than this!*

# STATISTICS
# AND TRIVIA

## 1. The Commonwealth Games, Kuala Lumpur, Malaysia, 1998

### AUSTRALIA'S MATCHES IN GROUP B

*Group match, at PKNS, September 9*
Canada 60 (20 overs; DW Fleming 4-21) lost to Australia 1-61 (14 overs; ME Waugh 24*) by nine wickets

*Group match, at TNB, September 12*
Antigua 99 (30.1 overs; DW Fleming 5-24) lost to Australia 3-101 (18 overs; AC Gilchrist 43*)
by seven wickets

*Group match, at PKNS, September 15*
Australia 5-255 (SR Waugh 100*, TM Moody 76*) beat India 9-110 (37.4 overs; BE Young 4-23) by 145 runs

Semi-Final
*At TNB, September 17*
New Zealand 58 (26.3 overs; BE Young 4-4 including hat-trick, DW Fleming 3-23) lost to Australia 1-62
(10.5 overs; AC Gilchrist 43*) by nine wickets

**Final, Australia v South Africa, at PKNS, September 19** *(Toss: South Africa)*

**Australia**

| | | |
|---|---|---|
| ME Waugh | c Boucher b Pollock | 2 |
| +AC Gilchrist | c Rindel b Pollock | 15 |
| RT Ponting | c Dawson b Pollock | 2 |
| MG Bevan | run out | 13 |
| *SR Waugh | not out | 90 |
| DS Lehmann | c Boucher b Pollock | 26 |
| TM Moody | st Boucher b Adams | 3 |
| BE Young | c Benkenstein b Adams | 2 |
| GR Robertson | lbw b Boje | 2 |
| MS Kasprowicz | run out | 12 |
| DW Fleming | run out | 1 |
| Extras | (1b, 2lb,11w, 1nb) | 15 |
| **Total** | **(49.3 overs)** | **183** |

*Fall:* 10, 16, 28, 58, 121, 124, 142, 157, 176, 183.

*Bowling:* Pollock 9-2-19-4; Kallis 6-1-21-0; Dawson 8.1-1-27-0; Crookes 10-0-43-0; Boje 8-0-36-1; Adams 8-0-33-2; Benkenstein 0.2-0-1-0.

**South Africa**

| | | |
|---|---|---|
| AC Hudson | c Bevan b Robertson | 36 |
| MJR Rindel | c ME Waugh | |
| | b Lehmann | 67 |
| DN Crookes | c Moody b Robertson | 3 |
| JH Kallis | c Gilchrist b Lehmann | 44 |
| HH Gibbs | b Fleming | 9 |
| DM Benkenstein | not out | 2 |
| *SM Pollock | c Young b Lehmann | 2 |
| +MV Boucher | not out | 0 |
| Extras | (6b, 1lb, 10w, 4nb) | 21 |
| **Total** | **(6 wickets, 46 overs)** | **184** |

*Did not bat:* N Boje, PR Adams, AC Dawson.

*Fall:* 73, 86, 158, 172, 181, 183

*Bowling:* Fleming 10-1-44-1; Kasprowicz 5-0-34-0; Young 10-3-31-0; Robertson 10-2-28-2; Moody 4-0-15-0; Bevan 3-0-11-0; Lehmann 4-1-14-3.

**South Africa won by four wickets**

*Some Facts and Trivia from the Commonwealth Games*
• Cricket was included in the Commonwealth Games for the first time.
• All Test playing teams were represented except England, which declined an invitation, and West Indies, whose countries competed, as they did in all other events, as individual members of the Commonwealth.
• Placings in the groups were as follows:

| | 1st | 2nd | 3rd | 4th |
|---|---|---|---|---|
| A | Sri Lanka | Zimbabwe | Jamaica | Malaysia |
| B | Australia | India | Antigua | Canada |
| C | South Africa | Barbados | N. Ireland | Bangladesh |
| D | New Zealand | Pakistan | Kenya | Scotland |

- The International Cricket Conference ruled that matches in the tournament would not be recognised as official one-day internationals.
- In the other semi-final on September 16, Sri Lanka scored 130 and South Africa lost nine wickets in scoring 131, including an unbroken partnership of 35 for the last wicket.
- In the playoff for the bronze medal on September 18, New Zealand scored 7-212 and dismissed Sri Lanka in 44.4 overs for 161.
- Highest score for Australia in the tournament was 100 not out (off 102 balls) by SR Waugh v India; Best bowling for Australia in the tournament was 5-24 (off 9 overs) by DW Fleming v Antigua.
- Australia used the same 11 players in each match in the tournament.
- The 67 by MJR Rindel in the final was the highest score (and only half-century) against Australia in the tournament; best bowling against Australia in the tournament was also in the final, by SM Pollock who took 4-19.
- All matches involved a maximum of 50 overs per innings. Innings involved 50 overs unless otherwise stated.

## 2. Australia in Pakistan and Bangladesh, 1998

*Tour match, at Karachi, September 25, 26, 27, 28*
Australians 9-540 decl. (MJ Slater 221, SR Waugh 92, ME Waugh 66, RT Ponting 52, Ali Rizvi 4-160) and 2-194 decl. (JL Langer 101*) beat Karachi City Cricket Association 278 (Azam Khan 57) and 123 (SCG MacGill 6-34) by 333 runs.

**FIRST TEST, AT RAWALPINDI, OCTOBER 1, 2, 3, 4, 5**    *(Toss: Pakistan)*

Pakistan

| | | | | |
|---|---|---|---|---|
| Saeed Anwar | c Langer b MacGill | 145 | lbw b Miller | 19 |
| *Aamer Sohail | c Healy b McGrath | 4 | b McGrath | 13 |
| Mohammad Wasim | c Healy b Fleming | 1 | lbw b Fleming | 0 |
| Inzamam-ul-Haq | c Langer b McGrath | 14 | lbw b Fleming | 0 |
| Salim Malik | c Taylor b Miller | 10 | not out | 52 |
| Azhar Mahmood | c McGrath b MacGill | 16 | (7) c Langer b MacGill | 1 |
| +Moin Khan | c Fleming b MacGill | 39 | (6) c Taylor b MacGill | 18 |
| Wasim Akram | c Fleming b MacGill | 0 | c Healy b Miller | 15 |
| Mohammad Hussain | b MacGill | 1 | c Miller b MacGill | 17 |
| Mushtaq Ahmed | run out | 26 | lbw b MacGill | 0 |
| Saqlain Mushtaq | not out | 2 | lbw b McGrath | 7 |
| Extras | (5b, 2lb, 4nb) | 11 | (3lb) | 3 |
| Total | | 269 | | 145 |

*Fall (1):* 13, 18, 35, 50, 81, 140, 140, 147, 267, 269.
*Fall (2):* 24, 32, 32, 32, 66, 68, 94, 126, 128, 145.
*Bowling (1):* McGrath 26-3-88-2; Fleming 20-3-39-1; Miller 23-4-65-1; MacGill 22-5-66-5; Lehmann 4-1-3-0; SR Waugh 2-0-6-0.
*Bowling (2):* McGrath 15.5-6-24-2; Fleming 15-4-38-2; Miller 21-8-30-2; MacGill 21-7-47-4; Lehmann 3-2-3-0.

Australia

| | | |
|---|---|---|
| MJ Slater | c Mohammad Wasim b Mohammad Hussain | 108 |
| *MA Taylor | c Moin b Wasim Akram | 3 |
| JL Langer | lbw b Wasim Akram | 0 |
| ME Waugh | lbw b Mushtaq Ahmed | 0 |
| SR Waugh | c Mohammad Wasim b Aamer | 157 |
| DS Lehmann | b Mohammad Hussain | 98 |
| +IA Healy | c Mohammad Wasim b Saqlain | 82 |
| DW Fleming | b Wasim Akram | 8 |
| CR Miller | c and b Mushtaq Ahmed | 3 |
| SCG MacGill | b Saqlain | 21 |
| GD McGrath | not out | 3 |
| Extras | (19lb, 11nb) | 30 |
| Total | | 513 |

*Fall:* 11, 11, 28, 226, 352, 443, 459, 464, 504, 513.

*Bowling:* Wasim Akram 35-4-111-3; Azhar 13-1-36-0; Mushtaq Ahmed 41-7-115-2; Saqlain 41.5-9-112-2; Mohammad Hussain 20-3-66-2; Aamer 23-3-54-1.

**Australia won by an innings and 99 runs**

*Tour match, at Rawalpindi, October 8, 9, 10, 11*
Australians 355 (DS Lehmann 103, RT Ponting 88, Azhar Mahmood 4-83) and 298 (DS Lehmann 100 retired hurt, MA Taylor 63*, Shakeel Ahmed 7-71) drew with Rawalpindi 261 (Asif Mahmood 51) and 3-263 (Mohammad Naveed 115*, Ijaz Ahmed 60).

## SECOND TEST, AT PESHAWAR, OCTOBER 15, 16, 17, 18, 19 *(Toss: Pakistan)*

### Australia

| | | | | | |
|---|---|---|---|---|---|
| *MA Taylor | not out | 334 | (2) b Aamer | | 92 |
| MJ Slater | c Azhar b Shoaib | 2 | (1) lbw b Mushtaq | | 21 |
| JL Langer | c Moin b Azhar | 116 | c Yousuf b Mushtaq | | 14 |
| ME Waugh | c Salim b Aamer | 42 | b Shoaib | | 43 |
| SR Waugh | c Moin b Shoaib | 1 | not out | | 49 |
| RT Ponting | not out | 76 | lbw b Ijaz | | 43 |
| +IA Healy | | | not out | | 14 |
| Extras | (9lb, 3w, 16nb) | 28 | (4lb, 9nb) | | 13 |
| Total | (4 wickets, decl.) | 599 | (5 wickets) | | 289 |

*Did not bat:* DW Fleming, CR Miller, SCG MacGill, GD McGrath.

*Fall (1):* 16, 295, 418, 431
*Fall (2):* 39, 67, 170, 179, 269

*Bowling (1):* Shoaib 31-6-107-2; Mohammad 16-0-74-0; Mushtaq 46-3-153-0; Azhar 23-2-82-1; Aamer 42-8-111-1; Salim 16-0-63-0.
*Bowling (2):* Shoaib 16-2-68-1; Azhar 3-0-18-0; Mushtaq 20-1-59-2; Mohammad 10-2-42-0; Aamer 10-1-35-1; Salim 15-1-30-0; Ijaz 14-1-33-1.

### Pakistan

| | | |
|---|---|---|
| Saeed Anwar | c Healy b Miller | 126 |
| *Aamer Sohail | c Fleming b McGrath | 31 |
| Ijaz Ahmed | c Healy b MacGill | 155 |
| Inzamam-ul-Haq | c Healy b SR Waugh | 97 |
| Salim Malik | c Taylor b McGrath | 49 |
| Yousuf Youhana | c SR Waugh b MacGill | 28 |
| +Moin Khan | c Healy b Ponting | 0 |
| Azhar Mahmood | c Langer b McGrath | 26 |
| Mushtaq Ahmed | not out | 48 |
| Mohammad Zahid | lbw b Fleming | 1 |
| Extras | (5b, 9lb, 1w, 4nb) | 19 |
| Total | (9 wickets, decl.) | 580 |

*Did not bat:* Shoaib Akhtar

*Fall:* 45, 256, 371, 454, 500, 502, 521, 571, 580

*Bowling:* McGrath 36-8-131-3; Fleming 35.1-6-103-1; MacGill 42-5-169-2; Miller 38-12-99-1; ME Waugh 8-0-32-0; SR Waugh 8-1-19-1; Ponting 5-1-13-1.

**Match drawn**

## THIRD TEST, AT KARACHI, OCTOBER 22, 23, 24, 25, 26 *(Toss: Australia)*

### Australia

| | | | | | |
|---|---|---|---|---|---|
| *MA Taylor | c Inzamam b Arshad | 16 | (2) b Arshad | | 68 |
| MJ Slater | st Moin b Arshad | 96 | (1) c Yousuf b Arshad | | 11 |
| JL Langer | lbw b Shoaib | 30 | run out | | 51 |
| ME Waugh | c Inzamam b Shahid | 26 | st Moin b Shakeel | | 117 |
| SR Waugh | lbw b Shahid | 0 | c Moin b Shakeel | | 28 |
| DS Lehmann | b Shahid | 3 | c Ijaz b Wasim | | 26 |
| +IA Healy | c Moin b Arshad | 47 | c Shahid b Shoaib | | 3 |
| GR Robertson | c Yousuf b Shahid | 5 | c Wasim b Shakeel | | 45 |
| CR Miller | b Wasim | 0 | c Shahid b Shakeel | | 0 |
| SCG MacGill | not out | 24 | run out | | 10 |
| GD McGrath | c Shakeel b Shahid | 6 | not out | | 4 |
| Extras | (1b, 16lb, 10nb) | 27 | (4b, 8lb, 15nb) | | 27 |
| Total | | 280 | | | 390 |

*Fall (1):* 38, 105, 169, 169, 179, 189, 210, 211, 266, 280.
*Fall (2):* 27, 136, 152, 208, 284, 294, 357, 357, 369, 390.

*Bowling (1):* Wasim 22-4-51-1; Shoaib 14.2-3-39-1; Shakeel 24.4-9-48-0; Arshad 41-14-72-3; Shahid 23.3-6-52-5.
*Bowling (2):* Wasim 22-2-60-1; Shoaib 17-3-37-1; Arshad 56-14-141-2; Shahid 18-3-49-0; Shakeel 29.3-3-91-4.

## Pakistan

| | | | | | |
|---|---|---|---|---|---|
| *Aamer Sohail | c Langer b Miller | 133 | lbw b Miller | 25 |
| Shahid Afridi | c Taylor b McGrath | 10 | c Healy b Miller | 6 |
| Ijaz Ahmed | c Healy b McGrath | 5 | not out | 120 |
| Inzamam-ul-Haq | c Lehmann b McGrath | 9 | (7) not out | 21 |
| Salim Malik | c McGrath b MacGill | 0 | (4) lbw b Miller | 0 |
| Yousuf Youhana | b Robertson | 9 | (5) c ME Waugh b MacGill | 11 |
| +Moin Khan | c Slater b McGrath | 20 | (6) c MacGill b Lehmann | 75 |
| Wasim Akram | lbw b MacGill | 35 | | |
| Shakeel Ahmed | c Langer b McGrath | 1 | | |
| Arshad Khan | lbw b MacGill | 7 | | |
| Shoaib Akhtar | not out | 6 | | |
| Extras | (6b, 5lb, 1w, 5nb) | 17 | (2b, 2nb) | 4 |
| Total | | 252 | (5 wickets) | 262 |

*Fall (1):* 26, 40, 51, 54, 69, 116, 214, 239, 240, 252.
*Fall (2):* 20, 33, 35, 75, 228.
*Bowling (1):* McGrath 25-6-66-5; Miller 14-2-53-1; MacGill 25.4-5-64-3; Robertson 22-5-46-1; Lehmann 1-0-6-0; SR Waugh 2-0-6-0.
*Bowling (2):* McGrath 18-11-40-0; Miller 25-5-82-3; MacGill 17-2-66-1; Robertson 16-2-56-0; Lehmann 2-0-6-1; SR Waugh 8-5-10-0.

**Match drawn**
**Australia won series 1-0**

## AUSTRALIAN TEST AVERAGES v PAKISTAN, 1998

*Batting and Fielding*

| | mat | inn | n.o. | runs | high | 100 | 50 | avge | ct | st |
|---|---|---|---|---|---|---|---|---|---|---|
| MA Taylor | 3 | 5 | 1 | 513 | 334* | 1 | 2 | 128.25 | 4 | - |
| SR Waugh | 3 | 5 | 1 | 235 | 157 | 1 | - | 58.75 | 1 | - |
| IA Healy | 3 | 4 | 1 | 146 | 82 | - | 1 | 48.66 | 9 | - |
| MJ Slater | 3 | 5 | - | 238 | 108 | 1 | 1 | 47.60 | 1 | - |
| ME Waugh | 3 | 5 | - | 228 | 117 | 1 | - | 45.60 | 1 | - |
| DS Lehmann | 2 | 3 | - | 127 | 98 | - | 1 | 42.33 | 1 | - |
| JL Langer | 3 | 5 | - | 211 | 116 | 1 | 1 | 42.20 | 6 | - |
| SCG MacGill | 3 | 3 | 1 | 55 | 24* | - | - | 27.50 | 1 | - |
| GD McGrath | 3 | 3 | 2 | 13 | 6 | - | - | 13.00 | 2 | - |
| CR Miller | 3 | 3 | - | 3 | 3 | - | - | 1.00 | 1 | - |

*Played in two Tests:* DW Fleming 8 (3ct)
*Played in one Test:* RT Ponting 76*, 43; GR Robertson 5, 45.

*Bowling*

| | overs | maidens | runs | wickets | best | 5Inn | avge |
|---|---|---|---|---|---|---|---|
| SCG MacGill | 127.4 | 24 | 412 | 15 | 5-66 | 1 | 27.46 |
| GD McGrath | 120.5 | 34 | 344 | 12 | 5-66 | 1 | 28.66 |
| CR Miller | 121.0 | 31 | 329 | 8 | 3-82 | - | 41.12 |
| DW Fleming | 70.1 | 13 | 180 | 4 | 2-38 | - | 45.00 |

*Also bowled:* DS Lehmann 10-3-18-1; SR Waugh 20-6-41-1; ME Waugh 8-0-32-0; RT Ponting 5-1-13-1; GR Robertson 38-7-102-1.

*Some Facts and Trivia from the Test series v Pakistan*

- In the Test at Rawalpindi, Colin Miller made his Test debut, at 34 years of age, 12 years and 256 days after his first-class debut, becoming the 379th Australian Test cricketer.
- Australia's win at Rawalpindi was Australia's first Test win in Pakistan since November 1959. In 14 Tests in Pakistan since then, Australia had lost six and drawn eight.
- Australia's only previous Test series win in Pakistan was in 1959-60 (2-0 in a three-Test series).
- The following Australian batsmen scored hundreds during the series:

| | | | minutes | balls | fours | sixes | No. of Test hundreds |
|---|---|---|---|---|---|---|---|
| MJ Slater | 108 | Rawalpindi | 298 | 236 | 11 | 1 | 8 |
| SR Waugh | 157 | Rawalpindi | 392 | 326 | 15 | 1 | 15 |
| MA Taylor | 334* | Peshawar | 720 | 564 | 32 | 1 | 19 |
| JL Langer | 116 | Peshawar | 362 | 212 | 10 | - | 1 |
| ME Waugh | 117 | Karachi | 335 | 232 | 9 | - | 15 |

- SCG MacGill's 5-66 at Rawalpindi was his first five-wicket analysis in Tests, in his second Test.

- MA Taylor's 334 not out equalled DG Bradman's Australian Test record (334 v England, Leeds, 1930). It was the fifth Test triple-century for Australia, and also the highest score against Pakistan in Test cricket. It was the highest score by a Test captain. At 213, he became the fourth Australian to score 7000 Test runs (joining AR Border 11,174, DC Boon 7422 and GS Chappell 7110).
- Taylor's 92 in the second innings, for a match aggregate of 426, is the second highest total in a Test (the record is held by GA Gooch 456 — 333 and 123 — England v India, Lord's, 1990).
- The 279-run partnership for the second wicket at Peshawar by Taylor and Langer established a new record partnership for any wicket for Australia v Pakistan (the previous record was 259 for the second wicket by WB Phillips and GN Yallop — also two left-handers — at Perth in 1983-84).
- At Rawalpindi, IA Healy equalled RW Marsh's Test record 355 wicketkeeping dismissals by catching Mohammad Wasim in the first innings, and then broke it by catching Wasim Akram in the second innings. He completed the series with 362 dismissals (337 caught, 25 stumped) in 106 Tests.
- GD McGrath's 5-66 at Karachi was his 10th five-wicket analysis in Tests, in his 40th Test.

## AUSTRALIA IN THE WILLS INTERNATIONAL CUP IN BANGLADESH, 1998

*Quarter-final, at Dhaka, October 28*
India 8-307 (SR Tendulkar 141, AD Jadeja 71) beat Australia 263 (48.1 overs; ME Waugh 74, SR Tendulkar 4-38) by 44 runs.

## PAKISTAN V AUSTRALIA ONE-DAY SERIES IN PAKISTAN, 1998

*'Warm-up' match, at Karachi, November 4*
Australia 234 (48.2 overs; AC Gilchrist 72, DS Lehmann 55) beat Karachi XI 169 (47.5 overs) by 65 runs.

## GAME ONE, AT KARACHI, NOVEMBER 6    *(Toss: Pakistan)*

| Australia | | | Pakistan | | |
|---|---|---|---|---|---|
| +AC Gilchrist | c Azam b Shoaib | 45 | Salim Elahi | c ME Waugh b McGrath | 0 |
| ME Waugh | run out | 11 | Shahid Afridi | c and b McGrath | 6 |
| RT Ponting | c Shahid b Shoaib | 16 | *Aamer Sohail | c ME Waugh b Fleming | 5 |
| DS Lehmann | c Aamer b Arshad | 103 | Ijaz Ahmed | c Young b McGrath | 22 |
| *SR Waugh | c Shahid b Arshad | 10 | Yousuf Youhana | c Bevan b Julian | 92 |
| MG Bevan | c Aamer b Arshad | 83 | Azam Khan | c Gilchrist b Fleming | 3 |
| DR Martyn | c and b Wasim | 13 | +Moin Khan | b Julian | 16 |
| BP Julian | b Shoaib | 9 | Wasim Akram | c and b Bevan | 28 |
| BE Young | not out | 8 | Shoaib Akhtar | run out | 36 |
| Extras | (4b, 7lb, 10w, 5nb) | 26 | Arshad Khan | not out | 8 |
| Total | (8 wickets, 50 overs) | 324 | Kabir Khan | c McGrath b SR Waugh | 5 |
| | | | Extras | (5lb, 7w, 5nb) | 17 |
| | | | Total | (47.2 overs) | 238 |

*Did not bat:* DW Fleming, GD McGrath

*Fall:* 52, 78, 83, 113, 270, 304, 307, 324

*Bowling:* Wasim 10-0-48-1; Kabir 7-0-59-0; Shoaib 9-2-44-3; Shahid 9-0-63-0; Arshad 10-0-70-3; Aamer 5-0-29-0.

*Fall:* 0, 7, 19, 38, 41, 76, 130, 221, 224, 238.

*Bowling:* McGrath 8-1-35-3; Fleming 8-0-32-2; Young 10-0-66-0; Julian 10-2-31-2; Bevan 8-0-47-1; SR Waugh 3.2-0-22-1.

**Australia won by 86 runs**

**GAME TWO, AT PESHAWAR, NOVEMBER 8** *(Toss: Pakistan)*

| Pakistan | | |
|---|---|---|
| *Aamer Sohail | c Ponting b Julian | 15 |
| Asif Mahmood | c ME Waugh b Fleming | 14 |
| Ijaz Ahmed | c SR Waugh b Julian | 5 |
| Salim Malik | c Young b Julian | 8 |
| Yousuf Youhana | run out | 0 |
| +Moin Khan | lbw b Young | 41 |
| Azhar Mahmood | not out | 65 |
| Wasim Akram | c Ponting b McGrath | 34 |
| Shoaib Akhtar | not out | 8 |
| Extras | (11lb, 13w, 3nb) | 27 |
| **Total** | **(7 wickets, 50 overs)** | **217** |

*Did not bat:* Saqlain Mushtaq, Arshad Khan

*Fall:* 31, 41, 41, 43, 59, 137, 194

*Bowling:* McGrath 10-1-34-1; Fleming 10-1-41-1; Julian 10-3-40-3; SR Waugh 10-0-44-0; Ponting 4-0-21-0; Young 6-0-26-1.

| Australia | | |
|---|---|---|
| ME Waugh | b Saqlain | 19 |
| +AC Gilchrist | c and b Saqlain | 42 |
| RT Ponting | c Salim b Azhar | 55 |
| *SR Waugh | lbw b Saqlain | 0 |
| DR Martyn | c Moin b Wasim | 4 |
| MG Bevan | not out | 57 |
| DS Lehmann | not out | 26 |
| Extras | (2lb, 7w, 8nb) | 17 |
| **Total** | **(5 wickets, 48.1 overs)** | **220** |

*Did not bat:* BP Julian, BE Young, DW Fleming, GD McGrath

*Fall:* 63, 67, 71, 90, 172

*Bowling:* Wasim 10-0-32-1; Shoaib 9-0-56-0; Saqlain 10-1-35-3; Arshad 8.1-0-39-0; Azhar 9-0-46-1; Salim 2-0-10-0.

**Australia won by five wickets**

---

**GAME THREE, AT LAHORE, NOVEMBER 10** *(Toss: Pakistan)*

| Pakistan | | |
|---|---|---|
| *Aamer Sohail | c Gilchrist b Julian | 21 |
| Asif Mahmood | c Julian b McGrath | 0 |
| Ijaz Ahmed | b Lehmann | 111 |
| Salim Malik | run out | 2 |
| Yousuf Youhana | c ME Waugh b Julian | 100 |
| Shahid Afridi | run out | 40 |
| Wasim Akram | run out | 13 |
| +Moin Khan | c Bevan b McGrath | 0 |
| Azhar Mahmood | not out | 3 |
| Extras | (1b, 14lb, 8w, 2nb) | 25 |
| **Total** | **(8 wickets, 50 overs)** | **315** |

*Did not bat:* Shoaib Akhtar, Saqlain Mushtaq

*Fall:* 7, 50, 73, 235, 288, 303, 303, 315

*Bowling:* McGrath 10-0-58-2; Fleming 10-3-44-0; Julian 10-0-75-2; SR Waugh 6-0-31-0; Young 8-0-46-0; Symonds 2-0-14-0; ME Waugh 2-0-16-0; Lehmann 2-0-16-1.

| Australia | | |
|---|---|---|
| +AC Gilchrist | st Moin b Aamer | 103 |
| ME Waugh | lbw b Wasim | 13 |
| RT Ponting | not out | 124 |
| DS Lehmann | c Moin b Salim | 8 |
| *SR Waugh | b Saqlain | 30 |
| MG Bevan | not out | 6 |
| Extras | (1b, 12lb, 11w, 8nb) | 32 |
| **Total** | **(4 wickets, 48.5 overs)** | **316** |

*Did not bat:* A Symonds, BP Julian, BE Young, DW Fleming, GD McGrath

*Fall:* 25, 218, 237, 306

*Bowling:* Wasim 9-0-46-1; Shoaib 8-0-58-0; Saqlain 9.5-0-44-1; Azhar 2-0-23-0; Salim 7-0-54-1; Aamer 10-0-54-1; Shahid 3-0-24-0.

**Australia won by six wickets**
**Australia won series 3-0**

---

*Some Facts and Trivia from the Limited-Overs Matches in Bangladesh and Pakistan*

- All matches involved a maximum 50 overs per innings, with each bowler limited to a maximum of 10 overs. This would be the case for every one-day international played during 1998-99, including the World Cup.
- The Wills International Cup was a knockout involving all nine Test-playing teams. All matches were played at the Bangabandhu National Stadium in Dhaka. In the final on November 1, West Indies 245 (49.3 overs; PA Wallace 103; JH Kallis 5-30) lost to South Africa 6-248 (47 overs; WJ Cronje 61*) by four wickets.
- In the third match v Pakistan, Andrew Symonds became the 139th player for Australia in limited-overs internationals. This was the only instance of a player making his limited-overs international debut for Australia between January 1998 and September 1999.
- The 103 at Karachi was DS Lehmann's first hundred, in his 26th limited-overs international.
- The 103 at Lahore was AC Gilchrist's third hundred, in his 39th limited-overs international.
- The 124* at Lahore was RT Ponting's fifth hundred, in his 59th limited-overs international.
- The 8-324 at Karachi is a new record total for Australia in limited-overs internationals v Pakistan.
- The 193 partnership by Gilchrist and Ponting for the second wicket at Lahore is a new record partnership for any wicket by Australia in limited-overs internationals v Pakistan.
- The 4-316 at Lahore is Australia's highest total batting second in any limited-overs international.

**FIRST ASHES TEST, AT BRISBANE, NOVEMBER 20, 21, 22, 23, 24**   *(Toss: Australia)*

**Australia**

| | | | | |
|---|---|---|---|---|
| *MA Taylor | c Hussain b Cork | 46 | (2) b Cork | 0 |
| MJ Slater | c Butcher b Mullally | 16 | (1) c and b Fraser | 113 |
| JL Langer | lbw b Gough | 8 | c Mullally b Croft | 74 |
| ME Waugh | c Stewart b Mullally | 31 | not out | 27 |
| SR Waugh | c Stewart b Mullally | 112 | not out | 16 |
| RT Ponting | c Butcher b Cork | 21 | | |
| +IA Healy | c Mullally b Fraser | 134 | | |
| MS Kasprowicz | c Stewart b Mullally | 0 | | |
| DW Fleming | not out | 71 | | |
| SCG MacGill | c Stewart b Mullally | 20 | | |
| GD McGrath | c Atherton b Croft | 5 | | |
| Extras | (14lb, 1w, 6nb) | 21 | (1b, 1lb, 5nb) | 7 |
| Total | | 485 | (3 wickets, decl.) | 237 |

*Fall (1):* 30, 59, 106, 106, 178, 365, 365, 420, 445, 485.
*Fall (2):* 20, 182, 199

*Bowling (1):* Gough 34-4-135-1; Cork 31-6-98-2; Mullally 40-10-105-5; Croft 23-6-55-1; Fraser 28-7-76-1; Ramprakash 2-1-2-0.
*Bowling (2):* Gough 6-0-50-0; Cork 5-0-18-1; Mullally 14-4-38-0; Fraser 15-1-52-1; Croft 20-2-71-1; Ramprakash 2-0-6-0.

**England**

| | | | | |
|---|---|---|---|---|
| MA Butcher | c and b ME Waugh | 116 | lbw b MacGill | 40 |
| MA Atherton | c ME Waugh b McGrath | 0 | c Fleming b McGrath | 28 |
| N Hussain | c Healy b Kasprowicz | 59 | b MacGill | 47 |
| *+AJ Stewart | c Kasprowicz b MacGill | 8 | c Ponting b ME Waugh | 3 |
| GP Thorpe | c Langer b McGrath | 77 | c Langer b ME Waugh | 9 |
| MR Ramprakash | not out | 69 | st Healy b MacGill | 14 |
| DG Cork | c MacGill b McGrath | 0 | not out | 21 |
| RDB Croft | b Kasprowicz | 23 | not out | 4 |
| D Gough | lbw b McGrath | 0 | | |
| AD Mullally | c Kasprowicz b McGrath | 0 | | |
| ARC Fraser | c ME Waugh b McGrath | 1 | | |
| Extras | (1b, 9lb, 12nb) | 22 | (3lb, 1w, 9nb) | 13 |
| Total | | 375 | (6 wickets) | 179 |

*Fall (1):* 11, 145, 168, 240, 315, 319, 360, 373, 373, 375.
*Fall (2):* 46, 96, 103, 133, 148, 161

*Bowling (1):* McGrath 34.2-11-85-6; Fleming 27-5-83-0; Kasprowicz 29-7-82-2; MacGill 24-4-70-1; SR Waugh 3-0-17-0; Ponting 3-0-10-0; ME Waugh 8-1-18-1.
*Bowling (2):* McGrath 16-6-30-1; Kasprowicz 8-3-28-0; Fleming 7-2-12-0; MacGill 22-3-51-3; ME Waugh 14-0-55-2; Ponting 1-1-0-0.

**Match drawn**

**SECOND ASHES TEST, AT PERTH, NOVEMBER 28, 29, 30**   *(Toss: Australia)*

**England**

| | | | | |
|---|---|---|---|---|
| MA Butcher | c Healy b Fleming | 0 | c Ponting b Fleming | 1 |
| MA Atherton | c Healy b McGrath | 1 | c Taylor b Fleming | 35 |
| N Hussain | c Healy b McGrath | 6 | lbw b Fleming | 1 |
| *+AJ Stewart | b McGrath | 38 | c Taylor b Fleming | 0 |
| MR Ramprakash | c Taylor b Fleming | 26 | not out | 47 |
| JP Crawley | c ME Waugh b Gillespie | 4 | c Langer b Miller | 15 |
| GA Hick | c Healy b Gillespie | 0 | c Ponting b Gillespie | 68 |
| DG Cork | c Taylor b Fleming | 2 | lbw b Gillespie | 16 |
| AJ Tudor | not out | 18 | c Healy b Gillespie | 0 |
| D Gough | c ME Waugh b Fleming | 11 | lbw b Gillespie | 0 |
| AD Mullally | c Healy b Fleming | 0 | b Gillespie | 0 |
| Extras | (2lb, 2w, 2nb) | 6 | (8nb) | 8 |
| Total | | 112 | | 191 |

*Fall (1):* 2, 4, 19, 62, 74, 74, 81, 90, 108, 112.
*Fall (2):* 5, 11, 15, 40, 67, 158, 189, 189, 189, 191.

*Bowling (1):* McGrath 16-4-37-3; Fleming 14-3-46-5; Gillespie 7-0-23-2; Miller 2-0-4-0.
*Bowling (2):* McGrath 26-10-47-0; Fleming 19-7-45-4; Gillespie 15.2-2-88-5; Miller 10-4-11-1.

## Australia

| | | | | |
|---|---|---|---|---|
| *MA Taylor | c Stewart b Cork | 61 | (2) c Hick b Mullally | 3 |
| MJ Slater | c Butcher b Gough | 34 | (1) c and b Gough | 17 |
| JL Langer | c Crawley b Ramprakash | 15 | c Atherton b Tudor | 7 |
| ME Waugh | c Butcher b Tudor | 36 | not out | 17 |
| JN Gillespie | c Stewart b Mullally | 11 | | |
| SR Waugh | b Tudor | 33 | (5) not out | 15 |
| RT Ponting | c Stewart b Tudor | 11 | | |
| +IA Healy | lbw b Gough | 12 | | |
| DW Fleming | c Hick b Gough | 0 | | |
| CR Miller | not out | 3 | | |
| GD McGrath | c Cork b Tudor | 0 | | |
| Extras | (1b, 10lb, 13nb) | 24 | (3lb, 2nb) | 5 |
| **Total** | | **240** | **(3 wickets)** | **64** |

*Fall (1):* 81, 115, 138, 165, 209, 214, 228, 229, 240, 240.
*Fall (2):* 16, 24, 36

*Bowling (1):* Gough 25-9-43-3; Cork 21-5-49-1; Mullally 21-10-36-1; Tudor 20.2-5-89-4; Ramprakash 2-0-12-1.
*Bowling (2):* Gough 9-5-18-1; Mullally 9-0-24-1; Tudor 5-0-19-1.

**Australia won by seven wickets**

### THIRD ASHES TEST, AT ADELAIDE, DECEMBER 11, 12, 13, 14, 15 *(Toss: Australia)*

## Australia

| | | | | |
|---|---|---|---|---|
| MJ Slater | c Stewart b Headley | 17 | (2) lbw b Gough | 103 |
| *MA Taylor | c Hussain b Such | 59 | (1) lbw b Such | 29 |
| JL Langer | not out | 179 | c sub (BC Hollioake) b Such | 52 |
| ME Waugh | c and b Such | 7 | not out | 51 |
| SR Waugh | c Hick b Gough | 59 | c Hick b Headley | 7 |
| RT Ponting | c Hick b Gough | 5 | b Gough | 10 |
| +IA Healy | c Ramprakash b Headley | 13 | not out | 7 |
| DW Fleming | lbw b Headley | 12 | | |
| SCG MacGill | b Such | 0 | | |
| CR Miller | lbw b Headley | 11 | | |
| GD McGrath | c Stewart b Gough | 10 | | |
| Extras | (6lb, 13nb) | 19 | (12lb, 1w, 6nb) | 19 |
| **Total** | | **391** | **(5 wickets, decl.)** | **278** |

*Fall (1):* 28, 140, 156, 264, 274, 311, 338, 339, 354, 391.
*Fall (2):* 54, 188, 216, 230, 268

*Bowling (1):* Gough 29.5-4-103-3; Mullally 26-5-59-0; Headley 23-1-97-4; Such 38-8-99-3; Ramprakash 9-1-27-0.
*Bowling (2):* Gough 22-2-76-2; Mullally 16-6-18-0; Headley 18-1-78-1; Such 29-5-66-2; Ramprakash 12-1-27-0; Hick 1-0-1-0.

## England

| | | | | |
|---|---|---|---|---|
| MA Butcher | lbw b Miller | 6 | c Healy b Fleming | 19 |
| MA Atherton | c Taylor b MacGill | 41 | c ME Waugh b Miller | 5 |
| N Hussain | not out | 89 | lbw b Miller | 41 |
| *+AJ Stewart | c Slater b Miller | 0 | (6) not out | 63 |
| MR Ramprakash | c ME Waugh b McGrath | 61 | (4) b Fleming | 57 |
| JP Crawley | b McGrath | 5 | (7) c ME Waugh b McGrath | 13 |
| GA Hick | c Taylor b MacGill | 8 | (8) c Ponting b McGrath | 0 |
| DW Headley | lbw b MacGill | 0 | (5) c ME Waugh b Miller | 2 |
| D Gough | c Healy b MacGill | 7 | c Healy b McGrath | 3 |
| AD Mullally | b Fleming | 0 | c Healy b Fleming | 4 |
| PM Such | lbw b Fleming | 0 | lbw b McGrath | 0 |
| Extras | (1b, 3lb, 1w, 5nb) | 10 | (7b, 9lb, 14nb) | 30 |
| **Total** | | **227** | | **237** |

*Fall (1):* 18, 83, 84, 187, 195, 210, 210, 226, 227, 227.
*Fall (2):* 27, 31, 120, 122, 163, 221, 221, 231, 236, 237.

*Bowling (1):* McGrath 18-4-48-2; Fleming 10.5-2-34-2; Miller 23-6-71-2; MacGill 28-6-53-4; ME Waugh 3-0-17-0.
*Bowling (2):* McGrath 17-0-50-4; Fleming 21-3-56-3; Miller 24-1-57-3; MacGill 25-8-55-0; SR Waugh 2-1-3-0.

**Australia won by 205 runs**

**FOURTH ASHES TEST, AT MELBOURNE, DECEMBER 26 (No Play), 27, 28, 29**   *(Toss: Australia)*

**England**

| | | | | |
|---|---|---|---|---|
| MA Atherton | c Healy b McGrath | 0 | b Fleming | 0 |
| *AJ Stewart | b MacGill | 107 | c Slater b MacGill | 52 |
| MA Butcher | c Langer b McGrath | 0 | c Slater b MacGill | 14 |
| N Hussain | c Healy b Nicholson | 19 | (5) c Slater b Nicholson | 50 |
| MR Ramprakash | c McGrath b SR Waugh | 63 | (6) b Nicholson | 14 |
| GA Hick | c Fleming b MacGill | 39 | (7) b Fleming | 60 |
| +WK Hegg | c Healy b SR Waugh | 3 | (8) c MacGill b Nicholson | 9 |
| DW Headley | c Taylor b McGrath | 14 | (4) b McGrath | 1 |
| D Gough | b MacGill | 11 | c Slater b MacGill | 4 |
| ARC Fraser | not out | 0 | not out | 7 |
| AD Mullally | lbw b MacGill | 0 | c and b McGrath | 16 |
| Extras | (7lb, 1w, 6nb) | 14 | (2b, 4lb, 11nb) | 17 |
| Total | | 270 | | 244 |

*Fall (1):* 0, 4, 81, 200, 202, 206, 244, 266, 270, 270.
*Fall (2):* 5, 61, 66, 78, 127, 178, 202, 221, 221, 244.
*Bowling (1):* McGrath 22-5-64-3; Fleming 19-3-71-0; Nicholson 10-0-59-1; MacGill 19-2-61-4; SR Waugh 6-2-8-2.
*Bowling (2):* McGrath 20.2-5-56-2; Fleming 17-4-45-2; Nicholson 15-4-56-3; MacGill 27-3-81-3; ME Waugh 1-1-0-0.

**Australia**

| | | | | |
|---|---|---|---|---|
| *MA Taylor | c Hick b Gough | 7 | (2) c Headley b Mullally | 19 |
| MJ Slater | lbw b Gough | 1 | (1) lbw b Headley | 18 |
| JL Langer | c Hussain b Gough | 44 | c Ramprakash b Mullally | 30 |
| ME Waugh | lbw b Fraser | 36 | c Hick b Headley | 43 |
| SR Waugh | not out | 122 | not out | 30 |
| DS Lehmann | c Hegg b Gough | 13 | c Hegg b Headley | 4 |
| +IA Healy | c Headley b Fraser | 36 | c Hick b Headley | 0 |
| DW Fleming | c Hick b Mullally | 12 | lbw b Headley | 0 |
| MJ Nicholson | b Gough | 5 | c Hegg b Headley | 9 |
| SCG MacGill | c Hegg b Mullally | 43 | b Gough | 0 |
| GD McGrath | b Mullally | 0 | lbw b Gough | 0 |
| Extras | (4b, 6lb, 11nb) | 21 | (4b, 1lb, 4nb) | 9 |
| Total | | 340 | | 162 |

*Fall (1):* 13, 26, 98, 127, 151, 209, 235, 252, 340, 340.
*Fall (2):* 31, 41, 103, 130, 140, 140, 140, 161, 162, 162.
*Bowling (1):* Gough 28-7-96-5; Headley 25-3-86-0; Mullally 21.3-5-64-3; Ramprakash 2-0-6-0; Fraser 22-0-78-2.
*Bowling (2):* Gough 15.4-2-54-2; Headley 17-5-60-6; Mullally 10-4-20-2; Fraser 4-0-23-0.

**England won by 12 runs**

**FIFTH ASHES TEST, AT SYDNEY, JANUARY 2, 3, 4, 5, 1999**   *(Toss: Australia)*

**Australia**

| | | | | |
|---|---|---|---|---|
| *MA Taylor | c Hick b Headley | 2 | (2) c Stewart b Gough | 2 |
| MJ Slater | c Hegg b Headley | 18 | (1) c Hegg b Headley | 123 |
| JL Langer | c Ramprakash b Tudor | 26 | lbw b Headley | 1 |
| ME Waugh | c Hegg b Headley | 121 | c Ramprakash b Headley | 24 |
| SR Waugh | b Such | 96 | (7) b Headley | 8 |
| DS Lehmann | c Hussain b Tudor | 32 | (5) c Crawley b Such | 0 |
| +IA Healy | c Hegg b Gough | 14 | (6) c Crawley b Such | 5 |
| SK Warne | not out | 1 | c Ramprakash b Such | 8 |
| SCG MacGill | b Gough | 0 | c Butcher b Such | 6 |
| CR Miller | b Gough | 0 | not out | 3 |
| GD McGrath | c Hick b Headley | 0 | c Stewart b Such | 0 |
| Extras | (2lb, 9nb) | 11 | (3b, 1lb) | 4 |
| Total | | 322 | | 184 |

*Fall (1):* 4, 52, 52, 242, 284, 319, 321, 321, 321, 322.
*Fall (2):* 16, 25, 64, 73, 91, 110, 141, 180, 184, 184.
*Bowling (1):* Gough 17-4-61-3; Headley 19.3-3-62-4; Tudor 12-1-64-2; Such 24-6-77-1; Ramprakash 15-0-56-0.
*Bowling (2):* Gough 15-3-51-1; Headley 19-7-40-4; Such 25.5-5-81-5; Tudor 5-2-8-0.

**England**

| | | | | |
|---|---|---|---|---|
| MA Butcher | lbw b Warne | 36 | st Healy b Warne | 27 |
| *AJ Stewart | c Warne b McGrath | 3 | st Healy b MacGill | 42 |
| N Hussain | c ME Waugh b Miller | 42 | c and b MacGill | 53 |
| MR Ramprakash | c MacGill b McGrath | 14 | c Taylor b McGrath | 14 |
| GA Hick | c Warne b MacGill | 23 | b MacGill | 7 |
| JP Crawley | c Taylor b MacGill | 44 | lbw b Miller | 5 |
| +WK Hegg | b Miller | 15 | c Healy b MacGill | 3 |
| AJ Tudor | b MacGill | 14 | b MacGill | 3 |
| DW Headley | c McGrath b MacGill | 8 | c Healy b MacGill | 16 |
| D Gough | lbw b MacGill | 0 | not out | 7 |
| PM Such | not out | 0 | c and b MacGill | 2 |
| Extras | (8b, 8lb, 1w, 4nb) | 21 | (5lb, 1w, 3nb) | 9 |
| Total | | 220 | | 188 |

*Fall (1):* 18, 56, 88, 137, 139, 171, 204, 213, 213, 220.
*Fall (2):* 57, 77, 110, 137, 150, 157, 162, 175, 180, 188.

*Bowling (1):* McGrath 17-7-35-2; Miller 23-6-45-2; MacGill 20.1-2-57-5; Warne 20-4-67-1.
*Bowling (2):* McGrath 10-1-40-1; Miller 17-1-50-1; MacGill 20.1-4-50-7; Warne 19-3-43-1.

**Australia won by 98 runs**
**Australia won series 3-1**


## AUSTRALIAN TEST AVERAGES v ENGLAND, 1998-99

### Batting and Fielding

| | mat | inn | n.o. | runs | high | 100 | 50 | avge | ct | st |
|---|---|---|---|---|---|---|---|---|---|---|
| SR Waugh | 5 | 10 | 4 | 498 | 122* | 2 | 2 | 83.00 | - | - |
| ME Waugh | 5 | 10 | 3 | 393 | 121 | 1 | 1 | 56.14 | 10 | - |
| JL Langer | 5 | 10 | 1 | 436 | 179* | 1 | 2 | 48.44 | 4 | - |
| MJ Slater | 5 | 10 | - | 460 | 123 | 3 | - | 46.00 | 5 | - |
| IA Healy | 5 | 8 | 1 | 221 | 134 | 1 | - | 31.57 | 16 | 3 |
| DW Fleming | 4 | 5 | 1 | 95 | 71* | - | 1 | 23.75 | 2 | - |
| MA Taylor | 5 | 10 | - | 228 | 61 | - | 2 | 22.80 | 9 | - |
| DS Lehmann | 2 | 4 | - | 49 | 32 | - | - | 12.25 | - | - |
| RT Ponting | 3 | 4 | - | 47 | 21 | - | - | 11.75 | 4 | - |
| SCG MacGill | 4 | 6 | - | 69 | 43 | - | - | 11.50 | 5 | - |
| CR Miller | 3 | 4 | 2 | 17 | 11 | - | - | 8.50 | - | - |
| GD McGrath | 5 | 7 | - | 15 | 10 | - | - | 2.14 | 3 | - |

*Played in one Test:* MS Kasprowicz 0 (2 ct); JN Gillespie 11; MJ Nicholson 5, 9; SK Warne 2*, 8 (2 ct).

### Bowling

| | overs | maidens | runs | wickets | best | 5Inn | avge |
|---|---|---|---|---|---|---|---|
| JN Gillespie | 22.2 | 2 | 111 | 7 | 5-88 | 1 | 15.85 |
| SCG MacGill | 185.2 | 33 | 477 | 27 | 7-50 | 2 | 17.66 |
| GD McGrath | 196.4 | 53 | 492 | 24 | 6-85 | 1 | 20.50 |
| DW Fleming | 134.5 | 29 | 392 | 16 | 5-46 | 1 | 24.50 |
| CR Miller | 99.0 | 18 | 238 | 9 | 3-57 | - | 26.44 |
| MJ Nicholson | 25.0 | 4 | 115 | 4 | 3-56 | - | 28.75 |
| ME Waugh | 26.0 | 2 | 90 | 3 | 2-55 | - | 30.00 |

*Also bowled:* MS Kasprowicz 37-10-111-2; SR Waugh 11-3-28-2; RT Ponting 4-1-10-0; SK Warne 39-7-110-2.


### Some Facts and Trivia from the Ashes Series

- In the Test at Brisbane, MA Taylor played his 100th Test, becoming the fifth Australian to do so (after AR Border, DC Boon, SR Waugh and IA Healy).
- IA Healy's century in the first Test was his fourth in first-class cricket, and second at the Gabba. All four of his first-class centuries have come in Test cricket.
- GD McGrath's 6-85 at Brisbane was his 11th five-wicket analysis in Tests, in his 41st Test.
- The Test at Brisbane was the only match in the series which did not have a result, where England was 6-179, chasing 348, when heavy rain intervened after the tea interval on the fifth day.
- The second Test in Perth was the 108th career Test for both IA Healy and SR Waugh. This moved them into second place in the Australian all-time list, behind AR Border (156 Tests) and one ahead of DC Boon (107).
- DW Fleming's 5-46 at Perth was his first five-wicket analysis in Tests, in his seventh Test.
- JN Gillespie's 5-88 at Perth was his third five-wicket analysis in Tests, in his 10th Test.
- In the Test at Melbourne, Matthew Nicholson made his Test debut, at the age of 24, becoming Australia's 380th Test cricketer.

- When SR Waugh reached 43 in his first innings of the fourth Test, he reached 7000 Test career runs. He became the fifth Australian and 17th batsman to achieve this feat.
- In the Test at Sydney, MA Taylor equalled AR Border's record of 156 catches by a non-wicketkeeper when catching JP Crawley in the first innings, and took a record 157th catch when catching MR Ramprakash in the second innings.
- In the Test at Sydney, MA Taylor captained Australia for the 50th time, becoming the second Australian to do so (after AR Border, who led his country on 93 occasions).
- MA Taylor won all five tosses, joining Australian captains MA Noble (1909) and AL Hassett (1953) to perform this feat in a Test series v England.
- SR Waugh's 96 at Sydney was his ninth Test innings in the 90s. The previous record of eight such innings was held by AI Kallicharran (West Indies).
- D Gough's hat-trick at Sydney (first innings: IA Healy, SCG MacGill, CR Miller) was the ninth for England and the 23rd in Tests.
- In the Test at Sydney, GD McGrath became the 10th Australian to take 200 Test wickets by dismissing Stewart in the first innings.
- In the fifth Test, ME Waugh became the sixth Australian, excluding wicketkeepers, to complete 100 Test catches, when he caught N Hussain in England's first innings (after IM Chappell, RB Simpson, GS Chappell, AR Border and MA Taylor).
- MJ Slater's 123 at Sydney was 66.85% of the innings total, the second highest in Tests (C Bannerman scored 165 retired hurt out of 245 — 67.34% — of Australia's first innings v England, Melbourne, 1877).
- The following Australians scored hundreds in the series:

| | | | minutes | balls | fours | sixes | No. of Test hundreds |
|---|---|---|---|---|---|---|---|
| SR Waugh | 112 | Brisbane | 330 | 232 | 13 | - | 16 |
| IA Healy | 134 | Brisbane | 303 | 229 | 14 | - | 4 |
| MJ Slater | 113 | Brisbane | 190 | 139 | 13 | 1 | 9 |
| JL Langer | 179* | Adelaide | 491 | 351 | 13 | - | 2 |
| MJ Slater | 103 | Adelaide | 276 | 191 | 8 | 1 | 10 |
| SR Waugh | 122* | Melbourne | 315 | 198 | 13 | - | 17 |
| ME Waugh | 121 | Sydney | 293 | 205 | 10 | - | 16 |
| MJ Slater | 123 | Sydney | 271 | 189 | 11 | - | 11 |

- SCG MacGill's 5-57 at Sydney (first innings) was his second five-wicket analysis in Tests, in his eighth Test. His 7-50 in the second innings was his third five-wicket analysis in Tests, and his 12 wickets in the Test at Sydney are the most by an Australian in a Test since 1993-94, when SK Warne took 12-128 v South Africa, also at Sydney.
- Australia won their sixth successive Test series v England.
- An additional representative match was played at Hobart on December 19, 20, 21, 22: England 6-469 decl. (MA Atherton 210*, GA Hick 125) and 3-199 decl. (MA Butcher 103*) lost to an Australian XI 4-293 decl. (MTG Elliott 81, GS Blewett 169*) and 1-376 (GS Blewett 213*, CJ Richards 138*) by nine wickets. The 376 for victory was scored in 228 minutes off 55.2 overs.
- During 1998-99, SR Waugh was available for only one Sheffield Shield match: v Victoria at Sydney, December 19, 20, 21, 22. NSW 360 (SR Waugh 116; MWH Inness 4-69) and 4-362 (MJ Slater 113, ME Waugh 126) drew with Victoria 9-438 decl. (MP Mott 105, BJ Hodge 120). The 116 was SR Waugh's 50th century in first-class cricket.

## AUSTRALIA IN THE WORLD SERIES, 1999

*At Brisbane, January 10*
England 8-178 beat Australia 9-145 (36 overs; MG Bevan 56*, AD Mullally 4-18) on faster scoring rate.

*At Sydney, January 13*
Sri Lanka 9-259 (HP Tillekeratne 73, ST Jayasuriya 65) lost to Australia 2-260 (46.1 overs; AC Gilchrist 131, ME Waugh 63) by eight wickets

*At Melbourne, January 15*
England 179 (43.2 overs; GD McGrath 4-54) lost to Australia 1-182 (39.2 overs; ME Waugh 83*, RT Ponting 75*) by nine wickets

*At Sydney, January 17*
England 4-282 (GA Hick 108, N Hussain 93) beat Australia 6-275 (ME Waugh 85, DS Lehmann 76) by 7 runs

*At Hobart, January 21*
Australia 9-210 (ME Waugh 65, DS Lehmann 51) lost to Sri Lanka 7-211 (49.3 overs, MS Atapattu 82, RS Kaluwitharana 54) by three wickets

*At Adelaide, January 24*
Australia 270 (ME Waugh 57) beat Sri Lanka 190 (41.4 overs; RS Mahanama 55; GD McGrath 5-40) by 80 runs

*At Adelaide, January 26*
Australia 8-239 (ME Waugh 65, DR Martyn 59*, DS Lehmann 51) beat England 223 (48.3 overs; GA Hick 109) by 16 runs

*At Perth, January 31*
Australia 7-274 (MG Bevan 72*) beat Sri Lanka 229 (46.3 overs, ST Jayasuriya 50 retired hurt) by 45 runs

*At Sydney, February 5*
England 8-210 lost to Australia 6-211 (47 overs) by four wickets

*At Melbourne, February 7*
Australia 8-310 (AC Gilchrist 154, RT Ponting 61) beat Sri Lanka 267 (47.1 overs; AC Gunawardene 75, RS Kaluwitharana 68; S Lee 5-33) by 43 runs

*After 10 qualifying matches each: Australia seven wins, England five wins, Sri Lanka three wins*

*First Final, at Sydney, February 10*
Australia 8-232 (MG Bevan 69*) beat England 222 (N Hussain 58) by 10 runs

*Second Final, at Melbourne, February 13*
Australia 5-272 (DS Lehmann 71, DR Martyn 57, AC Gilchrist 52) beat England 110 (31.5 overs) by 162 runs

**Australia won finals series 2-0**

*Some Facts and Trivia from the World Series*
- Australia won the World Series for the 12th time in the 20 seasons of the tournament.
- SR Waugh played in two matches, on January 17 (his 250th limited-over international, only the second Australian to do so — after AR Border 273) and on January 21. In the other matches, Australia was led by SK Warne.
- During the series, MA Taylor announced his retirement from Test cricket, and SR Waugh was subsequently named captain of the team to tour the West Indies, becoming Australia's 40th Test captain.
- In the match on January 15, GD McGrath became the sixth Australian to take 100 wickets in limited-overs international cricket (after DK Lillee, SP O'Donnell, CJ McDermott, SR Waugh and SK Warne).
- AC Gilchrist's 154 v Sri Lanka at Melbourne, February 7, his fifth hundred in limited-overs internationals, set a new individual record for Australia in limited-over internationals, passing 145 (DM Jones v England in 1990-91 and RT Ponting v Zimbabwe in 1997-98). Nineteen players have scored 67 hundreds for Australia in limited-over internationals: the other 18 have all played Test cricket.
- GD McGrath's 5-40 v Sri Lanka, Adelaide, January 24, was his second five-wicket analysis in limited-over internationals (in his 80th match).
- S Lee's 5-33 v Sri Lanka, February 7, was his first five-wicket analysis in limited-over internationals (in his 14th match); he is yet to take more than four wickets in an innings in first-class or domestic limited-over cricket.

## 4. Australia in the West Indies, 1999

*Tour match, at St John's, Antigua, February 22, 23, 24*
Australians 156 (GS Blewett 52, R Hinds 4-23) and 4-209 decl. (RT Ponting 61*, GS Blewett 58) drew with West Indies Board XI 55 (AC Dale 7-24) and 4-121.

*Tour match, at Pointe-a-Pierre, Trinidad, February 27, 28, March 1*
President's XI 177 (DRE Joseph 64, SCG MacGill 6-46) and 185 (S Ragoonath 53, SCG MacGill 7-29) lost to Australians 368 (ME Waugh 106, SR Waugh 57, RD King 5-75, NAM McLean 4-111) by an innings and 6 runs

**FIRST TEST, AT PORT-OF-SPAIN, TRINIDAD, MARCH 5, 6, 7, 8**   *(Toss: Australia)*

**Australia**

| | | | | |
|---|---|---|---|---|
| MJ Slater | c Dillon b Collins | 23 | st Jacobs b Adams | 106 |
| MTG Elliott | lbw b Collins | 44 | c Joseph b Walsh | 0 |
| JL Langer | c Jacobs b Walsh | 5 | c Jacobs b Dillon | 24 |
| ME Waugh | lbw b Walsh | 2 | lbw b Ambrose | 33 |
| *SR Waugh | c Jacobs b Dillon | 14 | c Jacobs b Collins | 0 |
| GS Blewett | lbw b Ambrose | 58 | st Jacobs b Adams | 28 |
| +IA Healy | lbw b Walsh | 12 | lbw b Walsh | 0 |
| SK Warne | c Campbell b Ambrose | 21 | b Walsh | 25 |
| JN Gillespie | not out | 28 | c Lara b Ambrose | 22 |
| SCG MacGill | b Ambrose | 0 | b Walsh | 0 |
| GD McGrath | c Jacobs b Dillon | 39 | not out | 4 |
| Extras | (19lb, 4nb) | 23 | (4b, 7lb, 7nb, 1w) | 19 |
| Total | | 269 | | 261 |

*Fall (1):* 42, 51, 53, 74, 118, 153, 186, 203, 203, 269.
*Fall (2):* 7, 45, 126, 127, 192, 194, 227, 257, 257, 261.

*Bowling (1):* Walsh 31-9-60-3; Collins 23-8-45-2; Adams 14-2-41-0; Ambrose 27-15-35-4; Dillon 26.3-4-69-2.
*Bowling (2):* Walsh 25.2-2-67-4; Collins 21-2-72-1; Ambrose 18-8-25-2; Dillon 14-1-57-1; Adams 8-1-29-2.

**West Indies**

| | | | | |
|---|---|---|---|---|
| SL Campbell | lbw b McGrath | 9 | c ME Waugh b Gillespie | 0 |
| S Ragoonath | run out | 9 | lbw b Gillespie | 2 |
| DRE Joseph | lbw b McGrath | 50 | c Warne b McGrath | 5 |
| *BC Lara | run out | 62 | c ME Waugh b Gillespie | 3 |
| JC Adams | b MacGill | 13 | lbw b McGrath | 5 |
| +RD Jacobs | lbw b MacGill | 6 | lbw b McGrath | 19 |
| PT Collins | lbw b McGrath | 1 | (10) b Gillespie | 0 |
| RIC Holder | lbw b MacGill | 0 | (7) c ME Waugh b McGrath | 4 |
| CEL Ambrose | c Slater b McGrath | 0 | (8) lbw b McGrath | 6 |
| M Dillon | b McGrath | 0 | (9) run out | 0 |
| CA Walsh | not out | 0 | not out | 2 |
| Extras | (4b, 2lb, 11nb) | 17 | (4b, 1lb) | 5 |
| Total | | 167 | | 51 |

*Fall (1):* 16, 28, 116, 149, 156, 163, 163, 163, 167, 167.
*Fall (2):* 3, 8, 11, 16, 16, 31, 47, 47, 49, 51.

*Bowling (1):* McGrath 14-3-50-5; Gillespie 12-3-34-0; Blewett 1-0-1-0; MacGill 16-5-41-3; Warne 14-4-35-0.
*Bowling (2):* McGrath 10-3-28-5; Gillespie 9.1-4-18-4.

**Australia won by 312 runs**

## SECOND TEST, AT KINGSTON, JAMAICA, MARCH 13, 14, 15, 16  *(Toss: Australia)*

**Australia**

| | | | | |
|---|---|---|---|---|
| MJ Slater | c Jacobs b Walsh | 22 | (2) b Walsh | 0 |
| MTG Elliott | c Lara b Walsh | 0 | (1) lbw b Perry | 16 |
| JL Langer | c Jacobs b Walsh | 8 | c Jacobs b Perry | 24 |
| ME Waugh | b Perry | 67 | c Walsh b Ambrose | 21 |
| *SR Waugh | c Joseph b Collins | 100 | c Jacobs b Perry | 9 |
| GS Blewett | lbw b Walsh | 5 | c Lara b Perry | 30 |
| +IA Healy | run out | 6 | run out | 10 |
| SK Warne | c Joseph b Collins | 24 | c Joseph b Walsh | 23 |
| JN Gillespie | b Ambrose | 1 | c Jacobs b Walsh | 7 |
| SCG MacGill | c Joseph b Collins | 0 | c Joseph b Perry | 7 |
| GD McGrath | not out | 2 | not out | 11 |
| Extras | (1b, 3lb, 17nb) | 21 | (3lb, 16nb) | 19 |
| Total | | 256 | | 177 |

*Fall (1):* 8, 28, 46, 158, 171, 179, 227, 242, 248, 256.
*Fall (2):* 4, 36, 51, 63, 86, 107, 137, 157, 159, 177.

*Bowling (1):* Ambrose 17-9-33-1; Walsh 20-6-55-4; Collins 16.3-2-79-3; Perry 17-1-79-1; Adams 1-0-6-0.
*Bowling (2):* Ambrose 14-4-28-1; Walsh 18-3-52-3; Perry 26-8-70-5; Collins 8-0-24-0.

**West Indies**

| | | | | |
|---|---|---|---|---|
| SL Campbell | b McGrath | 12 | not out | 1 |
| S Ragoonath | lbw b Gillespie | 0 | not out | 2 |
| LA Roberts | c Warne b McGrath | 0 | | |
| *BC Lara | c Healy b McGrath | 213 | | |
| DRE Joseph | c Blewett b McGrath | 14 | | |
| PT Collins | c ME Waugh b MacGill | 13 | | |
| JC Adams | c Elliott b McGrath | 94 | | |
| +RD Jacobs | c Gillespie b Warne | 25 | | |
| NO Perry | not out | 15 | | |
| CEL Ambrose | b MacGill | 3 | | |
| CA Walsh | lbw b MacGill | 0 | | |
| Extras | (12b, 8lb, 22nb) | 42 | | |
| Total | | 431 | (0 wicket) | 3 |

*Fall (1):* 4, 5, 17, 34, 378, 398, 420, 427, 431, 431.

*Bowling (1):* McGrath 35-11-93-5; Gillespie 33-7-79-1; Warne 30-8-94-1; MacGill 22.3-3-84-3; Blewett 10-1-48-0; ME Waugh 2-0-13-0.
*Bowling (2):* McGrath 0.3-0-3-0.

Collins, 10, retired hurt in the first innings at 4-56 and resumed at 7-420.

**West Indies won by 10 wickets**

*Tour match, at St John's, Antigua, March 20, 21, 22, 23*
Australians 303 (JL Langer 134; CL Hooper 5-53) and 8-263 decl. (MTG Elliott 115) beat West Indies A 102 and 310 (CL Hooper 102, SC Williams 50, AC Dale 6-67) by 154 runs

## THIRD TEST, AT BRIDGETOWN, BARBADOS, MARCH 26, 27, 28, 29, 30 *(Toss: Australia)*

### Australia

| | | | | |
|---|---|---|---|---|
| MJ Slater | c Lara b Ambrose | 23 | (2) run out | 26 |
| MTG Elliott | c Jacobs b Walsh | 9 | (1) c Jacobs b Walsh | 0 |
| JL Langer | b Hooper | 51 | lbw b Ambrose | 1 |
| ME Waugh | b Ambrose | 0 | (5) lbw b Walsh | 3 |
| *SR Waugh | lbw b Perry | 199 | (6) b Collins | 11 |
| RT Ponting | c Hooper b Perry | 104 | (7) c Griffith b Walsh | 22 |
| +IA Healy | lbw b Walsh | 0 | (8) c Jacobs b Collins | 3 |
| SK Warne | c Lara b Perry | 13 | (9) lbw b Walsh | 32 |
| JN Gillespie | not out | 23 | (4) b Ambrose | 14 |
| SCG MacGill | run out | 17 | c Campbell b Walsh | 1 |
| GD McGrath | c Joseph b Hooper | 3 | not out | 8 |
| Extras | (4b, 10lb, 34nb) | 48 | (5lb, 1w, 19nb) | 25 |
| Total | | 490 | | 146 |

*Fall (1):* 31, 36, 36, 144, 425, 427, 429, 446, 483, 490.
*Fall (2):* 0, 12, 35, 46, 48, 73, 81, 134, 137, 146.
*Bowling (1):* Ambrose 31.3-7-93-2; Walsh 38-8-121-2; Perry 33-7-102-3; Collins 35.3-7-110-0; Hooper 15.4-4-50-2.
*Bowling (2):* Ambrose 20-2-60-2; Walsh 17.1-3-39-5; Collins 9-0-31-2; Perry 4-0-11-0.

### West Indies

| | | | | |
|---|---|---|---|---|
| SL Campbell | c SR Waugh b Gillespie | 105 | lbw b McGrath | 33 |
| AFG Griffith | run out | 0 | lbw b Gillespie | 35 |
| DRE Joseph | lbw b McGrath | 26 | lbw b MacGill | 1 |
| PT Collins | lbw b McGrath | 0 | lbw b McGrath | 0 |
| *BC Lara | c Healy b Gillespie | 8 | not out | 153 |
| CL Hooper | c Warne b McGrath | 25 | c Healy b Gillespie | 6 |
| JC Adams | c ME Waugh b McGrath | 0 | b McGrath | 38 |
| +RD Jacobs | c ME Waugh b Ponting | 68 | lbw b McGrath | 5 |
| NO Perry | lbw b Gillespie | 24 | lbw b McGrath | 0 |
| CEL Ambrose | not out | 28 | c Elliott b Gillespie | 12 |
| CA Walsh | c Slater b Warne | 12 | not out | 0 |
| Extras | (10b, 3lb, 20nb) | 33 | (8b, 13lb, 2w, 5nb) | 28 |
| Total | | 329 | (9 wickets) | 311 |

*Fall (1):* 1, 50, 50, 64, 98, 98, 251, 265, 291, 329.
*Fall (2):* 72, 77, 78, 91, 105, 238, 248, 248, 302.
*Bowling (1):* McGrath 33-5-128-4; Gillespie 28-14-48-3; Warne 15.5-2-70-1; MacGill 20-5-47-0; Ponting 4-1-12-1; ME Waugh 3-0-11-0.
*Bowling (2):* McGrath 44-12-92-5; Gillespie 26.1-8-62-3; Warne 24-4-69-0; MacGill 21-6-48-1; SR Waugh 5-0-19-0.

**West Indies won by one wicket**

## FOURTH TEST, AT ST JOHN'S, ANTIGUA, APRIL 3, 4, 5, 6, 7 *(Toss: Australia)*

### Australia

| | | | | |
|---|---|---|---|---|
| MJ Slater | c Joseph b Perry | 33 | (2) b Walsh | 44 |
| GS Blewett | c Jacobs b Collymore | 32 | (1) lbw b Ambrose | 7 |
| JL Langer | run out | 51 | b Hooper | 127 |
| ME Waugh | c Hooper b Walsh | 11 | c Jacobs b Ambrose | 65 |
| *SR Waugh | not out | 72 | c Jacobs b Ambrose | 4 |
| RT Ponting | lbw b Ambrose | 21 | not out | 21 |
| +IA Healy | c Hooper b Ambrose | 6 | c Adams b Hooper | 16 |
| AC Dale | c Hooper b Ambrose | 1 | (9) c Hooper b Walsh | 0 |
| SCG MacGill | c Joseph b Ambrose | 4 | (10) c Perry b Hooper | 2 |
| CR Miller | c Joseph b Adams | 43 | (8) c Lara b Walsh | 1 |
| GD McGrath | c Jacobs b Ambrose | 5 | b Walsh | 2 |
| Extras | (5lb, 19nb) | 24 | (2b, 1lb, 3w, 11nb) | 17 |
| Total | | 303 | | 306 |

*Fall (1)*: 60, 76, 96, 155, 211, 226, 232, 242, 295, 303.
*Fall (2)*: 15, 76, 223, 241, 265, 287, 288, 288, 296, 306.

*Bowling (1)*: Ambrose 29.5-6-94-5; Walsh 26-1-67-1; Collymore 25-6-49-1; Perry 15-5-36-1; Adams 6-1-18-1; Hooper 10-1-34-0.
*Bowling (2)*: Ambrose 27-10-55-3; Walsh 32.4-6-78-4; Hooper 30.4-7-69-3; Adams 8.2-2-13-0; Collymore 16-1-60-0; Perry 7-0-28-0.

### West Indies

| | | | | |
|---|---|---|---|---|
| SL Campbell | c ME Waugh b Miller | 8 | c Healy b McGrath | 29 |
| AFG Griffith | c Healy b Miller | 9 | lbw b MacGill | 56 |
| DRE Joseph | lbw b Dale | 28 | c Miller b Dale | 17 |
| *BC Lara | c Healy b McGrath | 100 | lbw b McGrath | 7 |
| CL Hooper | run out | 47 | lbw b Blewett | 12 |
| JC Adams | c Healy b Dale | 0 | st Healy b Miller | 18 |
| +RD Jacobs | lbw b MacGill | 4 | lbw b Blewett | 16 |
| NO Perry | b McGrath | 6 | c Slater b MacGill | 26 |
| CEL Ambrose | c Ponting b MacGill | 0 | b MacGill | 4 |
| C Collymore | not out | 11 | c MacGill bMcGrath | 6 |
| CA Walsh | lbw b McGrath | 3 | not out | 0 |
| Extras | (6nb) | 6 | (5b, 12lb, 3nb) | 20 |
| **Total** | | **222** | | **211** |

*Fall (1)*: 19, 20, 136, 176, 178, 192, 205, 206, 213, 222.
*Fall (2)*: 56, 58, 69, 87, 105, 145, 184, 190, 209, 211.

*Bowling (1)*: McGrath 27.2-9-64-3; Dale 18-7-67-2; Miller 17-5-39-2; MacGill 14-3-52-2.
*Bowling (2)*: McGrath 35.5-15-50-3; Dale 12-5-28-1; MacGill 26-8-80-3; Miller 21-10-27-1; Blewett 8-3-9-2.

Griffith, 10, retired hurt in the second innings at 0-25 and resumed at 4-87.

**Australia won by 176 runs**
**Series tied at 2-2**

### AUSTRALIAN TEST AVERAGES v WEST INDIES, 1999

*Batting and Fielding*

| | mat | inn | n.o. | runs | high | 100 | 50 | avge | ct | st |
|---|---|---|---|---|---|---|---|---|---|---|
| SR Waugh | 4 | 8 | 1 | 409 | 199 | 2 | 1 | 58.43 | 1 | – |
| RT Ponting | 2 | 4 | 1 | 168 | 104 | 1 | – | 56.00 | 1 | – |
| JL Langer | 4 | 8 | – | 291 | 127 | 1 | 2 | 36.38 | – | – |
| MJ Slater | 4 | 8 | – | 277 | 106 | 1 | – | 34.63 | 3 | – |
| GS Blewett | 3 | 6 | – | 160 | 58 | – | 1 | 26.66 | 1 | – |
| ME Waugh | 4 | 8 | – | 202 | 67 | – | 2 | 25.25 | 7 | – |
| JN Gillespie | 3 | 6 | 2 | 95 | 28* | – | – | 23.75 | 1 | – |
| SK Warne | 3 | 6 | – | 138 | 32 | – | – | 23.00 | 3 | – |
| GD McGrath | 4 | 8 | 4 | 74 | 39 | – | – | 18.50 | – | – |
| MTG Elliott | 3 | 6 | – | 69 | 44 | – | – | 11.50 | 2 | – |
| IA Healy | 4 | 8 | – | 53 | 16 | – | – | 6.62 | 7 | 1 |
| SCG MacGill | 4 | 8 | – | 31 | 17 | – | – | 3.88 | 1 | – |

*Played in one Test*: CR Miller 43, 1 (1 ct); AC Dale 1, 0.

*Bowling*

| | overs | maidens | runs | wickets | best | 5Inn | avge |
|---|---|---|---|---|---|---|---|
| GD McGrath | 199.4 | 59 | 508 | 30 | 5-28 | 4 | 16.93 |
| JN Gillespie | 108.2 | 36 | 241 | 11 | 4-18 | – | 21.90 |
| CR Miller | 38.0 | 15 | 66 | 3 | 2-39 | – | 22.00 |
| SCG MacGill | 119.3 | 28 | 352 | 12 | 3-41 | – | 29.33 |
| AC Dale | 30.0 | 12 | 95 | 3 | 2-67 | – | 31.66 |

*Also bowled*: GS Blewett 19-4-58-2; SK Warne 83.5-18-268-2; ME Waugh 5-0-24-0; RT Ponting 4-1-12-1; SR Waugh 5-0-19-0.

### Some Facts and Trivia from the Test series v West Indies

- SR Waugh became Australia's 40th Test captain, and the 18th to win his first Test as captain. The previous Australian to win his first Test as captain was KJ Hughes, against Pakistan in Perth in 1979.
- SR Waugh won his first four tosses as Test captain.
- GD McGrath's 30 wickets in the four Tests set a new series record for Australia in the West Indies, previously 26 (MHN Walker in 1973 in five Tests). McGrath finished the series with 232 wickets in 49 Tests, the sixth highest career aggregate for Australia. He has now taken five or more wickets in a Test innings on 15 occasions.
- In the fourth Test, ME Waugh, when 23 in Australia's second innings, reached 6000 Test career runs.

- McGrath's 10 wickets in the Test at Port-of-Spain was the second occasion on which an Australian has taken 10 wickets in a Test in the West Indies (NJN Hawke took 10 at Georgetown in 1965).
- In the third Test, SR Waugh, when he reached 190 in Australia's first innings, became his country's second leading rungetter in Test cricket, passing MA Taylor (who scored 7525 runs in 104 Tests). At the end of the series, SR Waugh stood at No. 10 on the all-time list, with 7622 runs at 50.81, behind AR Border (11,174), SM Gavaskar (10,122), GA Gooch (8900), Javed Miandad (8832), IVA Richards (8540), DI Gower (8231), G Boycott (8114), GS Sobers (8032) and MC Cowdrey (7624).
- The following Australians scored hundreds in the series:

| | | | | minutes | balls | fours | sixes | No. of Test hundreds |
|---|---|---|---|---|---|---|---|---|
| MJ Slater | 106 | Port-of-Spain | | 285 | 205 | 12 | - | 12 |
| SR Waugh | 100 | Kingston | | 251 | 165 | 11 | - | 18 |
| SR Waugh | 199 | Bridgetown | | 509 | 374 | 20 | 1 | 19 |
| RT Ponting | 104 | Bridgetown | | 376 | 292 | 10 | - | 3 |
| JL Langer | 127 | St Johns | | 396 | 307 | 8 | 1 | 3 |

- Only four players had previously scored 199 in a Test innings: Mudassar Nazar, Pakistan v India, Faisalabad, 1982-83; M Azharuddin, India v Sri Lanka, Kanpur, 1986-87; MTG Elliott, Australia v England, Leeds, 1997; ST Jayasuriya, Sri Lanka v India, Colombo, 1997.

## ONE-DAY INTERNATIONAL SERIES, AUSTRALIA IN THE WEST INDIES, 1999

### GAME ONE, AT KINGSTOWN, ST VINCENT, APRIL 11   *(Toss: Australia)*

**West Indies**
| | | |
|---|---|---|
| SL Campbell | b Lee | 62 |
| S Chanderpaul | c Reiffel b Fleming | 7 |
| *BC Lara | c Bevan b Lee | 16 |
| +JC Adams | run out | 30 |
| SC Williams | b Reiffel | 0 |
| KLT Arthurton | st Gilchrist b Warne | 10 |
| PV Simmons | c ME Waugh b Fleming | 25 |
| HR Bryan | lbw b Warne | 0 |
| NO Perry | c Ponting b Julian | 9 |
| M Dillon | not out | 13 |
| CA Walsh | b Fleming | 2 |
| Extras | (1b, 8lb, 6nb, 20w) | 35 |
| Total | (48.1 overs) | 209 |

*Fall:* 21, 58, 134, 135, 146, 150, 152, 182, 204, 209.

*Bowling:* Fleming 9.1-1-41-3; Reiffel 10-1-34-1; Julian 9-0-51-1; Lee 10-0-44-2; Warne 10-3-30-2.

**Australia**
| | | |
|---|---|---|
| ME Waugh | b Bryan | 28 |
| +AC Gilchrist | c Adams b Dillon | 2 |
| RT Ponting | c Williams b Dillon | 23 |
| DS Lehmann | run out | 24 |
| *SR Waugh | b Bryan | 10 |
| MG Bevan | c Adams b Bryan | 1 |
| S Lee | b Bryan | 5 |
| BP Julian | b Perry | 35 |
| SK Warne | b Arthurton | 11 |
| PR Reiffel | not out | 9 |
| DW Fleming | run out | 0 |
| Extras | (4lb, 9w, 4nb) | 17 |
| Total | (41.5 overs) | 165 |

*Fall:* 6, 57, 60, 99, 100, 106, 109, 144, 157, 165.

*Bowling:* Walsh 8-1-37-0; Dillon 10-1-45-2; Bryan 10-1-24-4; Arthurton 9-1-33-1; Simmons 1-0-7-0; Perry 3.5-0-15-1.

**West Indies won by 44 runs**

### GAME TWO, AT ST GEORGE'S, GRENADA, APRIL 14   *(Toss: Australia)*

**Australia**
| | | |
|---|---|---|
| +AC Gilchrist | c Chanderpaul b Hooper | 17 |
| ME Waugh | c and b Hooper | 41 |
| DR Martyn | b King | 28 |
| DS Lehmann | not out | 110 |
| *SR Waugh | c Lara b King | 0 |
| MG Bevan | not out | 72 |
| Extras | (6lb, 8w, 6nb) | 20 |
| Total | (4 wickets) | 288 |

*Did not bat:* S Lee, BP Julian, SK Warne, PR Reiffel, DW Fleming

*Fall:* 30, 85, 108, 116

*Bowling:* Ambrose 10-0-47-0; King 10-0-53-2; Hooper 10-0-66-2; Arthurton 8-0-43-0; Bryan 7-0-41-0; Simmons 5-0-32-0.

**Australia won by 46 runs**

**West Indies**
| | | |
|---|---|---|
| S Chanderpaul | c Lee b Fleming | 0 |
| SL Campbell | b Lee | 46 |
| *BC Lara | b Fleming | 9 |
| +JC Adams | b Warne | 40 |
| CL Hooper | c and b SR Waugh | 17 |
| SC Williams | c sub (TM Moody) b Warne | 25 |
| KLT Arthurton | b Lee | 0 |
| PV Simmons | c Lee b Reiffel | 39 |
| HR Bryan | lbw b Warne | 6 |
| CEL Ambrose | run out | 23 |
| RD King | not out | 12 |
| Extras | (3lb, 14w, 8nb) | 25 |
| Total | (47.3 overs) | 242 |

*Fall:* 3, 18, 102, 125, 135, 140, 175, 183, 215, 242.

*Bowling:* Fleming 8-1-45-2; Reiffel 8-0-53-1; Julian 7-0-49-0; Martyn 2-0-5-0; Warne 10-2-39-3; Lee 6-0-22-0; SR Waugh 3.3-0-13-1; ME Waugh 3-0-13-0.

## GAME THREE, AT PORT-OF-SPAIN, TRINIDAD, APRIL 17    *(Toss: Australia)*

**Australia**

| | | |
|---|---|---|
| ME Waugh | run out | 74 |
| +AC Gilchrist | c Ambrose b Perry | 43 |
| S Lee | lbw b Perry | 7 |
| DR Martyn | run out | 29 |
| DS Lehmann | c Hooper b Simmons | 40 |
| *SR Waugh | b Simmons | 2 |
| MG Bevan | not out | 29 |
| TM Moody | b Perry | 2 |
| SK Warne | not out | 5 |
| Extras | (3lb, 6w, 2nb) | 11 |
| **Total** | **(7 wickets)** | **242** |

*Did not bat:* DW Fleming, GD McGrath

*Fall:* 108, 123, 128, 194, 201, 210, 215

*Bowling:* Ambrose 10-2-40-0; Bryan 10-0-50-0; Perry 10-0-45-3; Hooper 9-0-47-0; Arthurton 2-0-14-0; Simmons 9-0-43-2.

**West Indies**

| | | |
|---|---|---|
| SC Williams | lbw b Fleming | 4 |
| SL Campbell | b Lehmann | 64 |
| JC Adams | b Fleming | 82 |
| CL Hooper | b Fleming | 56 |
| *BC Lara | not out | 18 |
| PV Simmons | run out | 9 |
| KLT Arthurton | not out | 1 |
| Extras | (1lb, 9 w) | 10 |
| **Total** | **(5 wickets, 49 overs)** | **244** |

*Did not bat:* +RD Jacobs, NO Perry, CEL Ambrose, HR Bryan

*Fall:* 15, 124, 194, 225, 236.

*Bowling:* McGrath 1-0-1-0; Fleming 10-1-49-3; Moody 8-1-32-0; Martyn 3-0-16-0; Warne 9-0-59-0; Lee 7-0-39-0; Lehmann 4-0-17-1; ME Waugh 7-0-30-0.

**West Indies won by five wickets**

## GAME FOUR, AT PORT-OF-SPAIN, TRINIDAD, APRIL 18    *(Toss: Australia)*

**Australia**

| | | |
|---|---|---|
| +AC Gilchrist | lbw b Walsh | 25 |
| ME Waugh | b Ambrose | 18 |
| RT Ponting | c Jacobs b Walsh | 7 |
| DS Lehmann | b Ambrose | 12 |
| *SR Waugh | lbw b Dillon | 16 |
| MG Bevan | not out | 59 |
| S Lee | c Jacobs b Dillon | 1 |
| TM Moody | b Dillon | 4 |
| BP Julian | c Jacobs b Dillon | 0 |
| SK Warne | run out | 29 |
| DW Fleming | not out | 0 |
| Extras | (5b, 7lb, 5w, 1nb) | 18 |
| **Total** | **(9 wickets)** | **189** |

*Fall:* 39, 49, 66, 78, 91, 93, 103, 104, 181

*Bowling:* Ambrose 10-1-39-2; Walsh 10-0-37-2; Simmons 4.3-0-27-0; Dillon 10-5-20-4; Hooper 10-0-29-0; Perry 5.3-0-25-0.

**West Indies**

| | | |
|---|---|---|
| SL Campbell | lbw b Fleming | 13 |
| +RD Jacobs | run out | 29 |
| JC Adams | run out | 27 |
| CL Hooper | run out | 23 |
| *BC Lara | b Warne | 6 |
| SC Williams | b Warne | 0 |
| PV Simmons | c Gilchrist b Lee | 42 |
| CEL Ambrose | lbw b Warne | 4 |
| M Dillon | b Fleming | 2 |
| NO Perry | not out | 8 |
| CA Walsh | b Lee | 1 |
| Extras | (4lb, 8w, 2nb) | 14 |
| **Total** | **(46.2 overs)** | **169** |

*Fall:* 27, 60, 60, 97, 103, 116, 135, 149, 166, 169.

*Bowling:* Fleming 10-1-30-2; Julian 3-0-21-0; Warne 10-1-35-3; Moody 7-1-24-0; ME Waugh 5-0-16-0; SR Waugh 5-0-13-0; Lee 6.2-1-26-2.

**Australia won by 20 runs**

## GAME FIVE, AT GEORGETOWN, GUYANA, APRIL 21    *(Toss: Australia)*

**West Indies**

| | | |
|---|---|---|
| +RD Jacobs | c SR Waugh b Lee | 33 |
| SL Campbell | c and b Lee | 41 |
| *JC Adams | b Warne | 7 |
| CL Hooper | st Gilchrist b Warne | 8 |
| S Chanderpaul | c Moody b Lee | 27 |
| SC Williams | not out | 30 |
| PV Simmons | not out | 15 |
| Extras | (1b, 4lb, 4w, 3nb) | 12 |
| **Total** | **(5 wickets, 30 overs)** | **173** |

*Did not bat:* KLT Arthurton, HR Bryan, M Dillon, CA Walsh

*Fall:* 83, 84, 100, 101, 153

*Bowling:* Fleming 6-0-30-0; Reiffel 2-0-14-0; Moody 5-0-27-0; Lee 6-0-39-3; Warne 6-0-35-2; SR Waugh 5-0-23-0.

**Australia**

| | | |
|---|---|---|
| ME Waugh | c Adams b Dillon | 5 |
| +AC Gilchrist | run out | 44 |
| RT Ponting | b Dillon | 0 |
| DS Lehmann | b Hooper | 13 |
| *SR Waugh | not out | 72 |
| MG Bevan | b Simmons | 10 |
| S Lee | b Simmons | 0 |
| TM Moody | c Bryan b Dillon | 2 |
| SK Warne | not out | 19 |
| Extras | (3lb, 2w, 3nb) | 8 |
| **Total** | **(7 wickets, 30 overs)** | **173** |

*Did not bat:* PR Reiffel, DW Fleming

*Fall:* 26, 26, 50, 70, 116, 116, 119

*Bowling:* Walsh 6-0-32-0; Dillon 6-1-25-3; Bryan 6-0-27-0; Hooper 6-0-48-1; Simmons 4-0-25-2; Arthurton 2-0-13-0.

**Match tied**

**GAME SIX, AT BRIDGETOWN, BARBADOS, APRIL 24**  *(Toss: West Indies)*

| West Indies | | |
|---|---|---|
| SL Campbell | c Gilchrist b Warne | 24 |
| +RD Jacobs | c Julian b Warne | 68 |
| *JC Adams | c Gilchrist b Moody | 46 |
| CL Hooper | run out | 8 |
| S Chanderpaul | c Ponting b ME Waugh | 44 |
| SC Williams | st Gilchrist b Warne | 9 |
| KLT Arthurton | c Ponting b Fleming | 16 |
| HR Bryan | c and b Fleming | 6 |
| NO Perry | not out | 7 |
| M Dillon | not out | 1 |
| Extras | (6lb, 13w, 1nb) | 20 |
| **Total** | **(8 wickets)** | **249** |

*Did not bat:* RD King

*Fall:* 81, 107, 122, 183, 208, 214, 238, 241

*Bowling:* Fleming 9-0-53-2; Moody 8-0-49-1; Warne 10-1-28-3; Lee 3-0-27-0; ME Waugh 10-1-35-1; Julian 7-0-32-0; Lehmann 3-0-19-0.

| Australia | | |
|---|---|---|
| +AC Gilchrist | c Jacobs b Bryan | 64 |
| ME Waugh | c Adams b Dillon | 25 |
| BP Julian | c Adams b King | 31 |
| RT Ponting | run out | 43 |
| DS Lehmann | c Adams b King | 2 |
| *SR Waugh | c Jacobs b Perry | 5 |
| MG Bevan | not out | 35 |
| S Lee | not out | 19 |
| Extras | (10lb, 13w, 6nb) | 29 |
| **Total** | **(6 wickets, 48.3 overs)** | **253** |

*Did not bat:* TM Moody, SK Warne, DW Fleming

*Fall:* 70, 111, 153, 163, 171, 206

*Bowling:* Dillon 9.3-0-54-1; King 10-0-50-2; Bryan 9-0-58-1; Hooper 8-0-37-0; Perry 10-1-29-1; Arthurton 2-0-15-0.

**Australia won by four wickets**

---

**GAME SEVEN, AT BRIDGETOWN, BARBADOS, APRIL 25**  *(Toss: Australia)*

| Australia | | |
|---|---|---|
| ME Waugh | b King | 26 |
| +AC Gilchrist | c Ambrose b Dillon | 6 |
| RT Ponting | c Williams b Dillon | 1 |
| DS Lehmann | c Jacobs b Ambrose | 8 |
| *SR Waugh | c Jacobs b King | 30 |
| MG Bevan | run out | 34 |
| S Lee | b King | 47 |
| TM Moody | not out | 50 |
| BP Julian | b Arthurton | 20 |
| SK Warne | run out | 20 |
| DW Fleming | not out | 0 |
| Extras | (5lb, 3w, 2nb) | 10 |
| **Total** | **(9 wickets)** | **252** |

*Fall:* 6, 8, 29, 63, 80, 119, 175, 200, 250

*Bowling:* Ambrose 9-1-51-1; Dillon 10-2-36-2; King 9-0-59-3; Perry 5-0-22-0; Bryan 8-0-36-0; Arthurton 9-0-43-1.

| West Indies | | |
|---|---|---|
| SL Campbell | c Gilchrist b Bevan | 62 |
| +RD Jacobs | c ME Waugh b SR Waugh | 54 |
| *JC Adams | not out | 37 |
| S Chanderpaul | not out | 31 |
| Extras | (2b, 2lb, 8w, 1nb) | 13 |
| **Total** | **(2 wickets, 37 overs)** | **197** |

*Did not bat:* SC Williams, KLT Arthurton, HR Bryan, NO Perry, CEL Ambrose, M Dillon, RD King

*Fall:* 99, 153

*Bowling:* Fleming 7-0-25-0; ME Waugh 4-0-20-0; Moody 4-0-29-0; Warne 8-3-28-0; Lee 2-0-20-0; SR Waugh 3-0-17-1; Bevan 5-0-23-1; Julian 4-0-31-0.

**West Indies won by eight wickets**

(Target reduced to 196 off maximum 40 overs following interruption caused by crowd disturbance)

**Series tied at 3-3**

---

*Some Facts and Trivia from the Limited-overs Series v West Indies*

- DS Lehmann's 110* in the second match was his second hundred in limited-over internationals.
- Australian players have now scored three hundreds in 23 limited-over internationals in the West Indies (GR Marsh scored two in 1991).
- The 172-run unbroken partnership for the fifth wicket in the second match by DS Lehmann and MG Bevan set a new record for any wicket for Australia v West Indies in limited-over internationals. The previous record was 150 for the fourth wicket by AR Border and KJ Hughes at St Lucia, 1984.
- The innings total of 4-288 in the same match set a new record for Australia v West Indies in limited-over internationals. The previous record was 9-286 at Georgetown in 1995.

# 5. The World Cup, 1999

*Warm-up match at Cardiff, May 8*
Glamorgan 2-21 (10 overs) v Australians. Match abandoned

*Warm-up match at Worcester, May 10*
Worcestershire 7-162† (44 overs) lost to Australians 4-181 (34.1 overs; AC Gilchrist 86, ME Waugh 64) by six wickets

*Warm-up match at Taunton, May 12*
Australians 5-243 (MG Bevan 68*) beat Somerset 208† (45.2 overs) by 32 runs

*Note*
† indicates target revised after rain interruption. At Worcester, the Australians' target was increased to 178 off 44 overs; at Taunton the home side was set 241 runs from 47 overs.

## AUSTRALIA'S MATCHES IN GROUP B

### AUSTRALIA V SCOTLAND, AT WORCESTER, MAY 16 *(Toss: Australia)*

| Scotland | | |
|---|---|---|
| BMW Patterson | c Gilchrist b Fleming | 10 |
| IL Philip | c SR Waugh b McGrath | 17 |
| MJdeG Allingham | st Gilchrist b Warne | 3 |
| MJ Smith | c Bevan b Lee | 13 |
| *G Salmond | c Gilchrist b SR Waugh | 31 |
| GM Hamilton | b Warne | 34 |
| JE Brinkley | c Dale b Warne | 23 |
| +AG Davies | not out | 8 |
| JAR Blain | not out | 3 |
| Extras | (9lb, 22w, 8nb) | 39 |
| Total | (7 wickets, 50 overs) | 181 |

*Did not bat*: A Butt, NR Dyer

*Fall*: 19, 37, 52, 87, 105, 167, 169

*Bowling*: Fleming 9-2-19-1; Dale 10-2-35-0; McGrath 9-0-32-1; Warne 10-0-39-3; Lee 6-1-25-1; SR Waugh 6-0-22-1.

| Australia | | |
|---|---|---|
| +AC Gilchrist | c Philip b Butt | 6 |
| ME Waugh | c and b Dyer | 67 |
| RT Ponting | c Allingham b Blain | 33 |
| DS Lehmann | b Dyer | 0 |
| *SR Waugh | not out | 49 |
| MG Bevan | not out | 11 |
| Extras | (3lb, 4w, 9nb) | 16 |
| Total | (4 wickets, 44.5 overs) | 182 |

*Did not bat*: S Lee, SK Warne, DW Fleming, AC Dale, GD McGrath

*Fall*: 17, 101, 101, 141

*Bowling*: Blain 8-0-35-1; Butt 10-3-21-1; Brinkley 8-0-43-0; Hamilton 8.5-0-37-0; Dyer 10-1-43-2.

**Australia won by four wickets**

### AUSTRALIA V NEW ZEALAND, AT CARDIFF, MAY 20 *(Toss: Australia)*

| Australia | | |
|---|---|---|
| ME Waugh | lbw b Allott | 2 |
| +AC Gilchrist | c Astle b Allott | 14 |
| RT Ponting | c Harris b Astle | 47 |
| DS Lehmann | c Astle b Harris | 76 |
| *SR Waugh | c Astle b Harris | 7 |
| MG Bevan | b Allott | 21 |
| S Lee | run out | 2 |
| SK Warne | b Allott | 15 |
| DW Fleming | not out | 8 |
| AC Dale | not out | 3 |
| Extras | (10lb, 5w, 3nb) | 18 |
| Total | (8 wickets, 50 overs) | 213 |

*Did not bat*: GD McGrath

*Fall*: 7, 32, 126, 149, 172, 175, 192, 204

*Bowling*: Allott 10-0-37-4; Nash 8-1-30-0; Cairns 7-0-44-0; Larsen 10-2-26-0; Harris 10-0-50-2; Astle 5-0-16-1.

| New Zealand | | |
|---|---|---|
| MJ Horne | c Gilchrist b Dale | 5 |
| NJ Astle | c Ponting b Fleming | 4 |
| CD McMillan | c Fleming b Warne | 29 |
| *SP Fleming | b McGrath | 9 |
| RG Twose | not out | 80 |
| CL Cairns | c Dale b Fleming | 60 |
| +AC Parore | not out | 10 |
| Extras | (2lb, 11w, 4nb) | 17 |
| Total | (5 wickets, 45.2 overs) | 214 |

*Did not bat*: CZ Harris, DJ Nash, GI Allott, GR Larsen

*Fall*: 5, 21, 47, 49, 197

*Bowling*: Fleming 8.2-1-43-2; Dale 5-1-18-1; McGrath 9-0-43-1; Lee 6-0-24-0; Warne 10-1-44-1; SR Waugh 4-0-25-0; Bevan 3-0-15-0.

**New Zealand won by five wickets**

## AUSTRALIA V PAKISTAN, AT LEEDS, MAY 23 *(Toss: Australia)*

**Pakistan**

| | | |
|---|---|---|
| Wajahatullah Wasti | c SR Waugh b McGrath | 9 |
| Saeed Anwar | c Gilchrist b Reiffel | 25 |
| Abdur Razzaq | c Fleming b Warne | 60 |
| Ijaz Ahmed | lbw b Fleming | 0 |
| Inzamam-ul-Haq | run out | 81 |
| Yousuf Youhana | run out | 29 |
| *Wasim Akram | c Gilchrist b Fleming | 13 |
| +Moin Khan | not out | 31 |
| Azhar Mahmood | run out | 1 |
| Saqlain Mushtaq | not out | 0 |
| Extras | (1b, 5lb, 15w, 5nb) | 26 |
| **Total** | **(8 wickets, 50 overs)** | **275** |

*Did not bat:* Shoaib Akhtar

*Fall:* 32, 44, 46, 164, 216, 240, 262, 265

*Bowling:* Fleming 10-0-37-2; Reiffel 10-1-49-1; McGrath 10-1-54-1; Warne 10-0-50-1; SR Waugh 6-0-37-0; Martyn 2-0-25-0; Lehmann 2-0-17-0.

**Australia**

| | | |
|---|---|---|
| +AC Gilchrist | b Wasim | 0 |
| ME Waugh | c Moin b Abdur | 41 |
| RT Ponting | c Saeed b Saqlain | 47 |
| DS Lehmann | c Moin b Saqlain | 5 |
| *SR Waugh | b Shoaib | 49 |
| MG Bevan | c Ijaz b Wasim | 61 |
| DR Martyn | b Wasim | 18 |
| SK Warne | run out | 1 |
| PR Reiffel | c Wasim b Saqlain | 1 |
| DW Fleming | not out | 4 |
| GD McGrath | b Wasim | 0 |
| Extras | (7b, 10lb, 14w, 7nb) | 38 |
| **Total** | **(49.5 overs)** | **265** |

*Fall:* 0, 91, 100, 101, 214, 238, 248, 251, 265, 265.

*Bowling:* Wasim 9.5-1-40-4; Shoaib 10-0-46-1; Azhar 10-0-61-0; Saqlain 10-1-51-3; Abdur 10-0-50-1.

**Pakistan won by 10 runs**

---

## AUSTRALIA V BANGLADESH, AT CHESTER-LE-STREET, MAY 27 *(Toss: Australia)*

**Bangladesh**

| | | |
|---|---|---|
| Khaled Mahmud | lbw b McGrath | 6 |
| Mehrab Hossain | c Ponting b Moody | 42 |
| Faruk Ahmed | c Ponting b McGrath | 9 |
| Naim-ur Rahman | c Ponting b Moody | 2 |
| *Amin-ul Islam | b Fleming | 13 |
| Minhaj-ul Abedin | not out | 53 |
| Akram Khan | lbw b Warne | 30 |
| +Khaled Mashud | lbw b Moody | 17 |
| Enam-ul Hoque | not out | 17 |
| Extras | (2b, 10w, 7nb) | 19 |
| **Total** | **(7 wickets, 50 overs)** | **178** |

*Did not bat:* Manjural Islam, Hasib-ul Hossain

*Fall:* 10, 39, 47, 72, 91, 99, 143

*Bowling:* McGrath 10-0-44-2; Fleming 10-0-45-1; Moody 10-4-25-3; Julian 10-1-44-0; Warne 10-2-18-1.

**Australia**

| | | |
|---|---|---|
| ME Waugh | st Khaled Mashud b Enam-ul | 33 |
| +AC Gilchrist | st Khaled Mashud b Minhaj-ul | 63 |
| BP Julian | b Enam-ul | 9 |
| TM Moody | not out | 56 |
| RT Ponting | not out | 18 |
| Extras | (2w) | 2 |
| **Total** | **(3 wickets, 19.5 overs)** | **181** |

*Did not bat:* MG Bevan, DS Lehmann, *SR Waugh, SK Warne, DW Fleming, GD McGrath

*Fall:* 98, 98, 111

*Bowling:* Hasib-ul 4-0-24-0; Manjural 3-0-23-0; Khaled Mahmud 2.5-0-39-0; Naim-ur 2-0-17-0; Enam-ul 5-0-40-2; Minhaj-ul 3-0-38-1.

**Australia won by seven wickets**

---

## AUSTRALIA V WEST INDIES, AT MANCHESTER, MAY 30 *(Toss: Australia)*

**West Indies**

| | | |
|---|---|---|
| SL Campbell | c ME Waugh b McGrath | 2 |
| +RD Jacobs | not out | 49 |
| JC Adams | lbw b McGrath | 0 |
| *BC Lara | b McGrath | 9 |
| S Chanderpaul | b Warne | 16 |
| SC Williams | c ME Waugh b Moody | 3 |
| PV Simmons | b Fleming | 1 |
| CEL Ambrose | lbw b Warne | 1 |
| M Dillon | lbw b McGrath | 0 |
| RD King | lbw b Warne | 1 |
| CA Walsh | b McGrath | 6 |
| Extras | (3lb, 18w, 1nb) | 22 |
| **Total** | **(46.4 overs)** | **110** |

*Fall:* 7, 7, 20, 64, 67, 69, 70, 71, 88, 110.

*Bowling:* McGrath 8.4-3-14-5; Fleming 7-1-12-1; Moody 7-0-16-1; Julian 7-1-36-0; Warne 10-4-11-3; Bevan 7-0-18-0

**Australia**

| | | |
|---|---|---|
| +AC Gilchrist | b Ambrose | 21 |
| ME Waugh | c Jacobs b Ambrose | 3 |
| RT Ponting | c Chanderpaul b King | 20 |
| DS Lehmann | c Adams b Ambrose | 9 |
| *SR Waugh | not out | 19 |
| MG Bevan | not out | 20 |
| Extras | (4lb, 7w, 8nb) | 19 |
| **Total** | **(4 wickets, 40.4 overs)** | **111** |

*Did not bat:* TM Moody, BP Julian, SK Warne, DW Fleming, GD McGrath

*Fall:* 10, 43, 53, 62

*Bowling:* Ambrose 10-0-31-3; Walsh 10-3-25-0; Dillon 7.4-1-22-0; King 10-2-27-1; Simmons 3-2-2-0

**Australia won by six wickets**

## GROUP B TABLE (five matches each)

|  | *won* | *lost* | *points* | *net run rate* |
|---|---|---|---|---|
| Pakistan | 4 | 1 | 8 | +0.53 |
| Australia | 3 | 2 | 6 | +0.73 |
| New Zealand | 3 | 2 | 6 | +0.58 |
| West Indies | 3 | 2 | 6 | +0.50 |
| Bangladesh | 2 | 3 | 4 | -0.54 |
| Scotland | - | 5 | - | -1.93 |

## GROUP A TABLE (five matches each)

|  | *won* | *lost* | *points* | *net run rate* |
|---|---|---|---|---|
| South Africa | 4 | 1 | 8 | +0.86 |
| India | 3 | 2 | 6 | +1.28 |
| Zimbabwe | 3 | 2 | 6 | +0.02 |
| England | 3 | 2 | 6 | -0.33 |
| Sri Lanka | 2 | 3 | 4 | -0.81 |
| Kenya | - | 5 | - | -1.20 |

## 'SUPER SIX TABLE' AFTER GROUP MATCHES

|  | *points* | *net run rate* |
|---|---|---|
| Pakistan | 4 | +0.72 |
| Zimbabwe | 4 | +0.33 |
| South Africa | 2 | -0.35 |
| New Zealand | 2 | -0.40 |
| India | - | +0.03 |
| Australia | - | -0.35 |

*Notes*
- Each team in the 'Super Six' round of the World Cup would play against those teams that had qualified from the other group. Therefore, Australia's three matches would be against the three top teams from Group A.
- Each team carried forward to the Super Six points and run rate from their Group matches against the other teams who qualified from their Group. Therefore Pakistan carried forward four points — from their first-round wins against Australia and New Zealand — whereas Australia had no points to carry forward, having lost to New Zealand and Pakistan in the first round.
- The top four teams on the Super Six table after the completion of the Super Six matches would play in the semi-finals (1 v 4 and 2 v 3).

## AUSTRALIA'S MATCHES IN THE SUPER SIX

### AUSTRALIA V INDIA, AT THE OVAL, JUNE 4    *(Toss: India)*

**Australia**

| | | |
|---|---|---|
| ME Waugh | c Prasad b Singh | 83 |
| +AC Gilchrist | c Mohanty b Ganguly | 31 |
| RT Ponting | b Singh | 23 |
| DS Lehmann | run out | 26 |
| *SR Waugh | c Kumble b Mohanty | 36 |
| MG Bevan | c Mongia b Prasad | 22 |
| TM Moody | not out | 26 |
| SK Warne | not out | 0 |
| Extras | (14lb, 10w, 11nb) | 35 |
| **Total** | **(6 wickets; 50 overs)** | **181** |

*Did not bat:* PR Reiffel, DW Fleming, GD McGrath

*Fall:* 97, 157, 158, 218, 231, 275

*Bowling:* Srinath 10-2-34-0; Mohanty 7-0-47-1; Prasad 10-0-60-1; Kumble 10-0-49-0; Ganguly 5-0-31-1; Singh 7-0-43-2; Tendulkar 1-0-4-0

**India**

| | | |
|---|---|---|
| SC Ganguly | b Fleming | 8 |
| SR Tendulkar | c Gilchrist b McGrath | 0 |
| RS Dravid | c Gilchrist b McGrath | 2 |
| AD Jadeja | not out | 100 |
| *M Azharuddin | c SR Waugh b McGrath | 3 |
| RR Singh | c Reiffel b Moody | 75 |
| +NR Mongia | run out | 2 |
| J Srinath | c Gilchrist b SR Waugh | 0 |
| A Kumble | c Gilchrist b SR Waugh | 3 |
| BK Venkatesh Prasad | lbw b Fleming | 2 |
| DS Mohanty | run out | 0 |
| Extras | (3lb, 6w, 1nb) | 10 |
| **Total** | **(48.2 overs)** | **205** |

*Fall:* 1, 10, 12, 17, 158, 181, 186, 192, 204, 205.

*Bowling:* McGrath 10-1-34-3; Fleming 9-1-33-2; Reiffel 10-1-30-0; Moody 10-0-41-1; ME Waugh 1-0-7-0; Warne 6.2-0-49-0; SR Waugh 2-0-8-2

**Australia won by 77 runs**

## AUSTRALIA V ZIMBABWE, AT LORD'S, JUNE 9  *(Toss: Zimbabwe)*

### Australia

| | | |
|---|---|---|
| +AC Gilchrist | lbw b Johnson | 10 |
| ME Waugh | c Goodwin b Johnson | 104 |
| RT Ponting | b Olonga | 36 |
| DS Lehmann | retired hurt | 6 |
| *SR Waugh | b GJ Whittall | 62 |
| MG Bevan | not out | 37 |
| TM Moody | not out | 20 |
| Extras | (6lb, 13w, 9nb) | 28 |
| Total | (4 wickets; 50 overs) | 303 |

*Did not bat:* SK Warne, PR Reiffel, DW Fleming, GD McGrath

*Fall:* 18, 74, 226, 248

*Bowling:* Johnson 8-0-43-2; Streak 10-0-50-0; Olonga 7-0-62-1; GJ Whittall 4-0-24-1; Strang 10-1-47-0; AR Whittall 8-1-51-0; GW Flower 3-0-20-0

*Retirement:* Lehmann retired hurt at 2-97

### Zimbabwe

| | | |
|---|---|---|
| NC Johnson | not out | 132 |
| GW Flower | lbw b McGrath | 21 |
| MW Goodwin | c Moody b Bevan | 47 |
| +A Flower | c Gilchrist b Reiffel | 0 |
| *ADR Campbell | c Fleming b Reiffel | 17 |
| GJ Whittall | c ME Waugh b Reiffel | 0 |
| DP Viljoen | st Gilchrist b Warne | 5 |
| HH Streak | not out | 18 |
| Extras | (6lb, 13 w) | 19 |
| Total | (6 wickets; 50 overs) | 259 |

*Did not bat:* AR Whittall, PA Strang, H Olonga

*Fall:* 39, 153, 154, 188, 189, 200

*Bowling:* McGrath 10-1-33-1; Fleming 10-0-46-0; Warne 9-0-55-1; Reiffel 10-0-55-3; Moody 6-0-38-0; Bevan 5-1-26-1

**Australia won by 44 runs**

---

## AUSTRALIA V SOUTH AFRICA, AT LEEDS, JUNE 13  *(Toss: South Africa)*

### South Africa

| | | |
|---|---|---|
| G Kirsten | c Ponting b Reiffel | 21 |
| HH Gibbs | b McGrath | 101 |
| DJ Cullinan | b Warne | 50 |
| *WJ Cronje | lbw b Warne | 0 |
| JN Rhodes | c ME Waugh b Fleming | 39 |
| L Klusener | c Warne b Fleming | 36 |
| SM Pollock | b Fleming | 3 |
| +MV Boucher | not out | 0 |
| Extras | (7lb, 8w, 6nb) | 21 |
| Total | (7 wickets; 50 overs) | 271 |

*Did not bat:* N Boje, S Elworthy, AA Donald

*Fall:* 45, 140, 141, 219, 250, 271, 271

*Bowling:* McGrath 10-0-49-1; Fleming 10-0-57-3; Reiffel 9-0-47-1; Moody 8-1-56-0; Warne 10-1-33-2; Bevan 3-0-22-0

### Australia

| | | |
|---|---|---|
| ME Waugh | run out | 5 |
| +AC Gilchrist | b Elworthy | 5 |
| RT Ponting | c Donald b Klusener | 69 |
| DR Martyn | c Boje b Elworthy | 11 |
| *SR Waugh | not out | 120 |
| MG Bevan | c Cullinan b Cronje | 27 |
| TM Moody | not out | 15 |
| Extras | (6lb, 7w, 7nb) | 20 |
| Total | (5 wickets; 49.4 overs) | 272 |

*Did not bat:* SK Warne, PR Reiffel, DW Fleming, GD McGrath

*Fall:* 6, 20, 48, 174, 247

*Bowling:* Pollock 9.4-0-45-0; Elworthy 10-1-46-2; Donald 10-0-43-0; Klusener 10-0-53-1; Cronje 7-0-50-1; Boje 3-0-29-0

**Australia won by five wickets**

---

## FINAL SUPER SIX TABLE

| | won | no result | lost | points | total points | net run rate |
|---|---|---|---|---|---|---|
| Pakistan | 1 | - | 2 | 2 | 6 | +0.65 |
| Australia | 3 | - | - | 6 | 6 | +0.36 |
| South Africa | 2 | - | 1 | 4 | 6 | +0.17 |
| New Zealand | 1 | 1 | 1 | 3 | 5 | -0.52 |
| Zimbabwe | - | 1 | 2 | 1 | 5 | -0.79 |
| India | 1 | - | 2 | 2 | 2 | -0.15 |

*Note*
• 'total points' includes points carried forward from Group matches

## SECOND SEMI-FINAL, AUSTRALIA V SOUTH AFRICA, AT BIRMINGHAM, JUNE 17   *(Toss: South Africa)*

| Australia | | |
|---|---|---|
| +AC Gilchrist | c Donald b Kalllis | 20 |
| ME Waugh | c Boucher b Pollock | 0 |
| RT Ponting | c Kirsten b Donald | 37 |
| DS Lehmann | c Boucher b Donald | 1 |
| *SR Waugh | c Boucher b Pollock | 56 |
| MG Bevan | c Boucher b Pollock | 65 |
| TM Moody | lbw b Pollock | 0 |
| SK Warne | c Cronje b Pollock | 18 |
| PR Reiffel | b Donald | 0 |
| DW Fleming | b Donald | 0 |
| GD McGrath | not out | 0 |
| Extras | (1b, 6lb, 3w, 6nb) | 16 |
| Total | (49.2 overs) | 213 |

| South Africa | | |
|---|---|---|
| G Kirsten | b Warne | 18 |
| HH Gibbs | b Warne | 30 |
| DJ Cullinan | run out | 6 |
| *WJ Cronje | c ME Waugh b Warne | 0 |
| JH Kallis | c SR Waugh b Warne | 53 |
| JN Rhodes | c Bevan b Reiffel | 43 |
| SM Pollock | b Fleming | 20 |
| L Klusener | not out | 31 |
| +MV Boucher | b McGrath | 5 |
| S Elworthy | run out | 1 |
| AA Donald | run out | 0 |
| Extras | (1lb, 5 w) | 6 |
| Total | (49.4 overs) | 213 |

*Fall:* 3, 54, 58, 68, 158, 158, 207, 207, 207, 213.

*Bowling:* Pollock 9.2-1-36-5; Elworthy 10-0-59-0; Kallis 10-2-27-1; Donald 10-1-32-4; Klusener 9-1-50-0; Cronje 1-0-2-0

*Fall:* 48, 53, 53, 61, 145, 175, 183, 196, 198, 213.

*Bowling:* McGrath 10-0-51-1; Fleming 8.4-1-40-1; Reiffel 8-0-28-1; Warne 10-4-29-4; ME Waugh 8-0-37-0; Moody 5-0-27-0

**Match tied (Australia qualify for final due to higher position on Super Six table)**

## FINAL, AUSTRALIA V PAKISTAN, AT LORD'S, JUNE 20   *(Toss: Pakistan)*

| Pakistan | | |
|---|---|---|
| Saeed Anwar | b Fleming | 15 |
| Wajahatullah Wasti | c ME Waugh b McGrath | 1 |
| Abdur Razzaq | c SR Waugh b Moody | 17 |
| Ijaz Ahmed | b Warne | 22 |
| Inzamam-ul-Haq | c Gilchrist b Reiffel | 15 |
| +Moin Khan | c Gilchrist b Warne | 6 |
| Shahid Afridi | lbw b Warne | 13 |
| Azhar Mahmood | c and b Moody | 8 |
| *Wasim Akram | c SR Waugh b Warne | 8 |
| Saqlain Mushtaq | c Ponting b McGrath | 0 |
| Shoaib Akhtar | not out | 2 |
| Extras | (10lb, 13w, 2nb) | 25 |
| Total | (39 overs) | 132 |

| Australia | | |
|---|---|---|
| ME Waugh | not out | 37 |
| +AC Gilchrist | c Inzamam b Saqlain | 54 |
| RT Ponting | c Moin b Wasim | 24 |
| DS Lehmann | not out | 13 |
| Extras | (1lb, 1w, 3nb) | 5 |
| Total | (2 wickets; 20.1 overs) | 133 |

*Did not bat:* *SR Waugh, MG Bevan, TM Moody, SK Warne, PR Reiffel, DW Fleming, GD McGrath

*Fall:* 75, 112

*Bowling:* Wasim 8-1-41-1; Shoaib 4-0-37-0; Abdur 2-0-13-0; Azhar 2.1-0-24-0; Saqlain 4-0-17-1

*Fall:* 21, 21, 68, 77, 91, 104, 113, 129, 129, 132.

*Bowling:* McGrath 9-3-13-2; Fleming 6-0-30-1; Reiffel 10-1-29-1; Moody 5-0-17-2; Warne 9-1-33-4

**Australia won by eight wickets**

## AUSTRALIAN AVERAGES IN THE WORLD CUP

### Batting and Fielding

| | mat | inn | n.o. | runs | high | 100 | 50 | avge | S/R | ct | st |
|---|---|---|---|---|---|---|---|---|---|---|---|
| TM Moody | 7 | 5 | 4 | 117 | 56* | - | 1 | 117.00 | 130.00 | 2 | - |
| SR Waugh | 10 | 8 | 3 | 398 | 120* | 1 | 2 | 79.66 | 77.73 | 6 | - |
| MG Bevan | 10 | 8 | 3 | 264 | 65 | - | 2 | 52.80 | 67.51 | 2 | - |
| ME Waugh | 10 | 10 | 1 | 375 | 104 | 1 | 2 | 41.66 | 76.21 | 6 | - |
| RT Ponting | 10 | 10 | 1 | 354 | 69 | - | 1 | 39.33 | 66.54 | 6 | - |
| DS Lehmann | 9 | 8 | 2 | 136 | 76 | - | 1 | 22.66 | 79.06 | - | - |
| AC Gilchrist | 10 | 10 | - | 224 | 63 | - | 2 | 22.40 | 78.87 | 12 | 2 |
| DR Martyn | 2 | 2 | - | 29 | 18 | - | - | 14.50 | 64.44 | - | - |
| DW Fleming | 10 | 3 | 2 | 12 | 8* | - | - | 12.00 | 75.00 | 3 | - |
| SK Warne | 10 | 4 | 1 | 34 | 18 | - | - | 11.33 | 77.27 | 1 | - |
| BP Julian | 2 | 1 | - | 9 | 9 | - | - | 9.00 | 150.00 | - | - |
| S Lee | 2 | 1 | - | 2 | 2 | - | - | 2.00 | 25.00 | - | - |
| PR Reiffel | 6 | 2 | - | 1 | 1 | - | - | 0.50 | 20.00 | 1 | - |
| GD McGrath | 10 | 2 | 1 | - | - | - | - | 0.00 | 0.00 | - | - |
| AC Dale | 2 | 1 | 1 | 3 | 3* | - | - | - | 60.00 | 2 | - |

*Notes*
- n.o. = 'not out' innings, including Lehmann's retirement v Zimbabwe
- avge = batting average: runs scored per completed innings
- S/R = strike rate: runs scored per 100 balls faced.

*Bowling and Fielding*

| | overs | mdns | runs | wickets | best | 4Inn | avge | S/R | econ |
|---|---|---|---|---|---|---|---|---|---|
| SK Warne | 94.2 | 13 | 361 | 20 | 4-49 | 2 | 18.05 | 28.30 | 3.82 |
| GD McGrath | 95.4 | 9 | 367 | 18 | 5-14 | 1 | 20.38 | 31.88 | 3.83 |
| DW Fleming | 88.0 | 9 | 362 | 14 | 3-57 | - | 25.85 | 37.71 | 4.11 |
| SR Waugh | 18.0 | - | 92 | 3 | 2-8 | - | 30.66 | 36.00 | 5.11 |
| TM Moody | 51.0 | 5 | 220 | 7 | 3-25 | - | 31.42 | 43.71 | 4.31 |
| PR Reiffel | 57.0 | 3 | 238 | 7 | 3-55 | - | 34.00 | 48.80 | 4.17 |
| S Lee | 12.0 | 1 | 49 | 1 | 1-25 | - | 49.00 | 72.00 | 4.08 |
| AC Dale | 15.0 | 3 | 53 | 1 | 1-18 | - | 53.00 | 90.00 | 3.53 |
| MG Bevan | 18.0 | 1 | 81 | 1 | 1-26 | - | 81.00 | 108.00 | 4.50 |
| DS Lehmann | 2.0 | - | 17 | - | - | - | - | - | 8.50 |
| DR Martyn | 2.0 | - | 25 | - | - | - | - | - | 12.50 |
| ME Waugh | 9.0 | - | 44 | - | - | - | - | - | 4.88 |
| BP Julian | 17.0 | 2 | 80 | - | - | - | - | - | 4.70 |

*Notes*
- avge = bowling average: runs conceded per wicket taken
- S/R = strike rate: balls bowled per wicket
- econ = economy rate: runs conceded per over

## MOST RUNS IN THE WORLD CUP, 1999

| | team | runs | matches | innings | n.o. | high | 100 | 50 | avge | S/R |
|---|---|---|---|---|---|---|---|---|---|---|
| RS Dravid | India | 461 | 8 | 8 | 1 | 145 | 2 | 3 | 65.85 | 85.52 |
| SR Waugh | Aust | 398 | 10 | 8 | 3 | 120* | 1 | 2 | 79.66 | 77.73 |
| SC Ganguly | India | 379 | 7 | 7 | - | 183 | 1 | 1 | 54.14 | 81.15 |
| ME Waugh | Aust | 375 | 10 | 10 | 1 | 104 | 1 | 2 | 41.66 | 76.21 |
| Saeed Anwar | Pak | 368 | 10 | 10 | 1 | 113* | 2 | - | 40.88 | 72.01 |
| NC Johnson | Zimb | 367 | 8 | 8 | 1 | 132* | 1 | 3 | 52.42 | 52.42 |
| RT Ponting | Aust | 354 | 10 | 10 | 1 | 69 | - | 1 | 39.33 | 66.54 |
| HH Gibbs | SA | 341 | 9 | 9 | - | 101 | 1 | 2 | 37.88 | 73.01 |
| RG Twose | NZ | 318 | 9 | 9 | 5 | 80* | - | 3 | 79.50 | 74.64 |
| JH Kallis | SA | 312 | 8 | 8 | 2 | 96 | - | 4 | 53.00 | 66.38 |
| AD Jadeja | India | 285 | 8 | 7 | 1 | 100* | 1 | 1 | 75.19 | 75.19 |
| L Klusener | SA | 281 | 9 | 8 | 6 | 52* | - | 2 | 140.50 | 122.17 |

*Notes*
- The highest strike-rates achieved in the World Cup (qualification 50 runs) were by TM Moody (Aust, S/R: 130.00), L Klusener (SA, S/R: 122.17), Moin Khan (Pak, 10 matches, 242 runs, S/R: 111.01) and T Odoyo (Kenya, 5 matches, 117 runs, S/R: 100.00).
- The highest batting averages were as achieved by L Klusener (average: 140.50), TM Moody (117.00) and RD Jacobs (WI, 5 matches, 205 runs, average: 102.50)
- The most runs ever scored in a World Cup tournament is 523, by SR Tendulkar (India, 1996) in seven matches, average 87.16.

## HIGHEST INDIVIDUAL SCORES IN THE WORLD CUP, 1999

| Runs | Batsman | Position | Innings | Match |
|---|---|---|---|---|
| 183 | SC Ganguly | 2 | first | India v Sri Lanka, Taunton |
| 145 | RS Dravid | 3 | first | India v Sri Lanka, Taunton |
| 140* | SR Tendulkar | 4 | first | India v Kenya, Bristol |
| 132* | NC Johnson | 1 | second | Zimbabwe v Australia, Lord's |
| 120* | SR Waugh | 5 | second | Australia v South Africa, Leeds |
| 113* | Saeed Anwar | 1 | second | Pakistan v New Zealand, Manchester |
| 104* | RS Dravid | 3 | first | India v Kenya, Bristol |
| 104 | ME Waugh | 2 | first | Australia v Zimbabwe, Lord's |
| 103 | Saeed Anwar | 1 | first | Pakistan v Zimbabwe, The Oval |
| 101 | HH Gibbs | 2 | first | South Africa v Australia, Leeds |
| 100* | AD Jadeja | 4 | second | India v Australia, The Oval |

## Notes
• Highest Individual Scores for other teams were as follows:

| | | | |
|---|---|---|---|
| Bangladesh | 68* | Minhaj-ul Abedin | v Scotland, Edinburgh |
| England | 88* | N Hussain | v Kenya, Canterbury |
| | 88 | AJ Stewart | v Sri Lanka, Lord's |
| Kenya | 82 | MO Odumbe | v Sri Lanka, Southampton |
| New Zealand | 80* | RG Twose | v Australia, Cardiff |
| Scotland | 76 | GM Hamilton | v Pakistan, Chester-le-Street |
| Sri Lanka | 57 | RS Kaluwitharana | v England, Lord's |
| West Indies | 80* | RD Jacobs | v New Zealand, Southampton |

• The highest individual score in a World Cup match is 188*, by G Kirsten for South Africa v United Arab Emirates, Rawalpindi, 1996

## HIGHEST PARTNERSHIPS IN THE WORLD CUP, 1999

| Partnership | Batsmen, match |
|---|---|
| 318 for 2nd | SC Ganguly and RS Dravid, India v Sri Lanka, Taunton |
| 237 for 3rd | RS Dravid and SR Tendulkar, India v Kenya, Bristol |
| 194 for 1st | Saeed Anwar and Wajahatullah Wasti, Pakistan v New Zealand, Manchester |
| 176 for 1st | G Kirsten and HH Gibbs, South Africa v New Zealand, Birmingham |
| 161 for 6th | MO Odumbe and A Vadher, Kenya v Sri Lanka, Southampton |
| 159* for 2nd | N Hussain and GA Hick, England v Kenya, Canterbury |

## Notes
• The highest partnership for Australia in the World Cup, 1999 was 129 for the third wicket by ME Waugh and SR Waugh v Zimbabwe at Lord's. In fact, 152 runs were added for this wicket in two separate partnerships — ME Waugh and DS Lehmann added 23 before Lehmann retired hurt.
• The previous highest partnership in a World Cup match was 207 for the third wicket by ME Waugh and SR Waugh, Australia v Kenya, Visakhapatnam, 1996

## HIGHEST TOTALS IN THE WORLD CUP, 1999

| | | |
|---|---|---|
| 373 | (50 overs, 6 wickets) | India v Sri Lanka, Taunton |
| 329 | (50 overs, 2 wickets) | India v Kenya, Bristol |
| 303 | (50 overs, 4 wickets) | Australia v Zimbabwe, Lord's |
| 287 | (50 overs, 5 wickets) | South Africa v New Zealand, Birmingham |
| 282 | (50 overs, 6 wickets) | Australia v India, The Oval |
| 275 | (50 overs, 8 wickets) | Pakistan v Australia, Leeds |
| 275 | (50 overs, 8 wickets) | Sri Lanka v Kenya, Southampton |

## Notes
• The highest total achieved by a team batting second was 272 (49.4 overs, 5 wickets) by Australia v South Africa, at Leeds.
• The highest Total in a World Cup match is 398 (50 overs, 5 wickets) by Sri Lanka v Kenya, Kandy, 1996.

## LOWEST TOTALS (COMPLETED INNINGS) IN THE WORLD CUP, 1999

| | | |
|---|---|---|
| 68 | (31.3 overs) | Scotland v West Indies, Leicester |
| 103 | (41 overs) | England v South Africa, The Oval |
| 110 | (35.2 overs) | Sri Lanka v South Africa, Northampton |
| 110 | (46.4 overs) | West Indies v Australia, Manchester |

## Notes
• The lowest total scored by a team batting first and winning was 185 (9 wickets, 50 overs) by Bangladesh v Scotland, at Edinburgh.
• The lowest total off 50 overs was 178 (7 wickets) by Bangladesh v Australia, at Chester-le-Street.
• The lowest total in a World Cup match is 45 (40.3 overs) by Canada v England, Manchester, 1979.

## MOST WICKETS IN THE WORLD CUP, 1999

| | | mat | overs | runs | wkts | best | 4Inn | avge | S/R | econ |
|---|---|---|---|---|---|---|---|---|---|---|
| GI Allott | NZ | 9 | 87.4 | 325 | 20 | 4-37 | 2 | 16.25 | 26.30 | 3.70 |
| SK Warne | Aust | 10 | 94.2 | 361 | 20 | 4-29 | 2 | 18.05 | 28.30 | 3.82 |
| GD McGrath | Aust | 10 | 95.4 | 367 | 18 | 5-14 | 1 | 20.38 | 31.88 | 3.83 |
| L Klusener | SA | 9 | 75.5 | 350 | 17 | 5-21 | 1 | 20.58 | 26.76 | 4.61 |
| Saqlain Mushtaq | Pak | 10 | 83.4 | 379 | 17 | 5-35 | 1 | 22.29 | 29.52 | 4.52 |
| Shoaib Akhtar | Pak | 10 | 80.5 | 392 | 16 | 3-11 | - | 24.50 | 30.31 | 4.84 |
| AA Donald | SA | 9 | 82.0 | 325 | 16 | 4-17 | 2 | 20.31 | 30.75 | 3.96 |
| Wasim Akram | Pak | 10 | 90.4 | 342 | 15 | 4-40 | 1 | 22.80 | 36.26 | 3.77 |
| DW Fleming | Aust | 10 | 88.0 | 362 | 14 | 3-57 | - | 25.85 | 37.71 | 4.11 |
| Abdur Razzaq | Pak | 9 | 77.0 | 302 | 13 | 3-25 | - | 23.23 | 35.53 | 3.92 |
| Azhar Mahmood | Pak | 10 | 84.0 | 348 | 13 | 3-24 | - | 26.76 | 38.76 | 4.14 |
| NC Johnson | Zimb | 8 | 50.0 | 233 | 12 | 4-42 | 1 | 19.41 | 25.00 | 4.66 |
| CL Cairns | NZ | 9 | 69.5 | 333 | 12 | 3-19 | - | 27.75 | 34.91 | 4.76 |
| J Srinath | India | 8 | 73.2 | 313 | 12 | 3-37 | - | 26.08 | 36.66 | 4.26 |

Best bowling average (qualification five wickets):

| | average | matches | wickets |
|---|---|---|---|
| CA Walsh (WI) | 9.81 | 5 | 11 |
| RD King (WI) | 11.87 | 4 | 8 |
| CEL Ambrose (WI) | 13.42 | 4 | 7 |

*Notes*
- The best strike rates (qualification five wickets) were achieved by JAR Blain (Scotland, S/R: 22.30, five matches, 10 wickets), RD King (WI, S/R: 23.62) and RR Singh (India, S/R: 24.37, six matches, 8 wickets). The best economy rate (qualification five wickets) was 2.29 by CA Walsh (WI), then 2.35 by CEL Ambrose (WI).
- The previous record for most wickets in a World Cup tournament was 18 by RMH Binny (India, 1983, eight matches), CJ McDermott (Aust, 1987, eight matches) and Wasim Akram (Pak, 1992, 10 matches). Each of these teams won the respective tournament.
- There have been two hat-tricks taken in World Cup history, by Chetan Sharma, for India v New Zealand at Nagpur, 1987, and Saqlain Mushtaq, for Pakistan v Zimbabwe at The Oval, 1999

## FIVE WICKETS IN AN INNINGS

| | | | |
|---|---|---|---|
| 5-14 | (8.4 overs) | GD McGrath | Australia v West Indies, Manchester |
| 5-21 | (8.3 overs) | L Klusener | South Africa v Kenya, Amstelveen |
| 5-27 | (9.3 overs) | BK Venkatesh Prasad | India v Pakistan, Manchester |
| 5-31 | (9.3 overs) | RR Singh | India v Sri Lanka, Taunton |
| 5-35 | (10 overs) | Saqlain Mushtaq | Pakistan v Bangladesh, Northampton |
| 5-36 | (9.2 overs) | SM Pollock | South Africa v Australia, Birmingham |

*Notes*
- Best bowling for other teams were as follows:

| | | | | |
|---|---|---|---|---|
| Bangladesh | 3-31 | (10 overs) | Khaled Mahmud | v Pakistan, Northampton |
| England | 4-34 | (10 overs) | D Gough | v Kenya, Canterbury |
| Kenya | 3-56 | (10 overs) | T Odoyo | v Sri Lanka, Southampton |
| New Zealand | 4-7 | (3.1 overs) | CZ Harris | v Scotland, Edinburgh |
| Scotland | 4-37 | (10 overs) | JAR Blain | v Bangladesh, Edinburgh |
| Sri Lanka | 3-25 | (10 overs) | M Muralitharan | v South Africa, Northampton |
| West Indies | 4-25 | (10 overs) | CA Walsh | v Bangladesh, Dublin |
| Zimbabwe | 4-42 | (10 overs) | NC Johnson | v Kenya, Taunton |

- The best bowling analysis achieved in a World Cup match is 7-51 by WW Davis, West Indies v Australia, Leeds, 1983

## MOST DISMISSALS BY A WICKETKEEPER IN THE WORLD CUP, 1999

| | |
|---|---|
| 15 (11 ct, 4 st) | Moin Khan (Pak, 10 matches) |
| 14 (all ct) | RD Jacobs (WI, 5 matches) |
| 14 (12 ct, 2 st) | AC Gilchrist (Aust, 10 matches) |
| 11 (all ct) | MV Boucher (SA, 9 matches) |

*Notes*
- The most dismissals in a World Cup tournament is 16 (15 ct, 1 st) by PJL Dujon (WI, eight matches, 1983)
- The most dismissals in a World Cup innings: in 1999 was 5 (4 ct, 1 st) by NR Mongia, for India v Zimbabwe, at Leicester. This equalled the record for dismissals in an innings in a World Cup, joining SMH Kirmani (all caught, India v Zimbabwe, Leicester, 1983), JC Adams (4 ct, 1 st, West Indies v Kenya, Pune, 1996) and Rashid Latif (4 ct, 1 st, Pakistan v New Zealand, Lahore, 1996).

**MOST CATCHES (BY A FIELDER) IN THE WORLD CUP, 1999**

8  DJ Cullinan (SA)
6  RT Ponting (Aust), ME Waugh (Aust), SR Waugh (Aust), GA Hick (Eng.), GP Thorpe (Eng.), NJ Astle (NZ), Inzamam-ul-Haq (Pak)

*Note*
Cullinan's mark equals the previous record of eight catches in a World Cup tournament (by an fielder other than a wicketkeeper), set by A Kumble (India) in 1996.

### Some Facts and Trivia Involving Australia at the World Cup, 1999

#### Australia v Scotland, May 16

- SR Waugh became the second Australian to play in four World Cups (1987, 1992, 1996 and 1999), joining AR Border who played in 1979, 1983, 1987 and 1992 (25 matches).
- ME Waugh became the fourth Australian to play in three World Cups (1992, 1996 and 1999), following AR Border, SR Waugh and CJ McDermott (1987, 1992 and 1996).

#### Australia v Pakistan, May 23

- PR Reiffel claimed his 100th wicket in limited-over internationals when he captured the wicket of Saeed Anwar. He was playing in his 87th match. He became the seventh Australian and the 47th bowler to reach this mark.
- Inzamam-ul-Haq's 81 was the highest by a Pakistani in the World Cup against Australia, previously 76 by Aamer Sohail at Perth in 1992.

#### Australia v Bangladesh, May 27

- AC Gilchrist's 63 was the highest World Cup score by an Australian wicketkeeper, previously 52* by RW Marsh v West Indies, The Oval, 1975. The 63 was also the highest for Australia in limited-over internationals v Bangladesh, replacing PL Taylor's 54* at Sharjah, 1990.
- TM Moody became the fifth Australian to play in three World Cups (1987, 1992 and 1996), following AR Border, SR Waugh, CJ McDermott and ME Waugh.
- TM Moody scored the quickest half century in a World Cup match, in 28 balls, previously 29 balls by A Ranatunga, Sri Lanka v Kenya, Kandy, 1996. The previous quickest by a Australian in the World Cup, was ME Waugh in 32 balls v Zimbabwe, Hobart, 1992.

#### Australia v West Indies, May 30

- SK Warne conceded only 11 runs in his 10 overs, a new record for Australia in a World Cup match, previously MR Whitney 10-3-15-2 v Zimbabwe, Hobart, 1992. (In all limited-over internationals for Australia: MF Malone holds the record with 10-5-9-2 v West Indies, Melbourne on 1981-82.)
- RD Jacobs (WI) carried his bat, the first time this had been achieved in a World Cup match, and the fourth time in limited-over internationals.

#### Australia v India, June 4

- ME Waugh, when 41, became the highest run-scorer for Australia in World Cup matches, passing DC Boon's 815 in 16 matches.
- AC Gilchrist's four catches equalled GC Dyer's Australian record in the World Cup (Dyer took four catches v Pakistan, Lahore, 1987).

#### Australia v Zimbabwe, June 9

- Australia's 4-303 became the new highest score for Australia v Zimbabwe in limited-over internationals, previously 3-294 at Delhi, 1998.
- ME Waugh's 104 v Zimbabwe was his fourth hundred in the World Cup, a new record. Three other players have scored three World Cup hundreds: IVA Richards (WI), Rameez Raja (Pak) and SR Tendulkar (India). On 35, Waugh became the highest run-scorer for Australia in limited-over internationals, previously 6524 in 273 matches by Allan Border.
- ME Waugh reached his 100 off 115 balls, and hit 13 fours. In all he faced 120 balls.

#### Australia v South Africa, June 13

- SR Waugh reached his 50 off 47 balls, and 100 off 91 balls. In all, he faced 110 balls and hit 10 fours and two sixes.
- SR Waugh's 120* v South Africa was the highest score by an Australian captain in the World Cup; previously MA Taylor 74 v Sri Lanka (in the final), Lahore, 1996. It was the eighth century by a captain in the World Cup, following GM Turner (NZ) 2 in 1975, CH Lloyd (WI) in 1975, Imran Khan (Pak) in 1983, Kapil Dev (India) in 1983, IVA Richards (WI) in 1987 and MD Crowe (NZ) in 1992.
- SR Waugh became the seventh Australian to score a World Cup century, after A Turner, TM Chappell, DC Boon, GR Marsh, ME Waugh and RT Ponting. SR Waugh's hundred came from the No. 5 spot in the batting order; all the others bar Ponting's (who batted at three) were made by openers.

*Australia v South Africa, June 17*
- This was the first tie in a World Cup match.
- Australia has reached the semi-finals of the World Cup in four tournaments, and has never lost a semi-final.
- SR Waugh, when 46, became the highest run-scorer for Australia in the World Cup, overtaking the aggregate of 967 runs of ME Waugh. SR Waugh also became the fourth-highest run-scorer in the World Cup, following 1083 by Javed Miandad (Pak), 1059 by SR Tendulkar (India) and 1013 by IVA Richards (WI).

*Australia v Pakistan, June 20*
- Eight of the Australian team in the Final — ME Waugh, RT Ponting, SR Waugh, MG Bevan, SK Warne, PR Reiffel, DW Fleming and GD McGrath — played in the Final v Sri Lanka in 1996. The three 'missing' players from the 1996 Final were MA Taylor, IA Healy and SG Law, replaced by DS Lehmann, AC Gilchrist and TM Moody.
- This was SR Waugh's 33rd World Cup match, equalling the record of Javed Miandad (Pak) who played in the first six tournaments. Wasim Akram was playing in his 32nd Cup match. Next highest Australian is AR Border, with 25.
- SR Waugh, having played in the Finals in 1987 and 1996, became the first Australian to play in three Finals. Other players to play in three Finals are the West Indians, CG Greenidge, CH Lloyd, IVA Richards and AME Roberts, who played in 1975, 1979 and 1983.
- SK Warne, by dismissing Moin Khan, reached 200 limited-over international wickets in his 125th match, becoming the 11th bowler and second Australian (CJ McDermott, 203 wickets in 138 matches) to do so.
- SR Waugh, by catching Wasim Akram, completed his 14th World Cup catch, overtaking the 13 by A Kumble (India)
- AC Gilchrist, in taking 33 balls to reach 50, scored the quickest half century in a World Cup Final.
- ME Waugh, when 33, became the fourth batsman to score 1000 World Cup runs.
- Australia became the second team to win the Cup twice, after the West Indies, who won the first two tournaments, in 1975 and 1979. Australia also became the first team to appear in four finals (1975, 1987, 1996 and 1999), surpassing the West Indies and England, who had each previously appeared in three.
- Australia became the second team batting second to win a Cup final, after Sri Lanka in 1996. The first five Cup finals were won by the team batting first. Pakistan's 132 was their lowest score v Australia in limited-over internationals, previously 140, Adelaide, 1983-84. The total was the lowest score recorded in a Final; previously 140 by West Indies in 1983.
- The 1999 final was the briefest final, taking just 59.1 overs. The previous shortest final was the 1996 match, which involved 96.2 overs.

*General*
- SR Waugh, having been in the winning team in 1987, is the only Australian to be a part of two World Cup-winning teams, joining the West Indians, CG Greenidge, AI Kallicharran, CH Lloyd, DL Murray, IVA Richards and AME Roberts, who were in both winning teams in 1975 and 1979, as other cricketers to be dual-World Cup winners. The Australian team in the 1987 Final v England in Calcutta was DC Boon, GR Marsh, DM Jones, *AR Border, MRJ Veletta, SR Waugh, SP O'Donnell, +GC Dyer, TBA May, CJ McDermott and BA Reid; with reserves TM Moody, PL Taylor and AK Zesers. Australia 5-253 (DC Boon 75) beat England 8-246 (CWJ Athey 58) by 7 runs. In 1999, GR Marsh served as coach and AR Border served as a selector.
- SR Waugh has scored 978 World Cup runs, at an average of 48.90, including one century and six half-centuries. Only Javed Miandad (1083), SR Tendulkar (1059), IVA Richards (1013) and ME Waugh (1004) have scored more Cup runs.
- SR Waugh has taken 27 World Cup wickets, equal second-most by an Australian, after SK Warne (32) and level with CJ McDermott. SR Waugh's total is equal 10th on the all-time list, which is headed by Wasim Akram, with 43.
- Australia won all five tosses in the first round of the 1999 competition, and lost the toss in the remaining five matches.
- The following Australians received 'Man-of the-Match' Awards during the tournament — ME Waugh (v Scotland), TM Moody (v Bangladesh), GD McGrath (twice, v West Indies and v India), SR Waugh (v South Africa at Leeds) and SK Warne (twice, v South Africa at Birmingham and v Pakistan in the Final).
- S Lee played in first-round matches in 1996 and 1999, but is yet to play in a World Cup match in a subsequent round.
- For the second World Cup competition in a row, GD McGrath failed to score a run. In 17 World Cup matches, McGrath has batted three times, for two unbeaten noughts and one duck.

*A few other notable landmarks from the World Cup ...*
- Scotland made their limited-over international debut on May 16, becoming the 15th team to compete in the World Cup.
- Bangladesh, having made their limited-over international debut in 1988-89, became the 16th team to compete in the World Cup when they met New Zealand on May 17.
- Twenty-one venues were used during the World Cup, seven of which (including four in England and Wales) hosted a World Cup match for the first time. On May 21, the match at Dublin was the first limited-overs international played in Ireland. Three days later, the match at Edinburgh was the first limited-overs international in Scotland. On May 26, the match at Amstelveen was the first limited-overs international played in Holland and on continental Europe.

- SA Bucknor (WI) and DR Shepherd (England), who umpired the 1999 Final, also umpired the Final in 1996. SA Bucknor had also previously umpired the 1992 Final, for which DR Shepherd was unavailable (as England were playing). The only other umpire to appear in three World Cup Finals is HD Bird, who umpired the first three Finals.

## 6. Australia in Limited-Over Internationals, October 1998-June 1999

| Opponent | matches | won | tied | lost |
|---|---|---|---|---|
| Bangladesh | 1 | - | - | 1 |
| Pakistan | 3 | 3 | - | - |
| Australia | 12 | 9 | - | 3 |
| West Indies | 7 | 3 | 1 | 3 |
| World Cup | 10 | 7 | 1 | 2 |
| Total | 33 | 22 | 2 | 9 |

*Batting and Fielding*

| | mat | inn | n.o. | runs | high | 100 | 50 | avge | ct | st |
|---|---|---|---|---|---|---|---|---|---|---|
| MG Bevan | 30 | 26 | 14 | 929 | 83 | - | 9 | 77.41 | 7 | - |
| TM Moody | 12 | 9 | 5 | 175 | 56* | - | 2 | 43.75 | 3 | - |
| RT Ponting | 28 | 28 | 4 | 986 | 124* | 1 | 4 | 41.08 | 16 | - |
| ME Waugh | 33 | 33 | 2 | 1251 | 104 | 1 | 10 | 40.35 | 17 | - |
| DS Lehmann | 30 | 28 | 4 | 905 | 110* | 2 | 5 | 37.70 | 2 | - |
| AC Gilchrist | 33 | 33 | - | 1165 | 154 | 3 | 4 | 35.30 | 46 | 6 |
| SR Waugh | 23 | 21 | 4 | 600 | 120* | 1 | 3 | 35.29 | 9 | - |
| DR Martyn | 17 | 16 | 4 | 417 | 59* | - | 2 | 34.75 | 1 | - |
| BE Young | 5 | 2 | 1 | 26 | 18 | - | - | 26.00 | 2 | - |
| S Lee | 17 | 15 | 3 | 227 | 47 | - | - | 18.91 | 7 | - |
| SG Law | 3 | 3 | 1 | 31 | 20* | - | - | 15.50 | - | - |
| GS Blewett | 6 | 5 | - | 77 | 40 | - | - | 15.40 | - | - |
| BP Julian | 22 | 15 | - | 213 | 35 | - | - | 14.20 | 7 | - |
| SK Warne | 29 | 17 | 5 | 161 | 29 | - | - | 13.41 | 7 | - |
| MS Kasprowicz | 3 | 2 | 1 | 9 | 7 | - | - | 9.00 | - | - |
| AC Dale | 12 | 5 | 3 | 15 | 7* | - | - | 7.50 | 6 | - |
| DW Fleming | 25 | 8 | 5 | 16 | 8* | - | - | 5.33 | 4 | - |
| PR Reiffel | 9 | 3 | 1 | 10 | 9* | - | - | 5.00 | 2 | - |
| GD McGrath | 25 | 5 | 3 | 2 | 2 | - | - | 1.00 | 2 | - |
| A Symonds | 1 | - | - | - | - | - | - | - | - | - |

*Bowling*

| | overs | runs | wickets | best | 4Inn | avge | S/R | econ |
|---|---|---|---|---|---|---|---|---|
| GD McGrath | 226.0 | 917 | 51 | 5-14 | 2 | 17.98 | 26.58 | 4.05 |
| SK Warne | 270.1 | 1147 | 52 | 4-29 | 2 | 22.05 | 31.17 | 4.24 |
| S Lee | 92.3 | 464 | 18 | 5-33 | 1 | 25.77 | 30.83 | 5.01 |
| AC Dale | 109.0 | 366 | 14 | 2-25 | - | 26.14 | 46.71 | 3.35 |
| DW Fleming | 222.1 | 968 | 37 | 3-41 | - | 26.16 | 36.02 | 4.35 |
| PR Reiffel | 77.0 | 339 | 9 | 3-55 | - | 37.66 | 51.33 | 4.40 |
| MS Kasprowicz | 25.0 | 155 | 4 | 3-71 | - | 38.75 | 37.50 | 6.20 |
| MG Bevan | 49.2 | 242 | 6 | 2-9 | - | 40.33 | 49.33 | 4.90 |
| SR Waugh | 56.5 | 278 | 6 | 2-8 | - | 46.33 | 56.83 | 4.89 |
| GS Blewett | 15.1 | 95 | 2 | 2-6 | - | 47.50 | 45.50 | 6.26 |
| TM Moody | 83.0 | 381 | 8 | 3-25 | - | 47.62 | 62.25 | 4.59 |
| BP Julian | 162.0 | 828 | 17 | 3-40 | - | 48.70 | 57.17 | 5.11 |
| DS Lehmann | 30.0 | 176 | 3 | 1-16 | - | 58.66 | 60.00 | 5.86 |
| RT Ponting | 15.0 | 62 | 1 | 1-41 | - | 62.00 | 90.00 | 4.13 |
| ME Waugh | 53.0 | 192 | 2 | 1-11 | - | 96.00 | 159.00 | 3.62 |
| BE Young | 32.0 | 202 | 1 | 1-26 | - | 101.00 | 192.00 | 6.31 |
| SG Law | 2.0 | 8 | - | - | - | - | - | 4.00 |
| A Symonds | 2.0 | 14 | - | - | - | - | - | 7.00 |
| DR Martyn | 13.0 | 108 | - | - | - | - | - | 8.30 |